NAZI WIVES

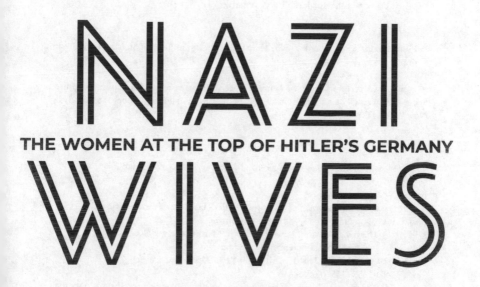

NAZI

THE WOMEN AT THE TOP OF HITLER'S GERMANY

WIVES

JAMES WYLLIE

ST. MARTIN'S GRIFFIN
NEW YORK

I would like to thank my agent, Sonia Land, at Sheil Land Associates Ltd for her unswerving commitment and support, and Gaia Banks and the foreign rights team for getting this book out into the world. Thanks are also due to Laura Perehinec at The History Press for her enthusiasm and dedication, to Alex Waite for helping turn my manuscript into a book, and to the whole The History Press team for their excellent work. Finally, I'd like to thank my friends and family; without their loyalty and generosity this book would not have been possible.

Published in the United States by St. Martin's Griffin, an imprint of St. Martin's Publishing Group

www.stmartins.com

The Library of Congress has cataloged the hardcover edition as follows:

Names: Wyllie, James, author.
Title: Nazi wives : the women at the top of Hitler's Germany / James Wyllie.
Other titles: Women at the top of Hitler's Germany
Description: First U.S. edition. | New York : St. Martin's Press, 2020. |
   Includes bibliographical references and index.
Identifiers: LCCN 2020028410 | ISBN 9781250271563 (hardcover) |
   ISBN 9781250271570 (ebook)
Subjects: LCSH: Women Nazis—Germany—Biography. | National socialism and women—
   History. | Hitler, Adolf, 1889–1945—Friends and associates. | Nazis—Biography. |
   National socialism—Social aspects—Germany. | Women—Political activity—Germany—
   History—20th century. | Germany—Politics and government—1933–1945. | Women—
   Germany—History—20th century. | Women—Germany—Biography.
Classification: LCC DD245 .W95 2020 | DDC 943.086092/52—dc23
LC record available at https://lccn.loc.gov/2020028410

ISBN 978-1-250-81596-5 (trade paperback)

Originally published in Great Britain by The History Press

First St. Martin's Griffin Edition: 2021

10 9 8 7 6 5 4 3 2 1

CONTENTS

INTRODUCTION

On the evening of 10 July 1937 the German-Jewish journalist Bella Fromm, who wrote the society column in a Berlin newspaper, went to the cinema to see the romantic comedy *Broadway Melody*. Loosely based on the 1929 original, it included the hit song 'You Are My Lucky Star', a bunch of characters trying to launch a Broadway show, farcical backstage intrigues and glamorous locations – penthouse apartments and rooftop pavilions – and a finale featuring two grand pianos gliding across the dancefloor next to a tap-dancing chorus line dressed in top hats and tails.

Arriving at the cinema, Bella parked her car and then suddenly noticed that she'd aroused the interest of two SS men. One of them noted down her licence plate while the other pointed his camera at her and 'took a quick snap-shot'. The reason for this level of surveillance became clear when several large automobiles with swastika pendants pulled up. Heinrich Himmler and his wife Margaret got out and entered the cinema, accompanied by their 'grim bodyguard'.[1] Once inside, Himmler and Margaret took their seats – flanked by his angels of death – and settled in for 101 minutes of fun and frolics. This surreal, almost comic scene is also rather unsettling given how Himmler is generally perceived: a humourless pedant and ruthless zealot obsessed by crackpot fantasies about a Germanic master race.

So why did he take Margaret to see a light-hearted MGM musical? Unlike others in the Nazi elite – including Hitler – Himmler wasn't a film buff eager to consume the latest Hollywood releases. Perhaps he fancied some carefree escapism to take his mind off the daily grind. Or did he view the film with a critical eye, regarding it as an example of the degenerate decadence of American society? Or maybe he was simply trying to please his wife. From the start, his long working hours and almost constant travelling had taken a heavy toll on their marriage. This was a rare opportunity to have a night out together. Dress up. Summon a fleet of cars and a uniformed escort. Treat her to a feel-good movie.

Sadly, we don't know if Margaret enjoyed *Broadway Melody*, or if she was pleased her husband had found time to indulge her; perhaps the most thrilling part of her evening was cruising the streets of the capital in an SS convoy, sending ripples of fear and awe through everyone who saw them speed past.

Among the thousands of books about Nazism barely a handful focus on the wives of the leading figures in Hitler's regime: Gerda Bormann, Magda Goebbels, Carin and Emmy Goering, Ilse Hess, Lina Heydrich and Margaret Himmler. While their men have left an indelible imprint on our collective memory the women who gave them vital support, encouragement and direction have largely remained relegated to the footnotes of history. While the overall experience of women in the Nazi period became a subject of serious study during the 1980s, opening up a whole field of enquiry and providing a complex and nuanced picture that challenged the stereotypes perpetuated by Nazi propaganda, the women at the very top of the system have been neglected.

Part of the reason for this is the nature of the source material, much of which has to be treated with caution. Although a lot more information has come to light in the last few decades, there are still considerable gaps and chunks of time missing from the diaries and letters that have survived, while the post-war autobiographies penned by several of the wives actively sought to portray their husbands as paragons of virtue and themselves as innocent bystanders; the memoirs and recollections of fellow travellers – each with their own agenda – have created an echo chamber of anecdotes, hearsay and gossip that make it harder to distinguish fact from fiction.

However, these sorts of issues affect any investigation into the past and are not sufficient to explain why historians have failed to give these women the prominence they deserve, thereby giving credence to their own claims that there was a clear distinction between their husbands' public and private lives. But this does not bear scrutiny. The Nazis set out to control every aspect of their citizens' existence – the food they ate, the clothes they wore, who they had sex with, what jokes they could tell, how they celebrated Christmas – making any separation between the public and the private meaningless. And despite their undoubted privilege, the wives were subjected to the same pressures as ordinary women. Their social lives were determined by political considerations. Friendships were jettisoned. Relationships – even with family members – abruptly terminated. Their behaviour was a factor in the struggles within the Nazi elite, particularly where Hitler was concerned; falling out of favour with the Führer could have serious implications for their husbands' careers.

Even though they might not have been privy to their husbands' daily decisions, the evidence of their murderous work was all around: the looted art on the walls; the furniture made from human skin and bones stashed in the attic; the fruit and vegetables taken from the local concentration camp gardens; the slave labour tilling their land. The rituals of family life – births, weddings, funerals – were inextricably linked to Nazi ideology. Perhaps this is why it has proved easier to take these women at face value and treat them as minor characters; treating them seriously means accepting that their husbands engaged in normal activities and experienced recognisably human emotions. Falling in and out of love. Worrying about the bills and their weight and where to send the kids to school. Planning dinner parties and picnics. Spending vacations sightseeing. Acknowledging that in many respects they were no different from the rest of us creates a form of cognitive dissonance: a deeply uneasy feeling.

Yet their story offers important insights into the nature of Nazi rule and the psychology of its leaders, providing a fresh perspective on the key events that shaped its rise and fall. The aim of this book is to chart their lives from the moment they became involved in the Nazi movement – in several cases before they even met their husbands – through the years of struggle, power, decline and destruction, and then into the post-war twilight of denial and delusion. While they enjoyed luxury lifestyles and VIP status, they also endured broken marriages, cheating husbands, suicide, assassination, desertion, impoverishment and incarceration. But despite all these trials and tribulations, their commitment to Hitler's cause never wavered.

Though they were each unique and fascinating individuals in their own right who coped differently with the demands placed on them, these women's backgrounds were strikingly similar. Well-educated, they all came from conservative middle-class families – representing the professions, business, the army and the lower gentry – where gender roles were rigidly defined; whatever her achievements, a woman's best hope was to find a good husband. Their parents, whether Protestant or Catholic, took religion seriously and their daughters were instilled with values that would shape their tastes, interests and political views: a belief in the supremacy of German culture, its music, art, literature and philosophy, the genius of its scientific achievements, its unbeatable army; devotion to the Kaiser and the state; a hatred of socialism and a fear that the unruly masses would devour them. As a result they had more in common with each other than they would ever have with a woman working in a factory.

They grew up in an era that saw the rapid transformation of Germany from a largely agricultural society to an industrial one, an uneasy trade-off between a democratic system and an imperial one, and a belligerent effort to establish Germany as a major global power with a large navy and a string of colonies. But despite the strident patriotism, there was also a pervasive feeling of crisis, of a country at war with itself, struggling to accommodate the pressures of modernity – not least the sharpening of class divisions – and surrounded by hostile neighbours.

The bourgeoisie were especially vulnerable to these stresses and strains, suffering from both an exaggerated sense of their own superiority and a nagging anxiety about the future.

The beginning of the First World War seemed to resolve these tensions, as the nation united in anticipation of glory. As the slaughter dragged on and on, the whole population was mobilised to support the war effort while blanket censorship and relentless propaganda made ultimate victory still appear inevitable, whatever the cost.

These women's young lives – at home and school – were monopolised by the conflict. Battlefield statistics and soldiers' stories entered the classroom. Priests prayed for success at the front. Everything from toys to playing cards were given a military theme. Mothers, particularly those from the middle classes, took part in a vast campaign of charity work, whether organising food drives or knitting socks and scarves for the men in the cold damp trenches.

The last year of the war delivered shock after shock to the already tottering system; the Bolshevik seizure of power in Russia threatened to spread revolution across its borders and inspire mutiny in the army; the failure of the massive do-or-die offensive on the Western Front that led to irreversible retreat; the collapse of Germany's main allies, Austro-Hungary and Turkey; the hunger, malnutrition and disease that wrecked civilian morale; the strikes and demonstrations; the calls for peace and the abdication of the Kaiser.

The chaos and violence that engulfed Germany in the wake of defeat and surrender continued into 1919, driving the country towards outright civil war. The radical left almost gained control before it was ruthlessly crushed by the *Freikorps* – right-wing paramilitary units made up of ex-soldiers and enthusiastic volunteers – who were given free rein by the embattled government of the new Weimar Republic, which was held responsible for the humiliating terms imposed by the Versailles Treaty.

As a result, these women became adults in profoundly insecure and volatile circumstances. Old certainties were gone. The civilised conventions of their parents' generation appeared increasingly irrelevant. Cut adrift, they each gravitated towards a self-styled saviour who promised them the world.

PART ONE

REACHING THE
SUMMIT

1

EARLY RUNNERS

In the spring of 1920, Ilse Pröhl moved into a respectable student hostel on the outskirts of Munich, determined to benefit from the educational opportunities opening up for German women. In 1900, the year Ilse was born, women were admitted to university for the first time. Eight years later, the first female versions of the *Gymnasium* – exclusive fee-paying high schools that trained their pupils for the university entrance exam known as the *Abitur* – opened their doors.

These *Gymnasia* were restricted to daughters of wealthy families, but this wasn't a problem for Ilse: her father was a respected doctor who treated members of the Prussian court in Berlin and became a chief military surgeon at the elite Potsdam garrison. Aged 14, Ilse took up a place at one of these prestigious high schools. A bright, energetic and popular pupil, she was particularly keen on music and literature. She also enjoyed hiking and camping, outdoor pursuits that were extremely popular among middle-class adolescents seeking to escape the soulless-ness of urban life. This back-to-nature movement began as an all-male activity but by the time Ilse got involved it was thoroughly mixed.

Her carefree teenage years were overshadowed by the First World War. Though a firm supporter of the armed forces and a convinced patriot, the full reality of the catastrophe occurring in northern France was brought home to her when her father, who had been posted to a rela-tively quiet sector of the front, was killed in the spring of 1917.

This painful loss was compounded by the shock of defeat and the upheavals that threatened to break Germany apart. Then, during her last year at the *Gymnasium*, her mother remarried – to a museum director – and the family moved to Munich before Ilse could complete the *Abitur*. Rather than stay at her new home, Ilse signalled her desire for independence by taking a room at the hostel.

One evening, Ilse ran into a fellow lodger, a tall young man wearing a threadbare, tattered uniform, who gruffly introduced himself as Rudolf Hess. She was immediately struck by his gaunt appearance: the thick eyebrows that seemed destined to meet in the middle, the sunken eyes and haunted expression. Despite his curt manner, she was instantly attracted to him. Whether the 26-year-old Hess had a similar reaction is impossible to say. Of all the senior Nazis, Hess was the most enigmatic. Dozens of experts, from psychiatrists to historians, have struggled to make sense of him. Hess even puzzled himself. In a letter to a friend he confessed that he felt torn between two opposing sides of his personality: one craved an almost monk-like existence contemplating the mysteries of the universe, while the other was a bloodthirsty barbarian hungry for battle.

Yet it was precisely this combination of the thinker with the man of action that appealed to Ilse. The frayed uniform he was wearing that fateful evening – which Ilse instantly recognised – belonged to the notorious von Epp *Freikorps* regiment that he'd joined in 1919 during the violent overthrow of Munich's left-wing government.

Hess was also a decorated veteran – with an Iron Cross for valour – who'd been wounded twice. At the hellish Battle of Verdun, during which he witnessed 'every horror of death imaginable',[1] he was hit by shrapnel; while leading an infantry charge in Romania he was shot in the chest. His recovery complete, Hess trained as a pilot, satisfying a long-held urge to fly, but the war was over before he could test himself in combat.

When the conflict began, Hess had been at a critical juncture in his life. He wanted to go to university, but his father wanted him to enter the family business, an import-export firm based in the Egyptian port city of Alexandria where Hess grew up in a palatial villa on the edge of the desert, an environment that contributed to his sense of otherworldliness. His father was a strict disciplinarian who thought the most important day of the year was the Kaiser's birthday. Hess felt closer to his mother, a gentle, intelligent woman who encouraged his early interest in astrology.

In 1908, when Hess was 14, the family returned to Germany; having only spent summers there, Hess was thrilled by his first sight of snow. Packed off to boarding school, he remained an outsider. A hard-working pupil, he passed the *Abitur* and reluctantly enrolled on a business course; his poor performance provoked a clash with his father that was only resolved when Hess enlisted in the army.

With the war over – and his father's business requisitioned by the British – Hess was free to pursue a degree in history and economics. While he flirted with the *Thule Society* (a semi-secret group interested in Aryan mythology and prehistoric Nordic civilisations) Hess's main intellectual influence was the 50-year-old geo-politics professor Karl Haushofer, who had managed to combine a military career with academic study: Haushofer developed the concept of *Lebensraum* after visiting Japan and concluding that a nation's chances of success depended on the amount of *living space* available to it. Though Haushofer didn't think Hess was particularly intelligent, he admired his strength of character. The professor – and the rest of his family – treated Hess like an adopted son. This close friendship, which included Ilse, endured for decades, with mixed results for all concerned.

Despite Hess's aversion to fun, Ilse decided to pursue him and they began spending time together. It was a platonic affair. Still a virgin, Hess showed absolutely no interest in sex: for the next few years, their relationship lacked a physical dimension. Instead, they consciously cultivated a spiritual connection based on their shared love of German culture, especially the writers and composers of the late eighteenth and early nineteenth century. Their favourite was the poet and philosopher Friedrich Hölderlin: his early work worshipped nature, his later work worshipped God. Ilse gave Hess a copy of Hölderlin's metaphysical novel *Hyperion* and added a lyrical inscription; their love was 'full of power and yet tender as their spirit', while their 'hearts beat stronger waves even than the trident of the Sea God who is ruler of the waves'.[2]

However, it was their shared response to Hitler that forged an unbreakable bond between them, both convinced they'd stumbled on the man destined to drag Germany out of the abyss and set it on the road to glory. Soon after they first met, Hess heard Hitler speak at a tiny gathering. Unable to contain his excitement, Hess ran back to the hostel and burst into Ilse's room, raving about this amazing man and his electrifying message. A few weeks later, Ilse accompanied him to another Nazi gathering and was equally impressed. Her unquestioning enthusiasm for Hitler's poisonous ideology is evident in a letter she wrote to a schoolfriend, in which she made no attempt to soften her views; 'we are anti-Semites. Constantly, rigorously, without exception. The two basic pillars of our movement – national, and social – are anchored in the meaning of this anti-Semitism.'[3]

By the autumn of 1920, Ilse had completed her *Abitur*, begun a part-time university course in German and library science, and started work at an antiquarian bookshop. Asides from occasional trips outside Munich to ramble in the countryside, she spent the majority of her spare time working for the Nazi movement; delivering leaflets, putting up posters, helping out with the party newspaper and acting as Hess's secretary while he attached himself to Hitler and put his body on the line during the frequent brawls between Nazi supporters and their left-wing opponents.

In recognition of their efforts, Ilse and Hess were granted the privilege of being around Hitler during his downtime, unwinding with his most trusted companions. Ilse – and many others – described how much Hitler enjoyed a good laugh; not one for telling jokes, Hitler did impressions and liked nothing better than listening to a well-told funny story as long as it wasn't about him.

Shy and sensitive, Gerda Buch was a dreamy, artistic child on the verge of adolescence when she first met Hitler, who promptly took her under his wing. 'Uncle Adolf' had a special interest in young people – girls in particular – and was keen to adopt a quasi-guardian role, taking responsibility for their cultural, political and moral welfare. At the time, his main focus was Henriette Hoffmann, the 9-year-old daughter of Heinrich Hoffmann, one of Hitler's closest associates who would become his personal photographer. Every afternoon, while Henriette practised the piano, Hitler would test her knowledge of German myths and folklore. Though he spent less time with Gerda, Hitler lavished her with attention whenever he visited her home.

The reason Hitler was such a regular presence in Gerda's life was her father, Walter Buch, a career soldier. Buch was 19 years old when he joined the army in 1902. Gerda was born in 1909, a year after Buch married her mother. By 1914 he was a first lieutenant, one of the small number of officers who wasn't from an aristocratic background. Serving on the Western Front, Buch gained one promotion after another until he commanded a whole battalion. In 1918, he resigned his commission – disgusted by the Allied peace terms that reduced his beloved army to a meagre 100,000 men – and joined the other disgruntled ex-soldiers milling round Munich, licking their wounds after the disbandment of the *Freikorps* and the collapse of the Kapp Putsch, a military coup launched in spring 1920 and defeated by the largest general strike in German history. Pointed in the direction of Hitler, Buch quickly fell under his spell, declaring that Hitler 'had been sent to the German people by the grace of God'.[4]

Buch was exactly the kind of recruit Hitler was looking for; a representative of the officer class with an untarnished reputation. Buch's natural home in the movement was the Sturmabteilung (SA), better known as the Brownshirts. Hitler needed experienced men like Buch to transform this undisciplined mob of street fighters into an effective paramilitary force. During the summer of 1923, Buch took charge of the 275 SA men based in Nuremberg – some 100 miles from Munich – and began preparing them for action. Once again, Buch would be away from home. Reflecting on her childhood, Gerda complained that her father was 'merely a visitor. He never stayed with us for any length of time.'[5] Ultimately, Buch's most significant contribution to his daughter's young life was introducing her to Hitler.

Before Buch took over in Nuremberg, the Brownshirts acquired a new overall leader, the ex-flying ace and war hero Hermann Goering, whose aerial exploits – he was awarded the prestigious Blue Max for twenty confirmed kills and took over the elite Richthofen squadron after the Red Baron's death – had won him considerable fame. Fighter pilots were genuine celebrities; portrayed as knights of the air engaged in chivalric duels, they excited the public's imagination, offering relief from the grim unglamorous reality of trench warfare. Hermann was in the top rank, a household name. Even though he'd been in Stockholm for the past few years, his reputation still preceded him.

Hitler certainly understood what a potential asset he was. Goering could open doors to the military elite and aristocracy; local power brokers who could help Hitler realise his immediate ambition, to use Munich as the starting point of a national revolution. When they were introduced in late 1922 – shortly after Goering had arrived there and seen Hitler perform at a rally – Hitler invited him to join the movement.

Over the years, Goering made various statements about his decision to align with Hitler. Whether it was a deeply felt act of submission to the chosen one or a calculated gamble on Hitler's ability to mobilise the masses, there's no doubt the fledgling Nazi party offered Goering an opportunity to be a big fish in a small pond. But it was Goering's new Swedish wife Carin who sealed the deal. Already a confirmed anti-Semite, Carin worshipped the ground Hitler walked on. To her, Hitler was like a mythical superhero from a Norse legend: Carin did everything in her power to cement the relationship between the two men.

The first encounter between Carin and her future husband resembled something out of a romance novel. It was a wild stormy night. An icy blizzard was raging. Yet Count Eric von Rosen – a wealthy Swedish explorer – was intent on finding somebody to fly him from Stockholm to his medieval-style castle around 60 miles away where his wife and her sister, the 31-year-old Countess Carin von Foch, were waiting for him. The only pilot prepared to risk such a hazardous journey was Goering. The hair-raising flight tested his skill and nerve to the limit; with visibility almost zero, he managed to land the plane on the frozen lake that lay by the castle. Once Goering had entered its imposing interior – adorned with Aryan-themed tapestries, Nordic sculptures, antique weapons and two huge wrought iron swastikas – and settled by a roaring fire with a brandy, he felt completely at home.

Goering spent much of his childhood at two castles (one in Bavaria, the other in Austria) owned by his godfather and guardian angel Hermann Ritter von Eppenstein, a respected physician. In 1893, while on a trip to Africa, von Eppenstein met Goering's father, a colonial governor, whose young attractive and pregnant wife was suffering from a high fever. With Goering ready to drop, the situation was critical: von Eppenstein stepped in and saved the day. After Goering's father had retired on a barely adequate civil service pension, von Eppenstein offered to take the family in. His motives weren't entirely altruistic: he was having an affair with Goering's mother. Under his castle roofs, she split her time between her rapidly ageing husband and her benefactor.

Von Eppenstein was extremely proud of his noble status – born Jewish, he'd become a Christian to further his medical career, thereby gaining access to influential members of the Prussian elite – and flaunted it whenever possible; fond of pageantry and playing lord of the manor, he hosted baronial banquets accompanied by minstrels in medieval garb.

Carin grew up in similarly baroque surroundings. Her father was an aristocratic colonel, her Anglo-Irish mother came from a brewing dynasty. Carin had four sisters and with the other female members of the family they combined to form their own pantheistic Christian society, the Edelweiss Club – with the flower as their emblem – that boasted its very own chapel, a small but beautifully decorated stone building where they worshipped, sang folk songs and performed séances. Every day during the First World War they knelt and prayed for a German victory.

Carin and Goering's rarefied, fantastical upbringings gave them a grandiose sense of themselves; like lead actors in some great drama. But life had left them both deeply frustrated. At the end of the war, Germany's air force had been banned by the Versailles Treaty, leaving Goering angry and bitter. Addicted to action – from an early age he was obsessed with all things military, as well as hunting and mountain climbing – he became an overnight sensation in Sweden as the star of aerial shows, performing daredevil stunts in front of open-mouthed audiences. But the novelty wore off; he ceased to be the toast of the town. Depressed, he took the gig shuttling civilians back and forth. The fact Goering accepted von Rosen's request, despite the danger, indicates how desperate he was for adventure.

Carin was trapped in a loveless marriage to Nils von Kantzow, an army officer. Wed at 21, she fell pregnant three years later and endured a traumatic birth; though she loved her son Thomas she was ill equipped to be a mother and yearned to escape the suffocating atmosphere of polite society. Having left her 7-year-old son and husband in Stockholm, she'd taken refuge at the count's castle.

From the moment she joined Goering in the grand hall, the two of them were transfixed by each other. Drawn irresistibly together, they began a semi-clandestine affair that rapidly escalated. Carin told her sister that she and Goering were like Tristan and Isolde: 'We have swallowed the love potion and are helpless'; and her letters to him were full of melodramatic declarations such as 'you're everything to me. There is no other like you', and burning desire: 'I kiss everything that is near you.'[6] Inevitably, her husband found out. Divorce was the only option. Carin lost custody of her son in exchange for von Kantzow's financial support.

Once Goering was established in Munich, Carin joined him. After a businesslike civil ceremony in Sweden, they tied the knot again with family and friends present. They lived in a two-storey villa in the suburbs that quickly became a gathering place for Hitler and his cronies. Carin's sister Mary – who would become something of a fixture in their lives – fondly recalled that Hitler seemed totally at ease in Carin's company while she positively shone in his presence.

By late spring 1923, Goering had assumed authority over the Brownshirts and set about whipping them into shape with parade-ground drills and regimental exercises. Writing home, Carin boasted that Goering had transformed 'a rabble … into a veritable army of light': thanks to him, thousands of SA men were now 'a band of eager crusaders ready to march at the Führer's orders'.[7]

2

FUGITIVES AND PRISONERS

arly afternoon, 8 November 1923: Carin was stuck in bed wrestling with a serious case of pneumonia that had made her dangerously ill. Her intensely passionate spirit was contained in a physically frail body. Thin, slightly built, with a raft of health problems, she was especially vulnerable to chest infections. Then her husband appeared with some surprising news. The long-talked-about national revolution was going to begin that night at a beer hall where three of the most powerful men in Bavaria – the state governor, the chief of police and a senior army figure – were hosting a large political meeting. The plan was deceptively simple and wildly ambitious: hijack the event, persuade the triumvirate to hand over the keys to the city, and, with the masses rallying to their standard, march on Berlin.

Hyperinflation had unravelled the fabric of German society; the occupation of the Ruhr by French troops – prompted by disputes over the reparations demanded by the Versailles Treaty – had re-energised the foot soldiers of the nationalist right; there were serious left-wing revolts in Saxony and Thuringia. Conditions seemed ripe. Yet, there was also a growing sense that the worst had passed. Worried they may have missed their chance, Hitler and his cohorts decided to act.

At 8.30 p.m. Hitler, with Hess at his side, stormed into the beer hall, followed soon after by Goering and a squad of SA men. The dignitaries were hauled off stage and the crowd brought to heel. In an upstairs room, a deal was hammered out. The three leading officials promised to support the coup.

By around 11 p.m. a strange calm had descended. Hess, who'd acquired his own set of hostages – including a chief justice, a police president and a Bavarian government minister – was ordered to transport them to a pre-prepared, isolated house 30 miles from Munich and await further instructions. Goering, confident that events were going their way, asked somebody to inform Carin that everything was under control.

It wasn't. After Hitler left the beer hall to monitor events elsewhere, the triumvirate managed to slip away into the night. They immediately mobilised the army and the police, who moved to secure key locations. By morning, it was clear the Putsch had failed.

Determined to make a symbolic gesture of defiance, Hitler, Goering, and the other main players assembled their troops – around 2,000 men – and with banners aloft set off for the town hall, which was guarded by armed police. After a brief stand-off, shots were fired. Hitler dislocated his shoulder in the confusion, which left fourteen Nazis and four police officers dead, while a bullet struck Goering in the thigh, just below the groin. Bleeding profusely, he was whisked away from the chaotic scene and taken in by an elderly Jewish woman who lived nearby. From there, he was moved to a private clinic.

Carin – who had received Goering's upbeat late-night message – was now confronted by the truth. Dragging herself off her sickbed, she rushed to his side. Clearly, he needed proper treatment. Fast. Yet if he stayed in Munich, his arrest was inevitable. So, Carin got him into a car and drove to the villa of an acquaintance near the Austrian border. The following morning, the 10th, they tried to cross but the customs officials recognised the fugitive and dragged him off to the nearest police station. Presumably because of Goering's severe condition, the police were confident he wouldn't escape and left him unguarded, but he slipped out through a window and into a waiting car. At the frontier, the driver used a false passport and concealed Goering under blankets in the back seat. The ruse worked, and they made it across. For now, he was safe from justice.

In all the confusion, Ilse still had no idea what had happened to her boyfriend. Hess had dutifully remained at his post, holed up in the countryside villa with the captives he'd taken from the beer hall, tension mounting with each passing hour. Finally, around mid afternoon, Hess got word of his comrades' ignominious defeat. Afraid the police might arrive any minute, he bundled several petrified and confused hostages into a car and embarked on a bizarre round-around through the surrounding forests while he figured out what to do.

In the end, he abandoned them and disappeared on foot, hoping to find a phone and call Ilse. When Hess eventually did get through to her, Ilse grabbed her bicycle and pedalled off to meet him. Taking turns on her bike, swapping every few miles, they headed back to Munich and Professor Haushofer's house. After a brief discussion, Hess opted to flee. By the next day, he was in Austria.

Meanwhile, Gerda's father was in Nuremberg trying to decide how to respond to the rapidly unfolding events. Though rumours of the Putsch had reached Buch the previous evening, he'd elected to stay put. During the morning, news of the debacle filtered through. Incensed by reports that Hitler had been seriously injured, Buch told his SA men that 'the blood of Hitler would be avenged by the blood of the Jews',[1] but then thought better of it. Instead, Buch was faced with an ultimatum: the authorities had ordered all SA units to disband. Avoiding arrest, Buch refused to comply for another two days before falling into line. Yet he was determined to prevent the SA from disintegrating altogether and on 13 November he was in Munich trying to pick up the pieces.

By then the former head of the SA was in Innsbruck. After a couple of nights at the Hotel Tyrol, a delirious Goering was rushed to hospital. The doctors got to work; his bullet wound closed but re-opened again. He was in constant agony, as Carin explained to her mother in a letter dated 8 December 1923: 'It hurts so much that he bites the pillow, and all I can hear are inarticulate groans … they are giving him morphine every day now, it does nothing to diminish the pain.'[2]

While Goering suffered, Hess was hiding out with various contacts and moving back and forth to Munich to see Ilse – who had fallen ill – and discuss with Haushofer whether or not he should give himself up. As the trial of Hitler and his co-conspirators was going better than Hess could have expected (the judge was sympathetic towards Hitler and let him use the witness stand as a soap box, garnering him both national and international press coverage) he was increasingly tempted to hand himself in.

The verdicts on 1 April 1924 settled the issue. Though guilty of treason – a crime that carried a life sentence – Hitler was given only five years; various technicalities reduced it even further to around eighteen months, and he was eligible for parole after six. Encouraged by this show of leniency, Hess took the plunge, handed himself in on 12 May, received the same sentence as Hitler and joined him in Landsberg prison about 40 miles west of Munich.

Hitler and Hess were confined in a special wing – known as 'The Fortress' – reserved for political prisoners and convicted duellists. Conditions there were extremely relaxed: no prison uniform, no mandatory haircuts. They were allowed to decorate their light, airy cells with pictures and flowers. They could buy tobacco and alcohol and had a daily ration of a litre of beer. With no duties to perform, they lived a life of leisure. They had access to the prison garden. Lunch was at midday, tea and coffee at around 4.30 p.m., supper at 6 p.m. Hot drinks and pastries were served before lights out at 10 p.m. The whole wing resembled a Nazi holiday camp.

Hess, like the other inmates, was permitted six hours' visiting time a week, and Ilse showed up every Saturday. Greeted on the stairs by Hess and Hitler – who would always indulge her with a kiss on the hand – they would then sit down for lunch together. One weekend, Ilse took her previously 'totally un-political' mother to see Hitler; won over by his gracious manners, she joined the party 'as soon as she got back to Munich'.[3]

Given all the free time on their hands, Hitler decided to use it productively and embarked on writing a book. After trying various titles, he plumped for *Mein Kampf*. Furnished with a typewriter, Hitler would bang away with two fingers then go over the results with Hess, who acted as critic and sounding board.

Hess's constant stream of letters to Ilse enthusiastically detailed the development of his emotional bond with Hitler as they mulled over the

progress of the manuscript. After reading Hess his First World War reminiscences, Hitler broke down in tears: 'Suddenly he dropped the page,
buried his head in his hands, and sobbed.'[4] He also confided in Hess
about his feelings regarding women and marriage; though he saw the
attraction, Hitler stated that he would only be able to fulfil his destiny if
he remained single, unencumbered by a wife and children.

All these revelations made Hess feel like he was being shown a rare
glimpse of Hitler's soul, and he shared these intimate moments with Ilse.
She responded by sending a collection of Hölderlin's poems to Hitler,
hoping to further inspire him. Unfortunately for her, Hitler never read
much poetry and he found Hölderlin's verse baffling. He was much
more interested in what Hess's mentor, Professor Haushofer, had to say
over the course of several visits he made to Landsberg, during which he
outlined his philosophy of *Lebensraum*: given the size of its population,
Germany could only survive and prosper if it grew beyond its current
borders and expanded eastwards.

Professor Haushofer later claimed that Hitler was simply not educated enough to grasp the complexity of his theories – 'Hitler never
understood these things and did not have the right outlook for understanding them'[5] – and wilfully misinterpreted their meaning. Haushofer
preferred mass migration to conquest and never endorsed the genocidal
violence that Hitler's racial imperialism demanded. But in Landsberg,
Professor Haushofer may well have planted a seed in Hitler's oddly
fertile brain. Over the coming years, his obsessive hatred of Jews and
Bolsheviks found expression in a grotesque vision of a sprawling
Eastern empire.

On 20 December 1924 – having spent eight and a half months in
jail – Hitler walked out of prison to be greeted by a beaten-up rented
car filled with well-wishers. Accounts vary as to whether Ilse was among
them, but she was definitely there a week later when Hess was released.
That evening, they met Hitler for dinner at his favourite restaurant and
had ravioli, the house speciality. Reunited, they faced an uphill battle to
get the movement back on its feet again.

Hitler was banned from any political activity and the party was
outlawed. His first task was to raise the morale of his most dedicated

followers. Almost immediately, Hitler reconnected with the Buch family. Gerda vividly remembered Hitler sitting by their 'tiled stove' as he reaffirmed his commitment to the struggle: 'If I saw the future as completely black, I wouldn't go on fighting.'[6]

In the meantime, Ilse and the music critic from the party newspaper were hard at work editing the very rough draft of *Mein Kampf* and turning it into a coherent text. On 18 July 1925, the first volume was finally ready for publication. By 1929, it had sold 23,000 copies; by 1932, nearly a quarter of a million; by 1945, 12 million.

One of the 350 people who visited Hitler in prison was Carin Goering. She turned up on 15 April 1924 with the intention of winning Hitler's support for her proposal; she and her husband would go to Italy and establish contact with Mussolini. Hitler was non-committal. Nevertheless, Carin left Landsberg re-inspired by her idol: 'He is a genius, full of love and truth and a burning faith.'[7]

It had been a tough winter. Though Goering had been released from hospital around Christmas, his condition continued to be serious and he was increasingly dependent on morphine. Money was tight, even though their hotel gave them a 30 per cent discount. The Austrian authorities were looking to expel their unwanted guest, and Italy appeared an attractive option. The couple landed in May 1924 and based themselves in Rome after brief stopovers in Venice and Florence.

At the time, Mussolini was busy consolidating his grip on the Italian state; Goering – and Hitler for that matter – were an irrelevance. Though Carin liked to pretend otherwise, Goering never got close to seeing *Il Duce*, his route blocked by a local fascist official who rebuffed his requests for an audience. Goering kept banging on his door, but to no avail.

Living hand-to-mouth in grotty lodgings, their situation became critical. Goering's weight ballooned. His morphine habit was now a full-blown addiction; he contemplated suicide. With her own health precarious, Carin knew they had to leave Italy before it was too late. Sweden was the obvious destination.

While nursing Goering was her main concern, Carin was worried that Hitler might forget about him. Before pitching up in Stockholm, Carin slipped across to Germany, saw Hitler and reassured him that a useful dialogue had been begun with Mussolini. She was careful not to reveal the full extent of Goering's spiral into drug-induced psychosis, his vicious mood swings, aggressive tantrums and erratic behaviour.

Back in Sweden, she contracted TB and was forced to pawn some of her possessions to feed his cravings. At her wits' end – and with her family's support – Carin had her husband admitted to a nursing home. Unable and unwilling to adjust to lower doses of painkillers, Goering ran amok, smashing medicine cabinets and assaulting staff. He was put in a straightjacket and carted off to the Långbro asylum. Locked in a cell and forced to go cold turkey, Goering's physical withdrawal was accompanied by nightmarish hallucinations and paranoid delusions. He ranted and raved about the Jews and their fiendish plots to kill him; according to his medical reports, he thought that a 'Jewish Doctor wanted to cut out his heart', and Abraham – from the Old Testament – was 'driving a red-hot nail into his back'.[8]

Yet Carin remained steadfast, convinced he'd recover. After ten weeks – and a brief relapse that led to another spell inside – he was fit enough to re-enter the world. Ashamed and reluctant to admit how far he'd fallen, Goering rarely spoke about this period in his life. Years later, he confessed to Carin's son that she saved him from oblivion.

3

MATCHMAKING

In the autumn of 1927, the government announced a general amnesty that meant Goering was able to return to Germany without fear of arrest: he found the party in the process of reconstruction and consolidation as it prepared itself to take a new route to power via the ballot box.

Hitler had spent much of his time since his release touring the country, uniting the fractured Nazi movement and reasserting his supreme leadership. Hess – who was now Hitler's personal secretary – stuck to him like glue wherever he went, leaving Ilse to her own devices. Though no less devoted to the Nazi cause, she was nevertheless losing patience with the snail-like progress of their relationship. After seven sexless years, Hess seemed no closer to popping the question. Despite shrugging off the delay – 'we were too busy to get married; he was away all the time and I was working'[1] – Ilse was contemplating moving abroad for a while. She'd completed her university course and her part-time job at the antiquarian bookshop was hardly enough to tie her to Munich. Which left Hess.

Ilse liked to claim that it was Hitler who settled the matter while the three of them were eating at the *Café Osteria*, one of his favourite hangouts. Ilse was debating her future when Hitler took her hand, placed it in Hess's and asked her if 'she'd ever thought about marrying this man?'[2] Her answer was obviously 'yes': unable to deny Hitler's wishes, Hess stopped procrastinating. After all – as he explained in a letter to his parents – Ilse was his 'good comrade' and 'loyal friend', they were 'fond of each other' and shared the same ideas about life. Compared to other women he'd encountered, she was 'an angel'.[3]

Having abandoned conventional religion, Ilse and Hess decided against a church wedding. On 20 December 1927, they got married at a small civil ceremony; Hitler and Professor Haushofer acted as witnesses. The newly-weds were very low on cash, but Ilse was able to obtain a loan through Winifred Wagner, mistress of the Bayreuth Festival that was held every year in the composer's honour. Winifred had briefly known Ilse before the war and they were re-introduced after Winifred befriended Hitler.

A huge Wagner fan, Hitler was delighted to make her acquaintance, while she regarded him with barely concealed awe. Her husband, Siegfried Wagner, was a bisexual bohemian twice her age who'd bowed to pressure from his mother –widow of Richard Wagner – to do the right thing and produce some heirs. Winifred had dutifully given birth to four children in rapid succession and together they provided Hitler with a kind of extended family. Her eldest daughter recalled how he would often drop by late at night and wake them in their nursery to tell them 'gruesome tales of his adventures'.[4]

Winifred was fond of Ilse and happy to help the young couple; in return, a grateful Hess kept her informed of Hitler's movements. With the money, Ilse and Hess got a small apartment in Munich. Not that co-habitation did anything to improve their sex life: Ilse complained to a friend that she 'felt like a convent girl'.[5]

Hess also insisted that she submit to the Nazis' new rules about female participation in the movement: she could retain her party membership – during this period around 8 per cent were women – but no more than that. Women were barred from taking on any official roles, while more mainstream conservative and right-wing parties had dedicated women's sections putting forward candidates for elections. Ilse could have joined one of the Nazi-orientated women's groups – like the German Women's Order (Deutscher Frauenorden, DFO) founded in 1923 – that were officially affiliated to the party in January 1928, but given her place in Hitler's hierarchy that option was closed to her.

However, this did not mean that Ilse was relegated to the sidelines. Her proximity to Hitler – who trusted her, respected her, and valued her loyalty – gave her a different but no less influential form of power. Her diplomatic skills and human touch were required when Hitler needed to find a solution to a tricky and sensitive personal matter; his relationship with his 19-year-old niece Geli Raubel.

Geli first caught Hitler's eye when she visited him in prison with her mother, who was Hitler's half-sister. Once she'd finished school, Geli was fully integrated into Hitler's inner circle after he invited her mother to become housekeeper at the modest cottage he was renting from Nazi sympathisers – who gave him a cut-price rate – near the small mountain town of Berchtesgaden; its spectacular location and tranquil atmosphere provided a perfect setting for long, lazy afternoons spent having picnics, swimming in lakes and strolling in forests. His entourage all embraced Geli; she was unpretentious, natural, light-hearted and full of fun. And she had a very positive effect on Hitler's moods. Ilse liked her. Hess thought she was sharp-witted. Heinrich Hoffmann called her 'an enchantress' who 'put everybody in the best of spirits';[6] even his daughter Henriette, who had every reason to resent Geli replacing her as Hitler's young protégée, found her 'incredibly charming'.[7]

In company, Hitler gave Geli the 'Uncle Adolf' treatment. Yet his feelings were far from pure; he'd become seriously besotted with her. The trouble was neither Geli nor Hitler's dashing chauffeur, Emil Maurice, realised this; they'd fallen for each other and were talking about marriage. Using her age as an excuse, a furious Hitler confronted Geli and demanded she drop Emil. Geli refused. Frightened of losing her, Hitler asked Ilse to broker a deal: the young lovers would have to wait two years to marry. In the meantime, they could only be together in Hitler's presence. Geli accepted these terms and on Christmas Eve 1937 she relayed them to Emil in a letter: 'Two whole years during which we may kiss each other only now and then and always under the watchful eye of Uncle Adolf.' Geli also acknowledged the key role Ilse played: 'She was so nice. She was the only person who believed that you really love me.'[8]

Hitler got what he wanted; within a few months Emil was gone and forgotten. In late 1929, Geli moved into a spare room in Hitler's new apartment. Ilse continued to take an interest in Geli's life, partly out of genuine concern, but mostly because Hitler needed a reliable source of information so he could keep track of Geli when he was away from Munich.

On 18 September 1927, Margaret Boden shared a three-hour train journey from Munich to Berlin with a bespectacled, unremarkable-looking young man called Heinrich Himmler. They struck up a conversation and by the end of the ride a connection had been made. Having gone their separate ways, they began exchanging letters, an almost daily habit that would continue throughout their relationship, largely because they were more often apart than together.

At 35, Margaret was eight years older than Himmler. From a comfortable land-owning family, she was just old enough to join the German Red Cross in 1914 and become a nurse. Established in the 1860s, it had 6,000 full-time angels of mercy available for duty when the First World War began. Nursing was considered a suitable vocation for women from upper- and middle-class backgrounds, like Margaret, and after completing her training she donned her uniform (which resembled a nun's habit) and was deployed to a field hospital. These were usually established in villages near the front, often in churches or schools, and furnished with 200 beds.

Vulnerable to shelling and air raids, the staff were rotated every six months. But no matter where Margaret went, she could not escape the cruel and heart-breaking parade of maimed, mutilated and traumatised casualties. The impact her experience of frontline nursing had on her is hard to quantify. How do you measure the loss of innocence? Of faith in the goodness of humanity? She was only 25 when the fighting stopped; from then on Margaret always seemed much older than her years.

Soon after the war, she got married. Very little is known about this union except that it was unsuccessful and the couple divorced after two years. In 1923, with financial help from her father, Margaret bought into a private clinic in Berlin run by a Jewish gynaecologist. As head nurse, her speciality was homeopathy – herbal cures and natural remedies.

Himmler was equally fascinated by alternative medicine. While he wasn't a technophobe, Himmler considered mass industrialisation to be an essentially alien force corrupting the essence of the German soul. He believed in revisiting peasant cultures and utilising the accumulated folk knowledge of earlier generations. More to the point, he had been afflicted by persistent and chronic stomach problems since childhood (during elementary school, he was off sick for 160 days) and the state of his guts was a recurring theme in their letters. Margaret put his condition down to stress and overwork – 'your stomach is just taking revenge for what you constantly put it through'[9] – and she recommended proper rest supplemented by doses of mustard, vinegar and onions.

Part of the attraction for Margaret could have been that Himmler reminded her of the young men she'd cared for during the war who often treated their nurses like surrogate mothers; in one letter she asked if Himmler had any pictures of himself as a little boy. Equally well, aside from finding her blonde hair and blue eyes very appealing, her sturdy frame and slightly severe manner gave her a matronly air that might have reminded Himmler of his doting mother. She'd always spoiled and indulged her sickly boy; she still sent him food parcels and did his washing.

Himmler's severe, stamp-collecting father was a head teacher at a well-respected *Gymnasium* – which Himmler attended – and he had tutored the son of Bavarian royalty, adding extra polish to the family name. Himmler grafted hard and did his best to live up to his father's high standards.

Aged 14 at the outbreak of the First World War, Himmler couldn't wait to be involved; yet in 1918, when he was finally old enough to begin basic training, he found it gruelling and was often homesick. The armistice came before he could be deployed at the front. Crestfallen, and reluctant to give up his uniform, he drifted in and out of various paramilitary groups, ending up in the SA in time to make a brief cameo appearance during the beer hall revolt.

By the mid 1920s he was working flat out for the party and had switched his allegiance from Gregor Strasser – who had emerged with a more left-wing orientated version of Nazism – to Hitler; Himmler's attachment to Hitler was total, a deep-seated emotional fixation that bordered on worship. Shortly before his train journey with Margaret, Himmler had been made deputy of the SS; formed to provide Hitler with an elite bodyguard, it was at that time a tiny fledgling outfit with no clear identity.

Though their early correspondence featured some tenderness and romantic word-play, it also revealed Margaret's essential pessimism – 'love without sorrow and worry is something I just cannot imagine' – and negative view of human nature. She was suspicious of new people and dreaded social interaction, yet at the same time felt a deep and crippling loneliness. Contemplating New Year's Eve, she bemoaned her fate: "Tomorrow is a dreadful day when everyone is having a party and I must be alone. It really is awful.'[10]

During their second rendezvous at a hotel in a snow-bound Bavarian town, a three-day stay just before Christmas, they became physically intimate. Margaret was not a particularly sexual person and Himmler was a virgin. A few years earlier, he'd sworn off women altogether, having read a quasi-scientific tract that urged young men to remain chaste and channel their abundant and valuable sexual energy into more useful activities. Choosing celibacy was a convenient way for Himmler to make a virtue out of his abject failure with women; sex both scared and fascinated him.

In his student diaries, Himmler often wrote about how appalled he was by young women who were too free with their bodies, while fantasising about what it might be like to surrender himself to such wild, uninhibited creatures; at the same time, he managed to alienate his two closest male companions by falling for their girlfriends, whose rejection of him led Himmler to conclude that they were morally suspect as well. From his perspective, Margaret was an ideal mate; she had some experience but not enough to make him feel totally inadequate in the bedroom. Whether or not they had intercourse is unclear, but their letters after they parted again reflect this shift in their relationship. They started using nicknames and terms of endearment; Himmler even dared to make references to her 'beautiful dear body'.[11]

Having crossed this line together, they decided to get married as soon as possible. But there were several stumbling blocks: Himmler was intensely busy doing his bit to boost the Nazis' chances in the upcoming

Reichstag elections – scheduled for 20 May – and their wedding plans depended on Margaret selling her share of the Berlin clinic and using the money to purchase a plot of land; they were going to become farmers. This was a long-cherished ambition of Himmler's. In the autumn of 1919, he began studying agriculture in Munich, a course that combined book learning with work on a farm. After graduating in August 1922, he got job for a fertiliser company, which lasted a year before he quit to join the Nazi party. Margaret was raised on her father's large farm and was familiar with dealing with livestock and growing crops.

However, the process of disengaging herself from her Jewish business partner took longer than expected. In her letters, Margaret made snide remarks at his expense, calling him 'riff-raff' and 'Jewish rabble'; to her, he was living proof that all Jews were equally untrustworthy, noting that 'the others are no better'.[12]

Though there is little evidence to suggest Margaret held the same twisted and outlandish views as her fiancé, she shared the prejudices of the social milieu she was raised in, including its engrained racism and snobbery. Margaret's anti-Semitism was an instinctive reflex, as was her fear and mistrust of the lower classes, whether rural or urban. Keen to educate her politically, Himmler sent her copies of his speeches and pamphlets, and well-known racist tomes, which she dutifully read and tried to sound enthusiastic about. But she was not an extremist and often found Himmler's violent language troubling: 'Why do you reach for the dagger in such a bloodthirsty way? After all, being a conservative is a nice thing to be.'[13]

Ultimately, they spent more time completing the puzzle books they both enjoyed than discussing the philosophical and historical roots of Nazism. Reluctant even to attend a party rally, she was jealous of Hitler's hold over him and openly expressed her dissatisfaction: 'If only you didn't have to go around with the Boss anymore. He takes up so much time.' Himmler responded by reminding her that he was a revolutionary, not a 'spineless civil servant'.[14]

With the May election over, and the negotiations about her exit from the clinic almost complete, they wed in a Berlin registry office on 3 July 1928. Margaret's father and brother acted as witnesses. None of

Himmler's family were present; his parents were committed Catholics and struggled to accept his son's marriage to a Protestant woman. There was no honeymoon. Himmler was off attending both the annual party rally and the Bayreuth Festival during August. The newly-weds managed a three-day break away in early September before he disappeared again.

The Reichstag election results – the party got less than 3 per cent of the vote – were a sharp reminder of how far the Nazis were from achieving their aims. Their dismal showing was largely due to the phoenix-like recovery of the Weimar Republic from the low point of 1923, boosted by large loans from America, agreement over sustainable reparation payments, the thawing of diplomatic tensions with Germany's European neighbours, and the public's overwhelming desire for something resembling normal life.

One of the dozen Nazi delegates to enter the Reichstag was a rejuvenated Goering. With Carin back from Sweden, he quickly accepted a key role in the party's development, attracting the great and good and tapping them for much-needed funds. However, to raise money he needed money, or at least the appearance of it. Luckily for him, his wartime achievements still counted for something: Lufthansa – Germany's largest civil aviation company – was looking to boost its profile and picked Goering as its representative, bankrolling him to the tune of 1,000 RM (Reichsmark) a month.

He and Carin moved into an opulent apartment. The couple were soon hosting soirees for the cream of society; aristocratic and royal representatives of Germany's former imperial dynasties; captains of industry and influential bankers. To their guests, Carin and her husband presented a respectable, moderate front, allaying fears about Hitler's intentions. A decorative, charming hostess, Carin became a different animal when entertaining her fellow Nazis, diving head-first into their debates and arguments. Though Carin was a woman, her interventions were tolerated, even welcomed – apparently Goebbels particularly enjoyed these discussions – because of her undoubted radicalism and ideological fervour. In a letter she wrote to her mother around that time Carin spat venom at her enemies: 'Every-day the Communists parade with their crooked noses and red flags with the Star of David.'[15]

One of Goering's other colleagues who also managed to get elected that year was Gerda's father. Since the Munich Putsch, Walter Buch had toyed with various careers – lawyer, teacher, and wine and cigar salesman – but never abandoned hope that Hitler would rise from the ashes. His faith was rewarded in November 1927. Due to the fact that his father had been a high court judge, Buch was put in charge of the USCHLA, the Nazi Party Court, set up to deal with internal disputes and breaches of discipline.

By then, Gerda had finished high school, passed her *Abitur*, and was about to become a kindergarten teacher, a logical career for someone whose chief interests were arts and crafts, reading German children's stories and playing folk music on her guitar. Her younger brother recalled that 'she was never happier than when she was with children, drawing with them or making lino cuts'.[16] However, the fact she'd chosen to enter such a caring, nurturing profession did not mean she'd rejected her father's politics. Having grown up around Hitler and his ideas, Gerda failed to develop a mind of her own: her worldview was completely shaped by Nazism, her belief absolute.

If anything, Gerda was more fanatical than her father, something that would become clear after she became involved with a stocky, thick-necked, roguishly handsome macho man called Martin Bormann, who was a relative latecomer to the movement, joining the party in February 1927. He was briefly a press officer in his local area, then moved into the SA, which is how he first came into contact with Gerda's father. Though most of the Nazi elite regarded Bormann as their social inferior, a boorish yob lacking culture – one rival compared him to a pig – his background was solidly middle class. His father's family were from humble roots but he made a career as a trumpeter in a military band and after leaving his regiment he entered the postal service as a clerk and worked his way steadily up the ladder.

In later life, Bormann spoke proudly of his father's achievements, but the truth is he barely knew him; Bormann's father died when he was 3.

His mother, faced with the prospect of raising Bormann, his younger brother Albert, and two stepchildren from her dead husband's previous marriage, quickly got hitched to her widowed brother-in-law – the director of a local bank – who had five children of his own. As a result, Bormann grew up in a very large family, but he didn't like any of his siblings and felt neglected by his stepfather, who he came to despise.

Nevertheless, there was enough money around to send the young Bormann to a private prep school; other than displaying a talent for arithmetic, he struggled with most subjects. Not academic enough for a traditional *Gymnasium*, at 14 Bormann went to a technical high school – slightly less prestigious but no less exclusive – and was leaning towards agricultural studies when he was called up in June 1918, too late to see any fighting.

Demobbed, Bormann decided not to return home and got a job as the foreman on a large estate of 810 acres, where the owner recognised his head for figures and put him in charge of the accounts and the payroll. His boss was an arch-nationalist who mostly hired ex-*Freikorps* men to work his land. In this milieu, Bormann got involved in a variety of extreme right-wing anti-Semitic associations.

On the night of 31 May 1923 Bormann's life took a significant turn when he was involved in the sadistic murder of a former employee, Walter Kadow, who'd run up considerable debts and run off without paying them. For some inexplicable reason, Kadow made the fatal mistake of returning to the scene of the crime. Spurred on by rumours that Kadow was a communist agent, Bormann planned a nasty surprise for him; he convinced half a dozen estate workers to kidnap Kadow and give him a thorough beating. The assailants got Kadow stupidly drunk and then – using a horse and cart provided by Bormann – carried him to a nearby forest where they fractured his skull with a tree branch, cut his throat, shot him twice in the head, stripped him naked, burned his clothes and buried his broken body.

Bormann was arrested alongside the murderers – who included Rudolf Höss, the future commandant of Auschwitz – and spent over six months awaiting trial. On 12 March 1924, they had their day in court. The killers were sentenced to ten years; Bormann, one year. In prison, he knuckled down and adapted to the draconian rules and mind-numbing labour. Bormann remembered that he had to 'paste together all sorts of paper containers for cigarettes, drugs, candy, and gut strings for instruments' in order to fill his quota of 1,500 cartons a day. At the same time, he took advantage of the lack of distractions to contemplate his 'own ideas, especially political ones'.[17] He left prison even more convinced that the enemies of the German people needed to be punished.

Bormann returned to the estate to pick up where he left off, but on arrival discovered that he wasn't welcome there any longer; the owner had found out that Bormann had been having an affair with his wife, Ehrengard. Though Bormann never openly acknowledged their relationship, he maintained a correspondence with Ehrengard for the next twenty years and would occasionally pay her visits, usually late at night.

Bormann possessed a relentless and unrestrained libido that he made no effort to control, seeking to satisfy his sexual hunger whenever and wherever he could without any regard for social convention. It's not difficult to grasp why Bormann found Gerda so irresistible; slender and long-limbed, strikingly attractive, she emitted the radiance of youth. Equally, an association with the daughter of such a prominent Nazi could only smooth his passage through the ranks of the party.

His rugged masculinity appealed to the inexperienced Gerda. Dating him would also be an act of rebellion against her father; Buch thought Bormann was a worthless ruffian. However, he decided not to interfere on the basis that Gerda's schoolgirl crush would pass as soon as she realised how incompatible they were.

But events got the better of Buch. Every Sunday, Bormann would drive his Opel to the Buch home just outside Munich and spend the afternoon with Gerda under her mother's supervision. In April 1929, after returning from one of their long walks, Bormann formally asked for her hand in marriage. With the engagement official, the couple were allowed a little more freedom and at some point around the beginning of August, Bormann took Gerda's virginity. She immediately fell pregnant.

They were married on 2 September, with Hitler and Hess acting as witnesses. In the wedding photograph, there is a sharp contrast between Gerda – dressed in white and wearing a veil and a myrtle wreath – and her jack-booted husband and the other guests, all in full uniform: yet none of the men in the picture had any doubt that Gerda belonged with them.

Some miles outside Munich, Margaret Himmler was also expecting a child. But her husband had other priorities; since becoming head of the SS on 4 January 1929 – when he famously declared that he'd shoot his own mother if Hitler asked him to – he was totally absorbed by his mission to create an elite force of racially pure warriors.

Though Himmler had overseen renovations to their modest house and the construction of the chicken hutches, he was soon gone, leaving her to manage the farm. Her situation was not unusual. Much of the burden of running Germany's small farms was shouldered by the wives – nearly 80 per cent of those employed in this type of agriculture were female family members – while their husbands sought more lucrative work in the cities. Aside from the poultry, Margaret had to tend to geese, rabbits, turkeys and a pig, plus a variety of fruit and vegetables; as time went on, the couple also hoped to cultivate healing herbs.

The pregnancy only made her life more onerous and demanding. From the road, Himmler ordered her not to work too hard, but maintaining the farm was an all-consuming task, especially if it was ever going to break even. Her health suffered. Both Margaret and the baby were at risk. When Himmler returned home from the party rally on 7 August 1928, she was in agony. Himmler whisked her off to a clinic and the following day their daughter Gudrun was delivered by Caesarean section.

Margaret remained in hospital for the next three weeks. On her release, Himmler hired a nanny to help her when he was away. Unfortunately, Margaret couldn't stand her – she was 'disrespectful and lazy'[18] – and requested a replacement, the first of many domestic servants who failed to live up to her expectations.

By the New Year, Margaret was back to the daily grind. She dug potatoes, chopped wood, trimmed branches, carted manure, harvested elderberries and cranberries and tended to the mushrooms sprouting in the cellar. All this physical labour took its toll, and she stopped having periods. In a letter, Himmler advised her to take hot baths and drink mulled wine with cinnamon, and speculated that the problem stemmed from 'her inner anxiety';[19] he completely failed to recognise that his prolonged absences were the main reason Margaret was so stressed out.

Gerda suffered no ill effects from her pregnancy. On 14 April 1930 she gave birth to a son who was named Adolf, for obvious reasons. Since Hess had taken Bormann under his wing, he and Ilse became the godparents. Eleven days later, Bormann was promoted and took control of the Party Aid Fund, which doled out insurance payments for the growing number of Nazis hurt or killed during violent confrontations with their opponents.

Aside from his official party duties, Bormann was successfully worming his way into Hitler's entourage and in 1930 Hitler gave him a task that required secrecy and discretion; checking out the ancestry of a 17-year-old girl whom Hitler had met at Heinrich Hoffmann's photographic studio, where she was working as an assistant. Hitler had taken a shine to her and wanted to know if she was from good Aryan stock. After completing a thorough investigation, Bormann was able to confirm that Eva Braun did not have a drop of Jewish blood.

4

ARRIVALS AND DEPARTURES

During the summer of 1930, the recently divorced Magda Quandt was looking for something to do. Her ex-husband had granted her a generous settlement: a spacious apartment in a fashionable part of Berlin, a healthy allowance and access to his country estate. Magda was sophisticated, multilingual, well-travelled, elegant, poised, at ease in elevated company and never short of male admirers; a life of gilded leisure beckoned.

She'd met her ex-husband, Gunther Quandt, in 1919 when he was 37 and she was 18. They spent a train journey together as she travelled from Berlin back to the elite finishing school she'd entered that year after passing her *Abitur*. Quandt was so overwhelmed by her that he kept showing up at Magda's college until they were granted sufficient time alone together for him to propose marriage. Flattered by the attention of such a successful man – Quandt had interests in textiles, chemicals and automobiles, including a controlling stake in BMW – Magda accepted. After a short grace period, they wed on 4 January 1921.

Magda's sudden plunge into married life suggested that she was seeking security after a disjointed childhood. Her mother divorced her father, an engineer, when Magda was 3, then remarried two years later. Magda's stepfather was a Jewish businessman whom she adored. The family moved to Brussels and Magda was sent to a strict Catholic convent school.

In 1914, Magda returned to Germany and was enrolled in a *Gymnasium*. During the war, her mother separated from Magda's stepfather. As a result, Magda was reunited with her biological father, who introduced her to Buddhism, while the older brother of a Jewish schoolfriend gave her a crash course in Zionism. Her genuine interest in both these wildly different philosophies withered when she became a housewife.

Magda inherited Quandt's two children from his first marriage. The couple then adopted three orphans, and in 1922 Magda gave birth to a son named Harald. Suddenly in charge of a large household and the servants that went with it, Magda did her best to cope while her husband focused on accumulating more and more wealth, locking himself in his study night after night, devising new ways to exploit Germany's see-sawing economy.

Quandt's idea of a good evening out was a formal dinner dance and home by ten; Magda was a stunning, lively young woman aching to sample what Berlin had to offer. The capital boasted the most spectacular and varied night-life in Europe, but Magda had to drag her heels at home. Perhaps sensing her restlessness, Quandt took her to London and Paris and together they made several transatlantic trips; a vacation to the USA and Mexico, and a longer visit to the east coast that combined business with pleasure; Magda was in her element, playing her part to perfection.

But opening Magda's eyes to the wider world only made the restricted nature of her Berlin existence more apparent. To make matters worse, her stepson – who was entering late adolescence – had developed a serious crush on her. Aware of the danger, Quandt and Magda decided to send him away to Paris to study. Shortly after his arrival there he was rushed into hospital suffering from acute appendicitis; sepsis set in following a botched operation, and within a few days he was dead.

The fraying connection holding the marriage together snapped. Soon after, Magda embarked on a torrid love affair with a young student. There are several competing theories about who he was, but no concrete evidence to support them. But those close to Magda agreed it was far more than a casual fling; she tried to break it off but couldn't, her feelings too strong to control. Quandt found out and divorce beckoned. Facing the prospect of losing everything – the divorce laws were heavily weighted towards the husband, especially if he was the injured party – Magda accidentally discovered some of Quandt's old love letters and used them to divert attention away from her and on to him. Fearing public embarrassment, Quandt gave her what she needed to continue living in style.

But Magda was dissatisfied and lacking purpose. Previously, she hadn't given much thought to politics, but in Berlin it was impossible to ignore the daily clashes between the Nazis and their opponents. Urged on by several friends, Magda attended a large Nazi rally where the main attraction was Joseph Goebbels.

Other than Hitler, Goebbels was the Nazis' most effective public speaker, peppering his invective with acerbic remarks and withering character assassinations, whipping up the audience as he went, bristling with aggression. He was extremely intelligent and highly educated, with a PhD in literature from Heidelberg University. Yet he was full of resentment and thwarted ambition; his attempts at being a writer – he produced several plays and a dire autobiographical novel – had proved fruitless, while his diminutive size, club foot and pronounced limp had marked him out for ridicule from a young age.

From a lower middle-class family where money was always tight (his father was a book-keeper in a factory) Goebbels was still able to attend a Christian-run *Gymnasium*; his parents were devout Catholics who hoped he'd enter the priesthood. Goebbels was a gifted student and his performance during his *Abitur* exams put him top of the class. Unfit for military service, he enrolled at the University of Bonn in April 1917, and studied there – and at several other institutions – before completing his doctorate in 1921. Three years later he joined the Nazi movement, attracted by its uncompromising attitude; Goebbels had nothing but contempt for the Weimar Republic, was thoroughly anti-Semitic and despised mainstream society.

Goebbels directed his anger at the upper class, the business elite and Jewish finance capital. Berlin based – where the movement adopted a more socialist stance, hoping to lure the city's working class away from the dreaded communists – he distinguished himself as an expert propagandist; his newspaper *Der Angriff* was a model of its kind. While initially uncertain about Hitler's credentials, by the late 1920s he was totally sub-servient to the Führer's genius: 'The born tribune of the people, the coming dictator.'[1]

Magda was inspired by the rally and Goebbels scorching rhetoric. She joined the party and dutifully read *Mein Kampf* and *The Myth of the 20th Century*, a rambling mishmash concocted by Alfred Rosenberg, the Nazi's self-appointed philosopher. Her early exposure to several all-embracing systems of thought – the Catholicism drilled into her by the Belgian nuns, her father's Buddhism, and her teenage friend's Zionism – had left her with a need to believe in something. She may not have fully realised it, but she'd always been searching for a cause to follow.

Magda quickly became leader of the local Nazi women's group, but her presence caused friction with the other members, who objected to taking orders from such an overprivileged lady. Frustrated, Magda set her sights higher and applied for work at Goebbels's propaganda depart-ment, where he couldn't fail to notice her. Struck by Magda's obvious class and beauty, Goebbels asked her to take responsibility for his private archive, hoping that working in such close proximity would make it easier for him to seduce her.

About six weeks before Magda entered Goebbels's life, the Nazis scored a spectacular breakthrough: on 14 September 1930 the party polled around 18 per cent of the vote in the Reichstag elections. The Wall Street Crash and the Depression that it unleashed ripped away the shaky foun-dations of the Weimar Republic, wiped out the centre ground of politics – pushing voters to the extremes – and concentrated power in the hands of a conservative clique around President Hindenburg, an ageing figure-head whose reputation rested on his exploits as one of Germany's most prominent military commanders during the First World War. Elected in 1925, he was meant to guarantee stability, but with the country plunged into deep despair, his influence proved largely malevolent.

In 1930, Hindenburg triggered Article 48 of the constitution, which gave him the authority to appoint the chancellor and govern without recourse to the Reichstag. Rather than deal with the eco-nomic emergency, the new cabinet simply poured oil on the flames by pursuing deflationary measures, sucking money out of the system;

banks folded, businesses went under and unemployment spiralled out of control. The immediate beneficiaries were the Nazis. For the first time they had the resources to mount a coordinated national campaign and their increased visibility, against a backdrop of mounting crisis, paid dividends.

Throughout the year, Goering had campaigned tirelessly. Despite persistent ill health, Carin gave her husband as much support as she could as he engaged in backstairs intrigues and addressed large crowds all across Germany. Her spirits lifted by the result, the couple staged a luxurious party on 13 October, attended by Hitler, Hess, Goebbels, and other prominent figures, to celebrate this transformation in their fortunes.

One of those flocking to Hitler's banner was the teenager Lina von Osten, whose older brother – already a confirmed Nazi supporter – persuaded her to accompany him to a party meeting and she left it a convert, energised by the dynamism of a movement geared towards the young; they would be the main beneficiaries of a bright new future. The party's anti-Semitism was also a factor. Lina loathed the Polish Jews who'd settled in her quiet corner of the world: to her, they were like an alien species.

Lina had seized the first opportunity she had to abandon her family home on the island of Fehmarn (on the north-eastern tip of Germany, facing the Baltic) and strike out on her own. Not that she disliked her parents, but her village was a parochial backwater, while her father's noble ancestry was a constant reminder of what was gone forever: descended from land-owning Danish aristocrats who had over time lost their extensive properties, her father was a humble teacher. During the hyperinflation of the early 1920s, Lina's family's assets dwindled even further and they had to move into the red-brick school building where her father worked.

Having decided to become a teacher herself – at the time, around a third of the teaching profession were women – Lina headed to the mainland port of Kiel to complete her training at a technical high school, staying at a boarding house for female students. As she neared the end of her course, Lina and a few friends attended a ball on 6 December 1930, and it was during what was otherwise a dull evening that Lina made the acquaintance of 27-year-old naval officer Reinhard Heydrich.

Much has been made of Heydrich's supposedly ideal Aryan physiognomy, at least in comparison to the other top Nazis. Tall, blond, with an athlete's build – a physically weak child, he'd taken up sports to get fitter and excelled at running, swimming and fencing – and no doubt impressive in a uniform, he also had an abnormally large head, narrow eyes, a slit for a mouth and jug ears. Lina found him intriguing – 'I felt sympathy for this purposeful yet reserved young man'[2] – and agreed to a rendezvous the next day. In her memoirs, she breathlessly described how Heydrich opened his heart to her over a series of long walks, a visit to the theatre and a meal in a restaurant, and then asked her to marry him during their third evening together.

Lina liked to suggest that their love was written in the stars and could not be denied; others have speculated that his sudden proposal was a necessary prelude to getting her into bed. But there is an alternative explanation. Heydrich was involved with another woman and though the evidence is somewhat confused it seems likely that she'd already had sex with him on the assumption that he'd do the decent thing. Was Heydrich in such a hurry to wed Lina because he was anxious to break free of this other entanglement? If so, his reprieve was only temporary: the jilted woman would come back to haunt him.

Beyond the powerful physical attraction between them, Lina and Heydrich shared some key characteristics. Both were fixed on escaping their backgrounds and forging a different destiny for themselves. They were stubborn and extremely ambitious. They each had a cold, calculating streak. Neither suffered fools gladly. Both had an inflated sense of their own worth and felt that the majority of people were inferior beings.

One of the things that set Heydrich apart was his musical talent. His father was a minor composer who ran a successful music school in their home town of Halle. Heydrich took up the violin at an early age and put in many hours of disciplined, dedicated and exacting practice. Not only did he develop a phenomenal technique – testimony to his work ethic and perfectionism – but his interpretations of classical pieces displayed a rare sensitivity and emotional range. Lina described him as an 'artist' who could 'translate feelings into sound'.[3]

Rather than follow in his father's footsteps, Heydrich chose the navy and joined up in 1922. Unpopular with his fellow cadets – who found him aloof and patronising – they considered his violin playing to be a sign of effeminate weakness, and constantly poked fun at him. But their insults bounced off Heydrich; he was used to being taunted. At school, his precociousness and persistent over-achievement made him a target from day one. All that mattered to him was whether his superiors thought he was officer material.

They did, and in 1926, after a six-month cruise, he was made a *Leutnant zur See* (ensign). In 1928, he became an *Oberleutnant zur See* (sub-lieutenant) and underwent special training as a wireless operator. Given further advancement was likely, Lina now saw no need to take up a teaching job; besides, nobody expected a professional woman to continue working after marriage. The couple visited both sets of parents and gained their approval. Then they hit the buffers: Heydrich's former girlfriend, distressed by the shabby way she'd been treated, was out for revenge.

The actual identity of this mystery woman is unknown; the general consensus is that her father was an important man with personal connections to the upper echelons of the navy. A complaint about ungentlemanly conduct – she accused Heydrich of trying to force himself on her – was made to the appropriate authorities and Heydrich had to appear before a naval court. All records of the proceedings were destroyed, though eye-witnesses contend that it was Heydrich's contemptuous and arrogant attitude that sealed his fate rather than the charges against him. On 30 April 1931 he was dismissed from the navy. Lina said that he was so shattered by the verdict that he had a total breakdown, locking himself in his room for days on end, smashing furniture and weeping uncontrollably, and she had to piece him back together again.

Whether true or not – and it's hard to imagine the man Hitler called 'Iron Heart' behaving like a hysterical child – the most startling thing about the whole incident is Lina's unswerving loyalty. Under the circumstances, nobody would have blamed her if she'd called off the engagement. She was only 19, so this was hardly her last chance of happiness. Clearly, Lina was convinced that with her guidance Heydrich could still rise to the top.

By late February 1931, Magda and Goebbels had begun sleeping together. From the start, the erotic charge between them was intense, a magnetic force that drew them together. Enraptured, Goebbels was walking on air: 'It's like I'm dreaming. So full of satisfied bliss.'[4] His sunny mood, however, did not last. The initial phase of the relationship was very volatile – if his diaries are anything to go by it was either agony or ecstasy without much in between – and they both had doubts about what they were doing. The trigger for screaming rows and agonised soul-searching was the re-emergence of Magda's younger lover.

One of the most corrosive aspects of Goebbels's character was his all-consuming jealousy. While it suited his gargantuan ego to be with a woman as desirable as Magda, he couldn't bear the thought of her with another man, despite the fact he rejected monogamy as an outdated bourgeois convention and made no secret of his own insatiable sexual appetite.

Magda was well aware of Goebbels's reputation as a shameless womaniser but he was also dynamic, motivated and obviously going places, while her young man had few tangible prospects. The lovesick student did himself no favours when he turned up at her apartment brandishing a gun and threatening to kill them both if Magda did not take him back. During a heated confrontation, he fired off one shot but the bullet whizzed past her and struck the doorframe instead. Magda called the police and had him carted away.

There were further complications when Magda was finally introduced to Hitler. However uncertain Magda was about Goebbels, there was no such ambiguity where Hitler was concerned. The feeling was mutual. In the spring of 1931, Magda and Goebbels spent some hours with Hitler and Otto Wagener, an ex-army *Freikorps* veteran and high-ranking SA man who for a while was a sort of special advisor to Hitler. Wagener observed 'the pleasure Hitler took in her innocent high spirits' and 'how her large eyes were hanging on Hitler's gaze'.

Afterwards, Hitler confessed to Wagener that Magda had made a big impression on him. Over the next few weeks, Hitler kept bringing her up in conversation. He told Wagener that Magda 'could play an important role in my life' and 'represent the feminine counterpart to my single-mindedly male instincts'. But what form could such a relationship take? Hitler believed that to perform his duties as the future leader of the Third Reich he had to appear single, dedicated solely to the welfare of his people, enduring self-enforced solitude for their benefit. Any contact with Magda would have to be as clandestine as possible; if she was with someone else it would be a lot easier to keep their liaison secret. Hitler remarked to Wagener that it was 'too bad she isn't married'.

Then, on a long walk alone together, Wagener relayed Hitler's thoughts to Magda and explained both Hitler's aversion to marriage and his desire to have a woman who could be like a wife to him; an intellectual, emotional and spiritual partner. Once Wagener was sure Magda understood what he meant – that if she wanted to form a special bond with Hitler she should consider marrying Goebbels – he asked Magda if she was prepared to accept the challenge. Magda didn't hesitate: 'For Adolf Hitler, I'd be prepared to take everything on myself.'[5]

Though Wagener's testimony lacks corroboration, there is no doubt that Magda was infatuated with Hitler. Perhaps with this bizarre *ménage à trois* in mind, she agreed to get engaged to Goebbels. They went public in July and marked the announcement with a small champagne-fuelled gathering alongside Hitler, Ilse and Hess, Wagener, and a few others. Yet Goebbels felt insecure about Magda's obvious feelings for Hitler, and he expressed his anxiety in an August diary entry: 'Magda loses herself a bit around the Boss ... I am suffering greatly ... I didn't sleep a wink.'[6] However, despite being tormented, Goebbels was too dependent on

Hitler's goodwill to confront him about it; ultimately, he was incapable of breaking up with his beloved leader.

Lina Heydrich liked to take the credit for pushing her husband into the Nazi fold; according to her, when they got together he had no political opinions of his own and considered most politicians to be incompetent, foolish civilians. Though it's true he'd not yet engaged with Nazism, all Heydrich's actions since late adolescence placed him firmly on the right of the ideological spectrum.

When his hometown was caught up in the post-war turmoil, Heydrich immediately signed up with the local *Freikorps* and acted as a messenger during clashes with the communists. The navy was virulently nationalistic and anti-Semitic, hostile to the Weimar Republic, bitterly opposed to the Treaty of Versailles and in favour of an authoritarian solution to Germany's problems. Heydrich didn't have far to travel to reach Nazism and Lina made sure he completed the journey.

In the spring of 1931 – while Heydrich was earning pocket money at a sailing club – his godmother spied an opening for him in the SS. Her son had joined Himmler's embryonic organisation and heard through the grapevine that he was looking for somebody to head up an intelligence-gathering section. Strings were pulled and Heydrich was granted an interview, much to Lina's delight.

However, at the last minute, Himmler cancelled due to illness. Heydrich decided to abandon his trip and reschedule but Lina, worried that he might not get another chance, telegrammed ahead to say he was still coming and then got him on the overnight train to Munich. Arriving the next morning, 14 June, Heydrich headed out to Himmler's home. Margaret opened the door, let Heydrich in and escorted him to her waiting husband.

Having Himmler at home was a rare treat for Margaret. Over the past year, she'd soldiered on with the farm, but the whole enterprise was close to collapse. The hens weren't laying well and she had to slaughter the geese because she couldn't afford to feed them any longer. The strain on her was palpable. But her husband was far too preoccupied to pay more than lip-service to her troubles. He had vastly increased SS membership and formalised its uniforms and rituals while carefully recruiting lawyers, academics, recent graduates and disaffected aristocrats for leadership positions. At the same time, he aspired to create a covert branch of the SS to monitor opponents.

The problem was that Himmler hadn't the faintest clue about intelligence work. As far as he knew, Heydrich had some experience in the field, based on his time in the navy, but he didn't realise that Heydrich had been engaged with purely technical stuff. So when Himmler asked him how he'd put together an intelligence unit, Heydrich fell back on his limited knowledge of espionage, based on the British spy novels he enjoyed reading. Himmler was impressed and offered him the job, beginning a partnership that would send millions to their deaths.

Since Geli Raubel had taken up residence in Hitler's Munich apartment – and his bed – she'd dabbled unsuccessfully in a number of things, including acting and singing, to fill her time while he was away. When Hitler was in town, she had no choice but to fall in with his routines and habits. Geli's social life revolved round his, whether it was a cosy lunch with Ilse and her husband, or paying Margaret Himmler a surprise visit. Margaret was shocked to find Hitler and Geli on her doorstep – 'I was speechless' – but enjoyed their stay: 'We had coffee together, which was very pleasant.'[7]

Often bored, Geli yearned to have a little fun. But that was easier said than done. Every year in the run-up to Lent, the Fausching Carnival was held in Munich and featured masquerades, dances, and street parades. Geli had persuaded Hitler to let her attend a fancy dress ball, on the condition that Heinrich Hoffmann and Hitler's publisher acted as chaperones. Despite this restriction, Geli was excited about going and had done a sketch of the type of dress she wanted to wear. While not overtly daring, it was relatively revealing. Hitler saw it and, according to Ilse, lost his temper; he yelled at Geli – 'you might as well go naked' – and started drawing an alternative design. Geli was so infuriated by his outburst that she grabbed the drawing 'and ran out the door, slamming it shut'.[8] Though Hitler apologised for his behaviour, she ended up going to the ball in a regulation white evening gown. With her two male escorts watching her every move, she was home by 11 p.m.

In the autumn of 1931, her frustration and unhappiness became too much to bear. Still only 23, she was a virtual prisoner who desperately wanted to escape. She begged Hitler to let her return to Vienna, where she'd grown up, and start afresh. Hitler wouldn't hear of it and bawled her out for even considering the idea; Geli knew then that he'd never let her break free.

On the evening of 18 September, while Hitler was in Nuremberg, Geli took the gun he'd given her for protection, placed the muzzle against her chest and fired. She fell to the floor. The bullet punctured her lung and lodged itself near the base of her spine. Lying face down, and in excruciating pain, Geli slowly bled to death.

The following morning, her body – which was already showing signs of rigor mortis – was most likely discovered by the housekeeper, though Ilse always insisted that her husband arrived there first, forcing the door to get in. Whether or not Hess found her, he was the one who had the thankless task of telling Hitler what had happened, managing to reach him on the phone as he was about to leave his hotel. Shocked and distressed, Hitler raced back to Munich – en route he got a ticket for driving at twice the speed limit – to face questions from the police, who had done a cursory search and spoken to witnesses, and the threat of scandal.

For forty-eight hours the rumours flew, left-wing newspapers cried murder, and it looked like Hitler's credibility was at stake. But then the fuss died down. The doctor who examined Geli was convinced she'd killed herself. The official investigation saw no reason to question his findings and the case was closed. Geli's corpse was transported to Austria and buried in Vienna. Hitler avoided the funeral, but made a solemn solo visit to her grave a week later. Geli's room in his apartment was left untouched.

Ilse was one of those who declared that Geli was Hitler's only true love and that after her death he was never the same again; he lost his capacity for joy and taking pleasure in simple things. However, this sentimental picture doesn't take into account the fact that Hitler had been seeing Eva Braun as well. He regularly dropped in on her at Hoffmann's studio, where she still worked, took her out to eat and occasionally to the cinema, and gave her presents. Geli was aware that Eva was on the scene; they accidentally bumped into each other during the 1930 Oktoberfest (sixteen days of funfairs and heavy drinking) and the two exchanged a few terse words and some spiteful glances. After Geli's suicide, Hitler and Eva's fairly innocent, mildly flirtatious relationship became a lot more serious; whether Eva realised it or not, she was about to step into Geli's shoes.

Though Goering wanted to be with Hitler in his hour of need, he was facing a crisis of his own. Since the beginning of the year, Carin's health had been in steep decline. By June 1931 she was in a sanatorium, her heartbeat weak, pulse faint, slipping in and out of consciousness, near death. Realising the end was near, she and Goering went on a last trip together in his new Mercedes, a present from Hitler. They travelled south to Bavaria and then into Austria, where Goering introduced her to his surrogate father, von Eppenstein, at his castle.

Then, on 25 September, Carin's mother died. She was determined to return to Stockholm for the funeral even though her doctors warned her it might kill her. Accompanied by her husband, they made the journey and were greeted at the station by her son Thomas – now in his late teens and fully reconciled with his mother – who remembered that 'she never looked lovelier'. It all proved too much, and Carin collapsed. Goering stayed at her bedside for days on end as she clung on; Thomas recalled how 'he would only steal away to shave or bathe or snatch a bite to eat … otherwise he spent all his time on his knees … holding her hand, stroking her hair, wiping the perspiration from her face and the moisture from her lips'.[9]

With Carin on the brink, Goering was suddenly required elsewhere; a meeting in Berlin with President Hindenburg, the man who ultimately held Germany's fate in his hands. Hindenburg was wary of Hitler but more sympathetic to Goering, the former war hero. Distraught, Goering didn't want to leave Carin, but she insisted he do his duty. Even then, her dedication to the cause outweighed all other considerations.

At 4 a.m. on 17 October, Carin passed away. Goering made it back for the funeral four days later, held at her family's private Edelweiss Chapel. Carin's death left a gaping hole in his heart that no amount of power or wealth could ever really fill.

The year ended with two weddings. The unresolved tensions between Magda and Goebbels over their relationship to Hitler had been laid to rest. Not long after Geli's death, there were a series of private meetings between Magda and Hitler, Goebbels and Hitler, and the three of them altogether, during which they reached an unspoken agreement. Magda and Goebbels would get married so they could stay close to Hitler and he could stay close to her. On 19 December 1931, Goebbels and Magda – who was probably already pregnant – tied the knot at a civil ceremony followed by a church service. Hitler was best man; when Magda thanked him with a kiss, his eyes were full of tears.

On 26 December Lina and Heydrich walked up the aisle; alongside family and friends were the local Nazi women's group – who'd provided a handmade swastika – and members of the SA and SS dressed in white shirts and black trousers (due to a temporary ban on both organisations they couldn't wear their full uniforms in public) who formed an honour guard outside the church, which was echoing to the strains of the 'Horst Wessel' song, the Nazis' favourite anthem.

Heydrich was now based in Munich, after a few months learning the ropes with the SS in Hamburg, renting a tiny flat from a sympathetic old lady and slowly constructing the framework for his intelligence unit, the Sicherheitsdienst des Reichsführers-SS (SD). His salary was poor – he earned less than a shop assistant – but just enough to enable Lina and him to begin their married life renting a small place in the suburbs of Munich.

Five days after their wedding, Himmler issued a set of guidelines to govern marriages within the SS. He wanted his SS clan to be descended from Nordic roots and free from racial impurities. All SS men would have to apply for a certificate that confirmed the biological suitability of their mates; anyone who married without it would be expelled. While Lina's Aryan heritage was flawless, Heydrich's own lineage would soon come under scrutiny.

5

BREAKTHROUGH

Despite the loss of their loved ones, both Goering and Hitler would find some consolation in the first few months of 1932. Though it's impossible to know for sure, most agree that Hitler began sleeping with Eva Braun early in the year.

Eva carried little of the traditional baggage with which an earlier generation of women had been burdened and in many respects she resembled the new breed of 'modern' women that shook up post-war German society: she smoked, followed the current dance crazes coming out of American jazz clubs, read fashion magazines and purchased the latest beauty products, idolised movie stars and celebrities, valued her independence – most young single women like Eva had jobs and usually worked in either retail, leisure or office administration – and had no intention of giving up her position at Hoffmann's, through which she'd acquired a serious interest in photography.

Yet in other ways, Eva embodied Hitler's ideal of natural womanhood. A true blonde, she was athletic and sporty – gymnastics and swimming – and kept herself in shape; she had almost no interest in politics or the state of the nation; she had few airs or graces and was refreshingly free-spirited; she was emotionally immature and easy for Hitler to manipulate. From her point of view, Hitler was courteous, often charming, indulgent and attentive, while his growing fame flattered and excited her. Eva hadn't yet grasped how cruel and indifferent Hitler could be towards those who dared get close to him.

That spring, a still heartbroken Goering renewed a brief acquaintance he'd made with a 38-year-old actress, Emmy Sonnemann, who was employed by the Weimar State Theatre. Goering was in town and after the show they ran into each other at the Kaiser Café; they went for a walk in a nearby park and Goering talked to Emmy at length about Carin and how her death had affected him: 'He spoke of his wife … with so much love and genuine sadness that my esteem grew for him with every word.' Next time he was in Weimar they met for lunch and before long Emmy received an invitation to a reception in Berlin, where she spent 'a thrilling evening'.

Emmy liked to portray herself as an artist with no feeling for politics and claimed she did her best to avoid discussing Goering's work: 'I needed a great effort to interest myself in any political subject.' She was much happier talking to him about 'the theatre, books, paintings and human relationships'.[1] The most important thing for Emmy was that Goering respected her, both as a woman and as an actress. She had caught the acting bug aged 12 when she saw a production of *The Merchant of Venice*. Her father, an affluent entrepreneur who owned a chocolate factory, was dead set against her treading the boards, but her mother was more sympathetic. Emmy's chance came when a prominent director announced he was opening an acting school in Hamburg – where she grew up – and was offering two scholarships. Emmy's mother assured her that if she got one, her father would allow her to become an actress. Emmy duly did, and after completing her training she began her career working in small regional theatres.

In 1914, Emmy met a fellow actor, Karl Köstlin, while she was performing the role of Margareta in Goethe's *Faust*. They married a year later when they were both appearing in Vienna. For the rest of the war, they were often apart as he was required to serve in the Austrian army. Though Emmy found him 'intelligent, distinguished and extremely cultured', the relationship lacked passion – 'we were no more than good friends'[2] – and in 1920 they amicably divorced. Two years later, she was in Weimar, around 150 miles south of Berlin, which became her base for the next ten years. Emmy played a wide range of leading roles in both the classics and works by more modern playwrights, including Ibsen and Oscar Wilde.

These were happy years for her; she had a three-room apartment, loved her work, enjoyed the company of her fellow actors and spent her down-time in Weimar's bars and restaurants. Her first encounter with Goering occurred when her theatre group were giving an outdoor performance at a private party, performing a play written by their host. Goering was there with Carin, who Emmy found fascinating: 'She looked ill, but there emanated from her a charm which I could not resist.'

From the start of her relationship with Goering, Emmy showed great sensitivity and tact when it came to Carin's lingering hold over him. Not that she had a lot of choice: the first present Goering gave Emmy was a photograph of his dead wife. When she visited his apartment, Goering showed her the room he kept as a shrine in honour of Carin's memory: 'Her beautiful eyes looked down from innumerable frames on every wall.'[3] Nevertheless, Emmy had made up her mind: she would bide her time, convinced that Goering was the right man for her. But neither Goering nor Hitler would have much room for romance in 1932, the year of elections, which not only included two Reichstag elections but also a presidential one. Hitler decided to run against Hindenburg and though nobody really expected him to win, it seemed an ideal way to establish himself as a legitimate contender for high office.

In Munich, the party machine – with Hess at the controls – was working overtime. While not permitted to directly engage in the push for power, Ilse was able to take an informal role, maintaining lines of communication with allies, donors and potential supporters in and out-side her social circle, which took in representatives of the city's cultural scene – writers, painters, philosophers – many of whom she'd got to know through the world of antiquarian books.

The first round of the presidential election saw Hitler get 30 per cent of the vote; Hindenburg got over 49 per cent. In the next round, Hitler added 2 million votes but Hindenburg increased his share to 53 per cent. While there was some lingering disappointment, the contest had allowed Hitler to play the statesman on the national stage. The priority now was to convert this goodwill into votes in the upcoming Reichstag election.

When Hitler wasn't on the campaign trail, zigzagging the country by plane, he divided his time in Berlin between his suite at the grand

Kaiserhof Hotel and Magda and Goebbels's apartment, which had become his unofficial HQ. By now, Hitler had adopted a fairly strict vegetarian diet – he still ate eggs but no dairy products – so Magda made sure there was always suitable food available; because of Hitler's paranoia about being poisoned, she even delivered meals to him when he was at the hotel.

The whole campaign was disfigured by extreme violence. Political meetings frequently descended into anarchy; on one occasion, Goering plunged into a massive punch-up wielding a sword. The SA and its communist equivalent, the Red Front Fighters' League, brawled in the streets. There were targeted attacks and random assaults. In late May, Margaret and Gudrun had to stay with friends for a while after an unknown gunman shot at their house. Taking the hint, Heydrich dispatched Lina to the countryside for a couple of months.

Lina's safety wasn't the only thing troubling Heydrich. In June, an SS man from Heydrich's home town accused him of concealing the fact that he had Jewish ancestors. Alarmed, Himmler ordered a comprehensive investigation, which revealed the source of the problem: Heydrich's paternal grandmother. Her second husband had a surname that happened to sound Jewish. While this was embarrassing, it wasn't fatal. Heydrich's bloodline was not tainted. He was free to resume his SS career.

Tempting though it might be to suggest that Heydrich's systematic and ruthless persecution of the Jews stemmed from an insecurity about his roots – during Heydrich's childhood his father was targeted by local anti-Semites and jealous colleagues would continue to try and undermine Heydrich by dredging up this racial slur – there is virtually no evidence that Heydrich was driven by self-loathing. Certainly, Lina never gave any credence to the idea that he was motivated by the need to atone for his suspect past.

If anything, Heydrich suffered from overconfidence; rather than operating from a position of weakness, constantly looking over his shoulder, Heydrich never felt the least bit vulnerable; as far as he was considered, he was practically invincible.

With all the election turmoil, Bormann – as manager of the Nazis' insurance fund – was extremely busy. Dealing with the mounting toll of deaths and serious injuries and the claims of compensation arising from them, Bormann gained a reputation for scrupulous honesty; despite the considerable sums passing through his hands – there were 3 million RM at his disposal – Bormann never dipped his fingers in the till.

Gerda had her hands full too; a year earlier she'd given birth to twin girls, one named after Ilse, the other after Bormann's former lover, Ehrengard, but the child died a few months later. There is no record of how Gerda felt about this loss but by the autumn of 1932 she was pregnant again. With her husband working flat out, Gerda was left to cope with their rapidly expanding family on her own; she received no help from her parents due to a definitive falling-out the couple had with her father, Walter Buch.

Exactly what prompted the break is hard to establish. Buch was non-committal about the reasons for the split, simply citing the bad feeling that had always existed between him and Bormann. A letter from Gerda to her husband – written near the end of the war – refers to the termination of contact between them without being specific. Whatever the cause, Gerda never regretted losing the father she felt she never had.

As for Bormann, he was well aware of his father-in-law's low opinion of him; he had no qualms about driving a wedge between Gerda and Buch. Besides, Bormann had become indispensable: he no longer needed Buch's patronage to progress. Bormann also kept his own relatives at a considerable distance; as a result, Gerda's many children would grow up without grandparents. Instead, they found an alternative family among the Nazi elite.

On 31 July, Germany went to the polls: the Nazis scored a stunning success, gaining over 37 per cent of vote. The country's economic situation was catastrophic – over a third of the workforce was out of a job – yet the government seemed incapable of doing anything about it. In these dire circumstances, Hitler's undoubted charisma and well-crafted image, combined with the simple, clear message that he alone was capable of uniting a shattered nation and restoring Germany's pride and power, attracted a wide range of people.

They were now the largest party in the Reichstag. With the exception of the urban working class – which on the whole remained committed to the left – the Nazis gathered votes from across the socio-economic spectrum; impoverished rural labourers and struggling farmers; shop-keepers and artisans; civil servants and professionals; financial wizards and the beneficiaries of inherited wealth.

Many women who had previously voted for middle-of-the-road conservative parties switched their allegiance to Hitler. Six months earlier the Nazis had merged all their existing women's associations into a single entity, the National Socialist Women's Organisation (NFS). Reflecting the party's increased share of the female vote, the NFS grew rapidly in size over the course of 1932, rising from just under 20,000 members to just over 100,000.

Given Hindenburg's aversion to the main socialist party, which had come in second, his options were narrowing; granting the Nazis a role in government seemed increasingly unavoidable, but Hitler wanted to be chancellor, and despite intense discussions in late July and early August, nobody was prepared to offer him the job. During the summer and autumn there was a growing sense that the Nazis had missed their chance.

With the Reichstag in a state of paralysis, new elections were held in November that only confirmed this disturbing feeling; the Nazi share of the vote was down by 4 per cent, an ominous sign that the party had reached the limits of its popular appeal. Hitler faced a dilemma; con-tinue to wait to be invited to rule and risk seeing his support slip away, or attempt a violent seizure of power and risk a civil war the Nazis had little hope of winning.

Back in Munich, Heydrich was also wrestling with a serious problem. The SD was chronically short of money; its very existence was at stake. In September, he and Lina moved out of their tiny apartment and into a two-storey villa. They took the first floor while the ground floor was occupied by Heydrich's seven-man SD team and all their paperwork. Lina described herself as 'look-out, cook and housewife'. As a security precaution, Lina acquired two dogs to raise the alarm, while the villa's position, set back from a large garden some distance from the main gate, meant she'd have time 'to hide anything incriminating'.[4] Lina did her best to manage the household on a meagre budget. Meat and fish were too expensive so she cooked cheap vegetable soups instead; the highlight of the week was a traditional Bavarian potato salad washed down with beer.

Heydrich reached out to Ernst Röhm, leader of the Brownshirts; since its inception, the SS, though notionally independent, was technically part of this sprawling organisation that under Röhm's direction had swollen in size and influence. Röhm was an ex-frontline soldier with little time for civilians; to him, the parliamentary path to power was a sideshow, merely the prelude to a blood-soaked revolution that would wipe the slate clean and turn Germany into a vast military camp.

Lina claimed that she was instrumental in getting Röhm's backing. Needing to watch every pfennig, Lina kept careful count of the number of matches available for lighting the basement boiler. When she noticed they kept disappearing, she figured somebody was pilfering them. So Lina decided to expose the thief. She bought some novelty exploding matches from a joke shop and mixed them in with the regular ones – but she hadn't considered the fact that Röhm and Himmler were about to arrive for a crucial tour of inspection.

Before she could intercede, Röhm reached for his cigars and lit one. There was a loud bang; Lina recalled that Röhm 'went as white as a sheet'[5] and Himmler dived for cover. Allegedly, Röhm was so amused by her audacity and ingenuity that he was glad to authorise some extra funding. This piece of welcome news coincided with the revelation that Lina was pregnant. Nine months later, Röhm would become the child's godfather.

On 1 January 1933, llse and her husband were among a select few who attended a performance of Wagner's *The Master Singer* at the Munich State Theatre with Hitler and his special guest, Eva Braun. It was the most public acknowledgement yet that she was Hitler's girlfriend. His decision to bring Eva out into the open was prompted by her attempted suicide a few months earlier.

Having given herself to Hitler, Eva endlessly waited for him to pay her some attention but Hitler was barely in Munich during 1932; even when he was, he had precious little time for her. Eva took his absences and silences personally, as a sign of rejection. Anxiety turned to despair. Like Geli before her, she had her own pistol. Leaving a scribbled farewell note, she pulled the trigger. The bullet lodged in her neck, just missing the artery. Bleeding profusely, Eva managed to call a doctor – Heinrich Hoffmann's brother-in-law – who came immediately and got her to hospital, where the bullet was successfully removed.

Whether, deep down, Eva actually intended to kill herself is open to question; was it a cry for help? Did she think that this was the only way to get Hitler to take notice of her? Whatever her motives, Hitler was shocked into action. He vowed that he'd take better care of her. The outing to the theatre – with intimate associates like Ilse – was his way of showing Eva that she mattered to him.

Goebbels was meant to be at the opera with them, until an emergency sent him hurrying back to Berlin. Though Magda had successfully delivered their first child – a daughter named Helga, born on 1 September – it had aggravated a pre-existing heart condition. Not yet fully recovered, Magda became pregnant again. On 23 December she had a miscarriage and went into hospital. With her condition stable, Goebbels thought it was safe to head down to Bavaria to spend Christmas and New Year with Hitler.

It wasn't. Hitler's cottage at Obersalzburg – a mountainous area of forests and farms – didn't have a phone, so on New Year's Day Goebbels went to the nearby town of Berchtesgaden and called the hospital in Berlin. Magda had got an infection and was running a terribly high fever; she was perilously close to death. Beside himself with worry, Goebbels caught the first available train and travelled overnight to the capital to be at her bedside. On arrival, he was relieved to discover that she was out of danger. Over the next few hectic weeks, Goebbels visited her as often as possible while she slowly regained her strength.

Goering spent Christmas with Emmy Sonnemann. Since its tentative beginnings, Emmy and Goering's relationship had made discreet but steady progress. She was regularly staying overnight at his apartment.

Yet Carin was never far from his mind; once Christmas was over, he left Emmy to spend New Year with Carin's family in Sweden. On his return, Goering played a critical part in the unfolding drama that would decide the Nazis' future, smoothing out wrinkles during tense negotiations with Hindenburg and his fellow conspirators, who were caught between the need to obtain popular consent for their administration and the urge to impose some form of dictatorship.

As the month wore on, the old general and his allies were increasingly inclined to disregard their reservations about Hitler. If they gave Hitler what he demanded, the mass support he commanded would shore up their crumbling position and help defeat the communist menace, which they genuinely feared. If they didn't, they risked an armed revolt; the SA were now over a million strong. They agreed it was better to have Hitler on the inside – where they might be able to control him – than standing outside hammering on their door.

On 30 January, Hitler was named chancellor. The plotters who believed they could neuter the Nazis by bringing Hitler into office seriously miscalculated when they also made Goering Minister of Prussia, the largest state in Germany and home to its capital. With the title came control over all its police forces; Goering would use them to devastating effect. That evening Nazi supporters joined the SA and the SS for a massed torchlit victory parade; Hitler, Goering, Goebbels, Hess and Himmler – who were both in town for the big day – stood on a balcony at the Kaiserhof Hotel and revelled in their triumph. Aside from Emmy – for whom Goering had reserved a room so she could watch the march – none of their women were there to see it. The next morning, Hess bought himself a new watch, and in a daze wrote to Ilse: 'Did I dream all this or am I awake?'[6]

On 2 February, Magda was discharged from hospital and returned home to find Hitler waiting to greet her. A few weeks later, on the evening of 27 February, Hitler was dining with her and Goebbels. Magda made the mistake of serving Hitler some carp. Irritated, he was telling her off – didn't she realise he couldn't eat fish – when the phone rang. Somebody was calling to tell them the Reichstag was on fire.

Goering was first on the scene; he had lushly decorated quarters – containing valuable and very flammable tapestries – right next to where the fire was raging. Panicked, he called Emmy, who'd returned to Weimar to resume her role in Goethe's *Faust*, before going in search of help. Speculation that the Nazis actually started the blaze persisted for decades afterwards but no definitive link was ever established. The Dutch arsonist charged with the crime, who had vague links with the left, remains the most likely culprit; he'd already tried to set light to several public buildings.

Moving fast, the Nazis insisted that the attack heralded the beginning of a full-blown communist revolt. The next day, Hindenburg signed an emergency decree that effectively suspended the rule of law and a massive crackdown – already under way in Prussia – was set in motion; thousands were detained and tortured. Goering was at the forefront, granting SA squads police powers and forming the Gestapo. Within weeks, the prisons were bursting at the seams and improvised camps sprung up to accommodate the overflow, a measure Goering was unashamedly proud of; in his political tract *Germany Reborn*, he casually remarked that 'it was only natural that in the beginning excesses were committed. It was natural that here and there beatings took place.'[7]

Meanwhile, elections were called for 5 March: Hitler wanted to win a majority so he could dismantle the Reichstag altogether. Hitler spent the evening with Magda and Goebbels; they went to see Wagner's *The Valkyrie* and then headed to the Reich Chancellery to listen to the results on the radio. Despite the pervasive threat of violence and intimidation the Nazis only won 44 per cent of the vote. However, by bullying a small nationalist party to join forces with them and persuading the Catholic Centre Party to cooperate, the Nazis were able to push through the Enabling Act, which gave Hitler the freedom to suspend the Reichstag and do as he pleased.

Ironically – given its status as the cradle of the movement – the one province resisting Nazi domination was Bavaria; its conservative nationalist leadership were refusing to budge. This was a source of intense frustration for Lina; it was tortuous watching her enemies being crushed everywhere except in her own backyard while her husband festered on the sidelines.

However, the Enabling Act had given Hitler the authority to steamroller provincial politicians. On 9 March, Ritter von Epp – whose

Freikorps unit Hess had joined all those years ago – was made Bavarian State Commissioner and Himmler was put in charge of the police. The gloves were off; over a few days, hundreds of socialists, communists and obstructive officials were beaten, humiliated and arrested.

In a letter to her parents, Lina could hardly conceal her glee, giving a detailed account of what happened when the 'SA and SS enjoyed themselves'. Among their victims was a prominent Jewish citizen: 'They beat him with dog whips, pulled off his shoes and socks, and then made him walk home barefoot.'[8]

Lina's sense of triumph was not yet shared by Magda and her husband; they were both anxious about his place in the new regime. While Goering ran rampant in Prussia, Goebbels had nothing tangible to show for his endeavours. He craved control over all Germany's media and cultural activity. Finally, Hitler granted his wish – with the exception of the press – and made him head of the Ministry of Propaganda and Popular Enlightenment on 14 March; under its authority, Goebbels went on to establish sub-sections to govern each area of cultural production – music, theatre, art, literature and film.

Basking in the glow of his new status, Goebbels took Magda to the Berlin State Opera on 16 May to see a performance of *Madame Butterfly*, accompanied by the film director Leni Riefenstahl and her date. Leni was a former dancer whose career had been curtailed by injury, and who had appeared in a number of movies before stepping behind the camera. She'd come to the attention of both Goebbels and Hitler after the premiere of her first feature, *The Blue Light*. Hitler requested a private audience and at the 1932 party rally Leni received an invitation to one of Magda's exclusive parties. Leni was impressed by Magda – 'a perfect hostess whom I instantly liked' – but found Goebbels repellent.

Having negotiated the paparazzi gathered outside and settled in their box, Leni ended up next to Goebbels, who proceeded to shove 'his hand under my gown; it touched my knee and was about to move up my thigh'.[9] Leni snapped her legs shut, squeezing his hand until he was forced to wriggle it free. According to her autobiography, this was not Goebbels's first attempt to breach her defences. While Leni is not the most reliable source, her description of Goebbels's behaviour matches the type of sexual harassment he inflicted on numerous actresses and starlets.

Though she is vague about dates, it's possible that Goebbels began pursuing Leni while Magda was in hospital fighting for her life. Much to Leni's annoyance, Goebbels began calling her on a daily basis. After she asked him to stop, he showed up at her apartment on two separate occasions; he begged, he grovelled, he bullied and threatened, but she managed to resist.

The night at the opera was not the final insult; that summer, Goebbels lunged at her while they were driving together and nearly sent the car off the road. From then on Goebbels kept his hands off her, realising that he was on a hiding to nothing. Had he been able to destroy her career, he would have. But Leni had Hitler's stamp of approval, and she was far too talented to be easily dismissed.

Whether Magda suspected anything is impossible to say; the fact that she remained friendly with Leni suggests she didn't. For the time being, Magda operated on the principle that what she didn't know couldn't hurt her: besides, there was no shortage of men who'd be more than willing to take Goebbels's place.

During all this turmoil and excitement, Margaret Himmler was focused on domestic matters. In February, she and her husband sold the farm and moved into an opulent Munich apartment located on the same street as Hitler's. She'd begun keeping a 'childhood journal', a daily record of Gudrun's development in which she both fretted over minor instances of ill-discipline and celebrated her daughter's mischievous antics. At the same time, Margaret used the journal to monitor and assess her own parenting skills.

Then, in March, they adopted a 5-year-old boy, Gerhard; his father was an SS man who'd been killed in a Berlin street fight a month earlier.

Aside from being a gesture that reflected well on Himmler, it provided him with a male child, something he knew Margaret could no longer give him: after the severe difficulties she experienced giving birth to Gudrun, the doctors advised her not to try again. Margaret was initially pleased by the new addition. He seemed 'bright' and 'very obedient'[10] and she hoped he'd be a good influence on Gudrun. Margaret's positive attitude didn't last. Soon, Gerhard was simply something else for her to worry about. Having satisfied his yearning for a son and saddled Margaret with further responsibilities, Himmler began planning the next phase of SS expansion. Not only did he want the SS to monopolise the machinery of terror and surveillance, he wanted absolute power over its victims too.

By the middle of March, there were over 10,000 prisoners crammed into the local jails. To release the pressure, an abandoned munitions factory on the outskirts of the town of Dachau, 16 miles north-west of Munich, became an improvised concentration camp. Within a matter of weeks, Himmler had placed it under SS jurisdiction.

By taking control of Dachau, Himmler was making a statement of intent; all of the Nazis' concentration camps should belong to him. Yet even in his wildest dreams, Himmler could not have imagined that his ambition to purge Germany of its ideological enemies would lead him to the gates of Auschwitz.

PART TWO

HIGH SOCIETY

6

FIRST LADY OF THE REICH

On 20 April 1933, Hitler spent the evening of his forty-fourth birthday at the Prussian State Theatre watching the premiere of a stirring piece of propaganda dedicated to him and first performed on the radio in the run-up to the March elections. The gala night went well and included Emmy's debut on the Berlin stage.

Emmy's promising start in this new era in German theatre was given added impetus by her friendship and professional alliance with the celebrated actor and director Gustav Gründgens, whose fame was based on his interpretation of Mephisto in Goethe's *Faust*. But after the Nazis' assumption of power, there was a real danger that everything he'd achieved would be taken away from him.

Gründgens was a bisexual who'd supported the communists and worked in left-wing theatre during the 1920s. But he was spared the same fate that many like him suffered because of his connection to Emmy, who felt 'tied' to him 'both artistically and personally'. Leaning on Goering, who as Prussian minister had inherited control of its theatres, concert halls and orchestras, Emmy persuaded him to take affirmative action on Gründgens's behalf. After renewing Gründgens's contract at the Prussian State Theatre, Goering elevated him to the position of overall director in 1934.

These arrangements provided a huge boost to Emmy's career. Up to that point – despite her successes – she'd been a provincial performer, but now she was propelled onto the national stage; as she later remarked, 'I had reached the summit of ambition for any actress in Germany.' With Gründgens at the helm, she formed a mutually beneficial creative partnership: 'He helped me develop whatever talent I had.'[1]

After briefly reprising her well-worn role in *Faust*, she and Gründgens opened the autumn season with the comedy *The Concert*, a farce about an old pianist intent on seducing his young female pupils while his long-suffering wife tries to get him to mend his ways. The production received good reviews and went on tour in the summer of 1934, first to Munich and then on to Hamburg. The Munich leg almost proved fatal: en route to Obersalzburg, Goering and Emmy's car collided with another vehicle. On impact, the steering wheel rammed into Goering's chest, breaking two ribs, and Emmy gashed her scalp when her head smashed into the windscreen. Though their injuries were nasty, they knew they'd had a lucky escape.

Returning to Berlin, Emmy and Gründgens chose another comedy, *Minna von Barnhelm*, with Emmy in the lead. A perennial classic, there were over 200 productions of it during the Third Reich. Emmy and Gründgens's version ran for nearly a year. In the Nazi period, comedy was by far the most popular genre in German theatres. Though the regime's efforts to draw audiences to its self-produced political satire were a dismal failure, the Nazis appreciated the value of comedy as a safety valve, a form of release and escape from the demands they placed on their citizens. There was no shortage of uncontroversial material to draw on, whether the work of contemporary playwrights with titles like *Honeymoon Without a Husband* and *Uproar in the Courtyard*, or old favourites by both German and foreign writers; *Twelfth Night* and *The Taming of the Shrew* were Shakespeare's most performed works, while Oscar Wilde's witty comedies of manners were in great demand, as was Bernard Shaw, whose *Pygmalion* was filmed in 1935 with Gründgens as Professor Higgins.

Emmy did not simply use her fame and recently won influence to her own advantage. Throughout the theatre world, Jewish artists were running scared – deprived of employment or forced into retirement – and Emmy, with Goering's assistance, stepped in whenever and wherever she could to help her fellow artists. Bella Fromm, the society columnist, wrote in her diary that 'Emmy has been wonderful in her loyalty to her non-Aryan friends'.[2]

However, there were limits to what she could achieve – and what Goering was capable of doing for her. Henny Porten had been a major star since before 1914; with a string of hits under her belt, she'd spent time in Hollywood and successfully made the transition from silent pictures to talkies. But her husband was Jewish and Porten refused to divorce him. As a result, nobody would hire her. Emmy reached out to Goering, who said he could do nothing. Emmy refused to accept 'no' for an answer and kept pestering him. Eventually, at his wits' end, Goering turned to his younger brother Albert – a fervent anti-Nazi – who worked in the Austrian film industry and managed to find her some gigs in Vienna.

Emmy's increasingly high profile was a direct challenge to Magda's status as the First Lady of the Reich. Once the Nazis had seized power, Magda was the obvious candidate to assume this role. On Sunday, 14 May 1933, she gave the first Mother's Day radio address. After a grassroots campaign to establish Mother's Day as a national holiday had gained momentum during the 1920s – with enthusiastic support from the Association of German Florists – the Nazis made it official.

In her speech, Magda proudly declared that the German mother 'instinctively' understood Hitler's 'noble spiritual and moral goals' and was prepared to be 'his enthusiastic supporter and fanatical warrior'.[3] The response to her broadcast was overwhelmingly positive and she received hundreds of letters from across the Reich. Her mailbag – which contained, among other things, requests for money and advice on relationships – swelled to such an extent that she hired two secretaries to deal with it all.

Magda and her children were constantly being photographed for magazines and periodicals as an example of the perfect Nazi family. Though she certainly performed the essential function required of

German women and continued to produce children – between 1934 and 1937, she had two more daughters and a son – motherhood didn't come naturally to her. In the dozens of images featuring Magda and her children, she always appeared slightly removed, distant even, impeccably groomed in her designer outfits.

In the late spring of 1933, reflecting her interest in fashion, Magda was made honorary president of the newly created German Fashion Institute, set up to encourage a unique national style, put an end to decadent foreign influences and drive Jews out of the business: this last ambition was especially problematic given that much of the industry was Jewish owned (70 per cent of Berlin's off-the-rack clothes were produced by Jewish firms) and many of the top designers favoured by both Magda and Emmy were also Jewish. Though the elite designers were protected because of their prominent customers, by the late 1930s the fashion business had been thoroughly Aryanised.

The other main aim of the Institute – to get German women to abandon the 'modern' look promoted by French fashion houses and Hollywood movies – was also fraught with problems. While splenetic criticism of foreign styles was widespread (as one Nazi commentator put it, 'the Parisian whores set the tone for the fashions offered to German women'[4]) efforts to convince them to adopt traditional folksy outfits like the dirndl, a Bavarian peasant costume, were not very successful. To further confuse matters, a Goebbels-sponsored journal featured regular photo-shoots with models in glamorous evening wear and swimsuits, plus a women's problem page; in an April 1934 edition it tackled the vexed question, short hair or long hair?

Magda embodied these mixed messages. Though the regime railed against cosmetics – everything from lipstick to false eyelashes – and favoured a 'natural' look (the SS periodical *The Black Corps* was fond of pictures of near-naked women in athletic poses) Magda used luxury brands like Elisabeth Arden toiletries, wore full make-up, and brushed her hair forty-two times before going out; in a public statement on the subject she said that 'the German woman of the future should be stylish, beautiful, and intelligent'.[5]

Magda also regularly made the front cover of *The Lady*, a high-end fashion magazine that held the German rights to *Vogue* and advertised clothes by Parisian designers like Chanel. On assuming her position at the Fashion Institute, Magda reaffirmed her commitment to making German women as 'feminine as possible'.[6]

Her husband was alarmed and swiftly moved to shut her down, instructing journalists that 'there is to be no mention made of Frau Goebbels in relation to the Fashion Institute'.[7] When the organisation held its first exhibition in mid August 1933, Magda was no longer involved. Goebbels may well have sacked her to prevent the ideological controversy her stance might have caused or because of the general hostility towards the wives of the top Nazis holding any public offices, but it is also possible that he was jealous and didn't want her stealing the spotlight.

Yet Goebbels continued to portray Magda as some kind of domestic goddess, a fairly futile exercise; after all, who could imagine her doing the washing up or scrubbing the floors? That's what the servants were for. Nevertheless, the Nazis went to great lengths to turn German women into super-efficient housewives, especially as their relentless drive to prepare the nation for war drained resources and materials out of the civilian economy and placed increasingly stringent limits on household goods. Butter, milk, eggs, sugar and coffee were all scarce, and there were shortages of textiles and furniture. Thousands of women attended courses lasting from a few days to a few weeks, covering such diverse topics as how to cook fish, provide a more sustainable alternative to the Sunday roast, turn old bed sheets into dresses, can and preserve food, and recycle their husband's suits as skirts or vests.

Deprived of a platform for her own ideas and uneasy about presenting herself as the housewife's choice, Magda did manage to find a domestic outlet for her frustrated creativity. She had a talent for interior design and decoration, and thanks to the number of residences the couple acquired, she had plenty to keep her busy. Even then, there was no escaping the demands of Nazi ideology, and in Magda's case, Hitler's views on art. Hitler loathed what he called 'degenerate art' – which essentially meant anything that was the slightest bit abstract or experimental – and was enraged when he saw that Magda had chosen a work by Emil Nolde, one of Germany's most prominent modernists, and hung it on the wall of Goebbels's official residence at the Propaganda Ministry. After Hitler threw a fit, the painting was quickly removed and stored discreetly away at the couple's lakeside property.

Despite being a contender for Magda's crown, Emmy still had to compete with Carin's legacy. In June 1934, Goering had Carin's remains transported from Sweden to Germany for reburial, prompted by the fact that her gravestone in Stockholm had been vandalised. Her zinc-lined coffin travelled by train under armed guard.* In every town it passed through, the church bells rang and the stations were draped in black. Arriving at Goering's new estate north of Berlin, the coffin was solemnly placed in an underground mausoleum, accompanied by the strains of Wagner's 'Twilight of the Gods'. Hitler laid a wreath and spoke a few words, paying tribute to the sacrifices Carin made for the movement.

Commentating on the ceremony, that month's edition of the Nazi's main newspaper for women extolled Carin's virtues: 'Let the life of this Nordic woman serve as a role model. We grow awe-struck, silent before so much self-evident loyalty and the inner greatness of a true woman.'[8] Her dutiful sister went on to write a glowing biography of Carin that became a bestseller; by 1943 it had sold 900,000 copies.

The site for her new resting place was in the grounds of Goering's country mansion, Carinhall, though the word 'mansion' hardly does it justice. Built to resemble a hunting lodge, it had a 150ft swimming pool, a movie theatre and a gymnasium in the basement, a map room, an office with a granite fireplace, a huge library, a vast banqueting hall serviced by uniformed footmen and surrounded by columns of red Veronese marble, state-of-the-art electronically controlled windows behind

---

* In 1991 a casket was discovered on the grounds of Carinhall, holding skeletal remains that were believed to belong to Carin Goering. In 2013 DNA evidence proved this theory to be correct and Carin was reburied in Sweden.

curtains that bore the letter *H* stitched in gold, a model railway with 60ft of track in the attic, and an imposing entrance hall lined with statues and paintings. Any awkwardness Emmy may have felt about occupying a home named after her lover's dead wife was trivial compared to the thrill of being the lady of the manor and living in the kind of splendour that was beyond the reach of even the top Hollywood actresses.

Then, in 1935 – perhaps following a nudge from Hitler – Emmy and Goering announced their engagement. Though the party staged at Carinhall to celebrate the announcement was hardly modest, it paled in comparison to the actual wedding. On 10 April, Berlin came to a standstill. In his dispatch to London, Eric Phipps, the British ambassador, described the scene: 'A visitor … might well have thought that the monarchy had been restored … the streets were decorated; all traffic was suspended … whilst two hundred military aircraft circled in the sky.'[9]

After a ceremony at the town hall, the 320 guests – who included Hitler and all the senior Nazi figures – moved to the cathedral and then on to a sumptuous feast. Emmy received a host of presents: the King of Bulgaria awarded her the country's highest honour along with a bracelet laced with sapphires, her hometown of Hamburg gifted her a solid silver ship, while the boffins at IG Farben – Germany's leading petro-chemical firm – gave her two synthetically produced gemstones.

The night before the nuptials, Emmy made her last stage appearance; whatever regrets she might have had, she recognised that it would be inappropriate for her to 'continue to act'.[10] In doing so, she was not only falling into line with the general prohibition against the top wives holding down jobs, but also the more general thrust of Nazi policy; a woman's place was at home, not at work.

However, like many of the regime's efforts to fit German women into the mould it had created for them, it was compromised by the overriding necessity of readying the country for war. With slight variations, the proportion of women in the workforce remained the same as in the Weimar period, at roughly a third. Reflecting the Nazis' priorities, there was a sharp decline in the level of female employment in the professions, including 15 per cent fewer high school teachers, but increases in agriculture, industry and office work. The majority of these working women were single; only about 35 per cent were married.

Emmy's retirement did not mean that she ceased to take an interest in the theatre world – she also became involved in defending and promoting her favourite classical musicians and conductors – or to exert her influence, especially when it came to Gründgens. In 1936, some critics expressed the opinion that Gründgens's production of *Hamlet* was ideologically suspect. Knowing that a bad review could land him in a concentration camp, Gründgens lost his nerve and fled to Switzerland. Alarmed by his sudden disappearance, Emmy sent her husband after him, and Goering was able to convince Gründgens to return; Goering even had the journalists involved arrested by the Gestapo and forced one of them to apologise to Gründgens in person. Nevertheless, Gründgens still felt vulnerable and decided to cultivate Goebbels as well. That same year, he married the screen star Marianne Hoppe. The relationship served a dual purpose; wedlock would help silence the rumours about his sexuality, while being with a movie actress brought him into Goebbels's orbit. Gründgens skilfully worked both sides of the fence and survived the Nazi era unmolested.

Firmly established as the Nazis' first couple, Emmy and Goering bestrode Berlin's social scene with considerable swagger, exhibiting their shared love of theatrical display; Goering was no less a performer than Emmy, and was well-known for his outlandish dress sense – he'd often greet visitors sporting a toga and Turkish slippers – and his habit of wearing a dizzying array of colourful and elaborate uniforms bestrewn with the medals he kept awarding himself as head of Germany's air force, the Luftwaffe.

His ever-changing wardrobe was a constant source of amusement for the general public, who never tired of inventing jokes about his fanciful attire; gags that were more affectionate than mean-spirited as his preposterous vanity made him appear more human and more relatable than the other Nazi leaders: 'Your Excellency,' reports Goering's adjutant, 'a pipe has burst in the Air Ministry!' Goering turns to his wife and cries out, 'Emmy, quick! Get me my Admiral's uniform!'[11]

A typical example of their ostentatious behaviour was the party they held to celebrate Goering's forty-third birthday on 12 January 1936. Over 2,000 guests paid 50 marks – the money went to charity – to attend the bash at the Berlin State Opera; there was a full orchestra playing waltzes and sanitised jazz tunes, an endless stream of champagne and a tombola – prizes included miniature tanks and machine guns made of marzipan, and a diamond-encrusted brooch in the shape of a swastika. Tellingly, Magda cried off sick, while Hitler, who had no wish to be upstaged, stayed at home.

The Goerings' reputation for behaving like an emperor and empress from ancient times was further enhanced by their decision to raise lions at home. Borrowing them from the Berlin Zoo, and returning them when fully grown, Emmy treated her lions as if they were harmless pets or very small children: 'Whenever a new lion cub came to us he was always greatly alarmed when we first put him in the bath-tub. But they soon got to know that they were washed once a week and let themselves be soaped all over.'[12]

For Emmy, all the roleplaying in which she indulged served to conceal the ugly truth of what Goering actually did for a living: his turbocharged Luftwaffe saw its first action in the Spanish Civil War fighting alongside Franco's right-wing armies and was responsible for the flattening of the small town of Guernica. Henriette Hoffmann – who married Baldur von Schirach, the Hitler Youth leader, in 1932 – made a psychologically acute observation about Emmy's flight into a fantasy world: 'She would have been content if … the uniforms had been stage costumes, her palace the scenery, the noise of war the sound effects behind the scenes and her magnificent presents only props. She never wanted reality.'[13]

Attempting to keep up with them were Magda and Goebbels. Certainly, most of those who encountered Magda on the endless round of receptions, diplomatic soirees and formal occasions found her enchanting – with the notable exception of Bella Fromm, who claimed she'd never seen 'such ice-cold eyes in a woman', full of 'determination and inordinate ambition'.[14]

But everywhere Magda turned, Emmy and her husband were there or thereabouts, putting their imprint on events and outdoing the competition. One of the highlights of the social calendar was a day out at the races. The Berlin Racecourse was run by the elite Union Club – founded in 1867 – and had 500 fee-paying members. The club expanded rapidly under the Nazis with bigger stands, more horses, off-track facilities that included a salon and a clinic for the animals, and a special enclosure reserved for high-ranking female punters like Magda and Emmy, where the ladies could eat, drink and gamble without being interfered with.

Goebbels attempted to put his stamp on the club by arranging an annual fashion show there – with help from Bella Fromm, of all people – but Goering easily trumped him by offering the largest cash prize ever awarded to the winner of the Berlin Grand Prix – renamed the Grand Prix of the Capital of the Third Reich – which was the premier race of the year.

The fact was that no matter how hard Goebbels and Magda tried to shine, they could never match Goering's vast income; behind Hitler, he was the second-richest Nazi. Most military experts believed that air power would prove decisive in the next major war and Goering's air force was a major beneficiary of Hitler's rearmament programme. Goering had the ultimate say over aircraft design and production; he awarded contracts and allocated the vast resources coming in from state and private investment. This enabled him to shamelessly siphon off a fortune from the Luftwaffe budget and illicit bribes from firms in exchange for contracts.

In 1936, his empire grew dramatically when Hitler made him the head of the Four-Year Plan, which was meant to gear the whole economy towards total war and encourage self-sufficiency in several key commodities: iron, steel, petrol and rubber. Hitler had lost patience with his economics minister, who was dragging his feet over the pace of rearmament. By creating the Four-Year Plan office and giving it to Goering – despite his complete lack of qualifications and relevant experience – Hitler was undermining the influence of the minister and promoting a man as hell-bent on war as he was. Once in charge of this sprawling conglomerate, Goering was able to commit larceny on a massive scale;

among the contributors to Goering Inc. were German companies like BMW and Bosch, the Swedish firms Electrolux and Ericsson, and the American corporations Standard Oil and General Motors.

Though Goebbels was no less corrupt than Goering, his sources of revenue were nowhere near as substantial. He and Magda had an official residence at the Propaganda Ministry and a house in Berlin, plus two lakeside properties not far from the city; the largest was at Schwanenwerder, an English-style country house with stables for the ponies and a four-bedroom guest annexe; the second, bankrolled by the state, was at Lanke, a slightly smaller manor house, but no less grand.

But Goering and Emmy had three Berlin addresses: the ever-expanding Carinhall, a large cottage at Obersalzburg, and Goering had inherited both his godfather's castles. Goebbels may have bought a sailing boat – which he was extremely proud of – but Goering had two massive yachts, *Carin I* and *Carin II*, while the chunk of forest Goebbels purchased could hardly compare with the 100,000 acres surrounding Carinhall, which Goering used as his private hunting ground. Guests to their respective homes would also be treated to better food – both in terms of quality and quantity – at Emmy and Goering's table: the meals served at the Goebbels residences were notoriously stingy and guests would often fill up beforehand.

Emmy and her husband even had better vacations. Both couples made frequent trips abroad, combining business with pleasure, some for only a couple of days, others more extended visits. Yet Goebbels mostly travelled alone as Magda was often either pregnant or recovering from giving birth. She saw Rome and northern Italy a few times, and joined her husband – and several other couples – on a ten-day jaunt to Greece in September 1936. After brief stopovers in Budapest and Belgrade, the group flew to Athens, where they were greeted by cheering crowds and a buffet lunch. Next up was a meeting with the king and a sit-down with the prime minister, followed by some free time to go sightseeing. Goebbels marvelled at the glories of antiquity – the Acropolis, the Parthenon, the amphitheatre at Delphi – but Magda felt under the weather, defeated by the heat. Then, on a four-day boat trip to various islands and their ancient sites, she came down with a severe case of seasickness.

Emmy, on the other hand, enjoyed numerous excursions on her yachts, whether gliding down the Rhine or sailing in the Adriatic. There were also state visits to potential allies. In the spring of 1939, she and Goering went to Libya and stayed at the summer house of the fascist governor Marshall Balbo, who'd waged a brutal war against indigenous rebels to secure Italian domination.

The day after their arrival, there was a huge welcoming party with 'big flood-lit fountains and Moorish guards' that reminded Emmy of 'a story from the Arabian Nights'. Other highlights of the trip were a military parade and camel riding in the desert, which Emmy compared to being 'in a ship on a rough sea'. The following year, they were in the Balkans as guests of both the Bulgarian and Serbian royal families, spending time at 'a real fairy tale castle by the sea-side'.[15]

The one tangible advantage Magda and Goebbels had over their rivals was their unique relationship with Hitler. This triangular arrangement continued to function uninterrupted after the seizure of power: Hitler frequently dropped in on Magda and the children, they celebrated their birthdays together, shared trips to the coast and had long discussions late into the night. On Magda and Goebbels's fifth wedding anniversary, as a token of his affection, Hitler gave them a mid-nineteenth-century oil painting by Carl Spitzweg that alluded to his own marital status; entitled *The Eternal Bridegroom*, it depicted a middle-aged gentleman offering flowers to a young maiden.

Goebbels was also a regular fixture at the lunches Hitler held at the Reich Chancellery, where he was expected to assume the role of court jester. Goebbels's talent for sarcasm was legendary and Hitler relished the way he would select a victim then mercilessly shred them with his razor-sharp tongue. At the same time, Hitler 'often asked Frau Goebbels to invite a few young actresses to tea, and he took a delight in attending these tea-parties'.[16]

Hitler had a guarded attitude towards Emmy; he didn't disparage or criticise her, but he was never relaxed around her either – maybe he sensed her lack of ideological commitment or was unsettled by the fact that she didn't treat him like some kind of demi-god. There was none of the intimacy or the meeting of minds that he experienced with Magda.

However, this special connection was nearly permanently broken during the 1935 party rally in Nuremberg. The cause of this falling out was the appearance of Eva Braun at the event, the first time she'd been introduced to Magda and many other of the leading Nazi personalities. This very public airing of Hitler's secret relationship occurred in similar circumstances to the trip to the theatre at the beginning of 1933; Eva had once again tried to kill herself.

Eva had seen a fair bit of Hitler during 1934, which lulled her into a false sense of security and made his neglect of her in the early part of 1935 much harder to bear. On 6 February, he forgot her birthday. For weeks on end, he didn't even call. She finally got to see him for two hours on 2 March. The next day he returned to Berlin without saying goodbye. Through the rest of March and all of April, she was left to her own devices. It was becoming unbearable.

A record of Eva's suffering is provided by the twenty-two pages of her diary – the only portion of it to survive – which cover this period. On 4 March she was 'on tenterhooks' as she clung to the forlorn hope that he might appear at her door. A week later, she bitterly complained that 'he only needs me for certain purposes'. On 29 April, she mournfully acknowledged that 'love seems not to be on his agenda at the moment'.[17]

Eva didn't know that Hitler was resting up after a minor surgery to remove a cyst from his throat. Towards the end of May, and still in the dark about his condition, Eva's moods fluctuated wildly and reached a near-hysterical peak on the 28th; that evening she took an overdose of sleeping pills. Her younger sister found her in time and a sympathetic doctor came to Eva's rescue.

Hitler realised he had to make amends and let Eva take her place among the other leading wives at the party rally that September. Perhaps not realising Eva's actual significance to Hitler – it wasn't unusual for him to have a young woman in tow – Magda made some negative remarks about her. One of Hitler's bodyguards recalled that Magda was 'completely shocked' by 'this capricious and dissatisfied looking girl sitting on the VIP rostrum'.[18] Word got back to Hitler. Furious, he refused to see Magda socially for over six months. Given the strength of her feelings for Hitler – his chauffeur rather caustically remarked that when Magda was with Hitler you could 'hear her ovaries rattle'[19] – it was torture for her to be denied contact with him and no doubt contributed to her growing dissatisfaction with her marriage. Without the regular visits from Hitler, the issues she had with Goebbels were harder to shrug off.

Goebbels suffered too, paranoid about losing favour with the man who meant everything to him; together, he and Magda tried to woo him back. They reserved a small cottage in the grounds of their Schwanenwerder property for Hitler's exclusive use. Finally, on 19 April 1936, Hitler came to see it for himself, and he and Magda were reconciled. Even so, this welcome development was not enough to lift her spirits. Only a few weeks after the reunion with Hitler, Goebbels made a note in his diary about her miserable state of mind: 'she weeps and is terribly sad' and 'sometimes has her moods: like all women'.[20]

Also causing a stir at the 1935 party rally – and friction with Eva – were two aristocratic English sisters, Unity and Diana Mitford, from the sort of vaguely artistic, eccentric and unconventional upper-class family that the writer Evelyn Waugh captured so well. Diana was the mistress of Oswald Mosley, an ex-Labour politician who founded the British Union of Fascists in 1932. However, it was Unity, the younger of the two, who fell hardest for Nazism, and particularly for Hitler.

Speculation raged at the time about whether Unity was romantically involved with Hitler. Diana didn't think so, saying that 'her admiration and even affection for him was boundless, but she was not in love', and she believed that Hitler simply appreciated Unity's fun-loving personality; Heinrich Hoffmann said Unity was both an example of Hitler's ideal woman, and potentially useful 'for propaganda purposes'. Hitler hoped to exploit Unity's 'blind devotion to him'[21] as part of the ongoing campaign to ensure British neutrality in the war he was determined to fight. But for that purpose, Hitler seemed to prefer Diana – whom he treated to a number of one-to-one meetings – not fully realising that her relationship with Mosley compromised her credibility back in the UK.

Once Unity had arrived in Munich in 1934 – and she and Diana had lurked in the wings of the party rally – she behaved like a deranged fan. She stalked Hitler, following his daily movements, learning his habits and patterns, waiting for the moment when he would acknowledge her presence, which he finally did at the Café Osteria on 9 February 1935. Now Unity had finally established contact, she convinced Diana to join her in Munich. The two of them received mixed reactions from the Nazi faithful; there was much grumbling about their low-cut dresses and liberal use of lipstick. Friedelind Wagner, Winifred's oldest daughter, was slightly more charitable; she said Diana was 'truly beautiful in a cool blue-eyed English way' and noted that Unity was 'an attractive girl' except when she smiled and 'revealed the ugliest set of teeth I have ever seen'.[22]

Magda was the only one who really warmed to Unity and appreciated her lively sense of humour. Whenever Unity was in Berlin they hung out together; they went shopping, watched movies and attended the opera. Magda also liked Diana, and she returned the compliment; as she put it in her autobiography, 'I became very fond of Magda Goebbels and her children'.

Magda went out of her way to help Diana and Oswald Mosley get married in Germany. Diana was a divorcee – her ex-husband was a member of the hugely wealthy Guinness family – and Mosley was recently widowed; they were both keen to avoid the negative publicity they'd receive if they got hitched at home. Diana asked Magda for help 'with all the form-filling'[23] and on 6 October 1936 the wedding went ahead. The ceremony was held in Goebbels's private rooms at the Propaganda Ministry. Diana was dressed in a pale gold tunic, and Hitler gave the newlyweds his blessing and a signed photograph in a silver frame; afterwards, Magda treated them to a wedding feast and presented Diana with leatherbound editions of Goethe's collected works.

A couple of months earlier, Hitler had personally invited the sisters to the 1936 Olympic Games – he provided them with a chauffeur-driven limo to ferry them back and forth to the stadium – and they stayed with Magda and Goebbels. For their amusement, Diana and Unity taught the couple the English parlour game 'Analogies'. Players had to guess the identity of a person by using an analogy; for example, what colour best represents them? In the case of Hitler, Goebbels's answer was 'fiery red'.[24]

During the Olympic Games, the Nazis engaged in a massive charm offensive; the streets of Berlin were cleared of anything that might spoil a visitor's day. Anti-Semitic propaganda was taken down, vagrants and petty thieves were systematically removed. For two weeks, with representatives of most of the participating nations descending on the capital, the main competitors for the title of First Lady of the Reich had a perfect opportunity to enhance their international prestige.

Setting the tone for the forthcoming events, Hitler presided over a banquet on the opening day of the Games. Goering picked up the baton and hosted an exclusive private lunch the following day – which featured kangaroo-tail soup on the menu – followed by a large and lavish official dinner on 6 August. Meanwhile, Goebbels and Magda were saving their energy for their big party, set for the 15th.

By then, Goering and Emmy had staged their final event in the grounds of the Air Ministry. After a splendid meal and a moonlit ballet, the arena was suddenly transformed into a fairground with roundabouts, a café and beer tents, while a procession of white horses, donkeys and actors dressed as peasants moved through the awe-struck crowd.

Two days later, Magda and Goebbels welcomed nearly 3,000 guests to Peacock Island, a magical wooded nature reserve connected to the mainland by pontoons. At first, it looked like the Goebbels' party might equal or even surpass their rivals' effort: the tree-lined pathways were illuminated by lamps, there were three orchestras providing dance music, an open barbecue and a spectacular fireworks display. However, as the night wore on – and young couples began disappearing into the bushes – things got increasingly out of control. The SS and SA men drafted in as security had been knocking back copious amounts of free alcohol and a minor disagreement turned into a riot; bottles and chairs were thrown and horrified guests scurried for cover. Ashamed, embarrassed and exhausted, Magda watched the dawn rise over the wreckage of broken glass, toppled tables and dishevelled survivors, and sobbed her heart out.

One fine morning in May 1937, Emmy claimed that she 'reached the peak of human happiness' when she and her husband opened a rest home for retired actors. Emmy had joined the board of governors of the Maria Seabach Foundation – established in the 1920s to provide accommodation for cash-strapped thespians – and convinced Goering to pump funds into the struggling organisation. Thanks to his generous donations, it was able to buy some land and build a new facility, situated in a picturesque forest location, which boasted thirty-five rooms, a large dining area and a library. Grateful for her contribution, the foundation took Emmy's name and under her direction it continued to thrive; the home was still taking in residents when Soviet troops arrived there in 1945.

Then, against all the odds, Emmy discovered that she was pregnant. Her joy was unconfined. Finally, she would join the other mothers of the Reich. Word of her condition spread fast and soon tongues were wagging all over Germany. Given that Emmy was 42 and Goering was 44 – and his marriage to Carin had been childless, even though the cause was her delicate constitution, not his alleged impotence – there was considerable doubt over the paternity. Emmy and Goering's sex life had already given rise to a number of wedding night jokes that focused on his performance in the bedroom (for example, that Emmy had stopped going to church after their honeymoon because she'd lost faith in the resurrection of the flesh), and now the gags flew thick and fast. Some were based on the wild rumour that Mussolini was the father – the Italian dictator spent time with the couple earlier that year – and some even accused his highly sexed son-in-law, Count Ciano, who was also said to have had a fling with Magda Goebbels, of doing the deed. More plausible were ones aimed at either the chauffeur or Goering's personal Luftwaffe adjutant: a senior airforce official asks Goering what they should do to celebrate if the baby is a girl. Goering replies 'A 100-plane fly-past'. And if it's a boy? 'A 1,000-plane fly-past'. And if there's no child? 'Court-martial my adjutant.'[25]

Goering liked to pride himself on his sense of humour and kept a notebook where he jotted down his favourite jokes, but with his manhood and Emmy's dignity at stake, he wasn't laughing any more. When a well-known Berlin night-club comic cut too close to the bone, Goering allegedly sent him for a short stay in a concentration camp. The accuracy of this oft-repeated story is hard to establish, and it is equally possible that it was Goebbels who cracked down on the hapless comic in 1936, dispatching him to Dachau before Goering got him released.

However, Goering was definitely very sensitive about the subject, and took exception to any suggestion he wasn't the father. When the founder and long-term editor of a rabidly anti-Semitic and shockingly crude Nazi tabloid made an indecent remark about Emmy in his paper, Goering tore him to pieces: the editor was dragged through the Party Court, barely escaped total excommunication and lost his place in the Nazi elite.

In the end, nothing could take away from Emmy and her husband's delight at the prospect of becoming parents. The only clouds on their horizon were health-related. There was concern that the pregnancy might aggravate Emmy's long-standing problems with sciatica, while Goering was having terrible trouble with his teeth and endured a series of dental procedures. To numb the pain, he was proscribed painkillers that contained a small amount of codeine. Though far less addictive than morphine, Goering carried on taking them once the course of treatment was complete, popping around five a day; not long after, he was up to ten a day.

On 29 October 1937, Magda and her husband held a glitzy reception at the Propaganda Ministry for the great and good of Germany's cultural scene. Guests included Hitler – who sat opposite Magda at dinner – the ubiquitous Heinrich Hoffmann, plus a bevy of famous film directors and well-known actors and actresses.

The whole evening was run with the precision of a military operation. Kicking off at 8.20 p.m., the various courses (a crab salad with asparagus, a clear soup, a main of goose with browned potatoes, dessert, a cheese platter with radishes on the side, and some fruit) were served at roughly ten-minute intervals. By 9.25 p.m. the guests had retired for coffee, pastries and cigars, before the VIPs were joined by less significant invitees for an hour-long concert featuring works by Schubert, Richard Strauss and Schumann.

Sitting at a top table was the 22-year-old Czech actress Lida Baarova, with whom Goebbels was having a passionate sexual relationship. As head of the movie industry, Goebbels was at the pinnacle of a booming business: during 1933–34, nearly 250 million cinema tickets were sold, and this had risen to 360 million in 1936–37. Fans queued up to enjoy the steady diet of comedies that accounted for over 50 per cent of all films produced; the biggest female star, Zarah Leander, specialised in rom-coms, playing women who had to choose between their jobs and finding a suitable husband.

With all that power came temptation, and Goebbels made vigorous use of the casting couch. While the more successful actresses were often able to fend him off without damaging their careers, the young hopefuls who rejected him suffered the consequences; Anneliese Uhlig was an up-and-coming star whose new film was pulled from the screens after she fought off his advances.

Goebbels's serial adulteries were common knowledge. Yet Magda continued to tolerate his excesses and turn a blind eye. In their Berlin home, Magda and Goebbels had separate bedrooms. One stormy night, Magda woke to discover the door connecting her room to his was locked, and in the morning she was confronted by the female guest who had shared her husband's bed. Magda let the incident pass without comment. In the end, she was convinced his one-night stands posed no threat to their marriage.

Equally, Magda was not above the odd dalliance herself; when provoked, she would taunt Goebbels with revelations about her own indiscretions. One such affair involved Kurt Ludecke, who had joined up with the Nazis in Munich in the early 1920s and then gone to the USA to build connections there. According to him, he first met Magda when she was in New York with her then husband Gunther Quandt and Ludecke renewed the acquaintance after his return to Germany in 1930.

Every so often, the two of them spent time alone together. Their last meeting was in 1936. Shortly after he was expelled from the movement for scandalous behaviour during his spell in America; Ludecke's powerful enemies included Gerda's father Walter Buch, who continued to be in charge of the Party Court. Ludecke made no direct reference to his liaison with Magda in his book *I Knew Hitler* (1937), but made no secret of his attraction to her, remarking on the 'warmth and charm with which nature had endowed her' and describing her as 'beautiful, cultured and intelligent'.[26]

Though Magda gained a measure of satisfaction from rubbing her husband's nose in it, his prolific infidelity was wearing her down, and things went from bad to worse after Goebbels encountered Lida Baarova. Born in Prague, Baarova had trained in the theatre and already had a number of screen credits before moving to Germany in 1934. With her dark hair, sultry look and seductive foreign accent she quickly became typecast as a sexy siren luring men to their doom; in her first German picture, released in 1935, she provokes a duel; in her second, a death at sea. Though these overblown melodramas were mediocre films she received positive reviews, and with a movie star boyfriend in tow, her career looked set to take off.

By 1936, Baarova was living with her celebrity partner in his villa close to Goebbels's home at Schwanenwerder, and she ran into him during a walk in the forest. From the start, Goebbels was extremely attracted to her – almost spellbound – and wasted no time letting her know how he felt. Baarova kept him at bay; she was involved with someone else and was well aware of Goebbels's reputation, but his persistence and the fact that his declarations of love seemed genuine – which they were – persuaded her to lower her defences.

Having consummated the relationship, Goebbels began energetically promoting Baarova's films. In 1937, she scored a big hit with *Patriots*. Set during the First World War, it followed the story of a German fighter pilot shot down in French territory. Taken in by a local theatre group, he has an affair with a French woman, played by Baarova, who must decide whether to hand him in or not. She does. Her lover is accused of spying; if convicted he faces the firing squad. Baarova's character makes an impassioned intervention and his life is spared. The critics ate it up, one reviewer gushing that Baarova was 'better than we have ever seen her'.[27]

Goebbels was in ecstasy and became more and more open about the relationship. Though he was playing with fire – and not just with Magda; according to the gossip hounds Baarova's partner, a hulk of a man, physically assaulted him – the propaganda maestro could not control himself. If Magda didn't want to attend a star-studded premiere, her husband would simply show up with Baarova on his arm.

Waking up to the danger, Magda confronted Goebbels and there were heated altercations. However, she was unable to summon enough energy to sustain her fightback. Earlier that year, she'd given birth to another girl – with the usual negative effects on her health – and friends noted that she seemed depressed. She was drinking and smoking more heavily. Then, in late autumn, she got pregnant again and lost the will to force the issue.

However, Goebbels didn't realise that his personal assistant had fallen hopelessly in love with Magda, couldn't bear to see his boss treating her so badly and was preparing to stab him in the back.

DOWN SOUTH

Gerda Bormann was in many ways the ideal Nazi wife. She didn't use cosmetics, had her blonde hair in a plait and wore traditional Bavarian dress, as did her children; in the few images of them that survived they look like they've just stepped off the set of *The Sound of Music*. At home, Gerda submitted without question to her husband's demands. She had no public profile and no place in the regime's publicity campaigns; at the party events she was obliged to attend, she remained hidden in the background. Most of all, she was a prodigious mother, producing children at a heroic rate: between 1933 and 1940, Gerda added five more to the two she already had.

As far as the Nazis were concerned, this was a woman's essential function: to drive population growth. Increasing the birth rate was an overriding goal and the regime mobilised its forces to achieve this aim: there were economic incentives and cash handouts for large families; the propaganda machine made films, broadcast radio shows and staged exhibitions that glorified motherhood; the medical profession and the scientific community – especially nutritionists and fertility experts – got in on the act; and the Gestapo policed those considered unfit to be mothers.

The regime also cracked down on abortion. During the Weimar period, it was reduced from a crime to a misdemeanour, but the Nazis introduced very harsh sentences and the number of convictions increased by 65 per cent. The policy towards contraception was more lenient, largely because the Nazis were worried about the spread of sexually transmitted diseases. Though frowned upon, condoms were available from vending machines at railway stations and in public toilets. A concerned Nazi doctor calculated that around 70 million condoms were sold every year.

Overall, Gerda was the exception rather than the rule. Though the birth rate increased – in 1933 there were just under fifteen live births per 1,000 people, which had risen to twenty by 1939 – it was still slightly less than it was in 1925, while the number of families with more than four children had dropped from a quarter in 1933 to a fifth in 1939. Lower-class women managing on tight budgets couldn't afford too many kids, and those women solvent enough not to work weren't prepared to give up the freedoms a smaller family gave them.

The Nazis knew they weren't meeting targets and launched a new initiative, the Honour Cross of the German Mother, a medal for the Reich's most productive women. Four offspring was enough to qualify for bronze, six or seven got you silver, while eight or over won a gold medal. Applicants were thoroughly vetted and their suitability assessed. Nevertheless, 3 million mothers were awarded the Honour Cross. Though Gerda's efforts were worthy of the top prize, she was not part of the grand inaugural ceremony held on the same day as Hitler's mother's birthday. Instead, Magda – who received a silver medal – was chosen to represent the leading wives.

Like Magda, Gerda didn't have to deal with her brood alone. There were nannies, cooks and cleaners. In the first few years after the Nazi takeover, the Bormanns' lifestyle was still relatively restrained. Because of his inexorable rise, by the mid 1930s they'd begun to enjoy the same privileged existence as other leading Nazis.

Bormann's career took a major leap forward thanks to Hess. On 21 April 1933, Hess was made Deputy Führer, and that year's Nazi party handbook outlined his duties: 'all matters of party leadership' and 'all the different aspects of the work performed inside the party' were 'under his supervision', as were 'all laws and decrees'.[1] Though this was a significant promotion for Hess, it didn't suit him. Hess was not a bureaucrat; he loathed paperwork and handed the vast bulk of the day-to-day business over to Bormann, who'd demonstrated his capabilities while managing the Nazis' insurance fund. In July of that year, Hess made Bormann his chief of staff. Bormann's power was unseen by the majority of Germans but no less real. The levers of the party were under his control; he delegated tasks, circulated directives to regional party bosses and dished out appointments. Before long, the whole structure was reliant on him. It helped that he had a brain like a filing cabinet where he stored a mine of information; Hitler knew he could depend on Bormann's memory – 'he never forgets anything' – and relentless efficiency, 'where others need all day, Bormann does it for me in two hours'.[2]

Bormann worked tremendously hard, existed on only a few hours of sleep a night, and pushed his subordinates to the limit. Christa Schroeder, Hitler's longest-serving secretary, wrote that Bormann 'expected from his staff the same enormous industriousness which distinguished himself'.[3] Demanding, impatient and unforgiving, Bormann was not a popular boss. His employees lived in fear of his quick-fire temper. According to Hitler's chauffeur, one minute Bormann could be charm personified, the next 'a sadist – belittling, offensive and wounding'.[4] Hitler knew Bormann was a terrible bully, but he got things done: 'I can rely on him absolutely and unconditionally to carry out my orders immediately and irrespective of whatever obstructions may be in his way.'[5]

By all accounts, Bormann behaved the same way at home, which gave rise to the widely held view that Gerda was an oppressed, brow-beaten housewife. A prominent Nazi characterised Bormann as 'the kind of man who takes delight in humiliating his wife in front of friends as if she was some lower form of being'.[6] If domestic standards slipped a fraction, or something was done incorrectly or landed in the wrong place, Bormann would lash out at Gerda. Hitler's valet said that everybody knew that Bormann terrorised his family: 'In moments of uncontrolled rage he would resort to physical violence against his wife and children.'[7] Bormann allegedly beat two of his children with a whip because they were frightened by a large dog, and kicked one for falling in a puddle.

It's hard to assess how Gerda felt about such degrading treatment. She'd didn't fight back. She didn't seek help. She didn't confide in anybody. Based on her Nazi ideology, Gerda believed it was her duty to obey her husband, and there's every indication that she was truly devoted to

Bormann. As far as her children were concerned, Gerda happily played with them, sang songs, drew pictures and read stories: it was their father's job to discipline and punish them. In a letter to him, in which Gerda contemplated the split with her own parents, she discussed her kids in a hard-headed and completely unsentimental way: 'Children are always selfish. They have their own interests and circles, and have no consideration for their parents.'[8]

In the early months of his rule, Hitler experimented with Reich Chancellery protocol by having one of the top Nazi wives on hand to welcome important guests and dignitaries. This system was dispensed with fairly quickly, but not before Ilse had demonstrated that she was totally unsuited to that sort of decorative role, especially when confronted by an awkward situation. Winifred Wagner's eldest daughter, Friedelind, was present for one such incident. A teenager at the time and something of a rebel, Friedelind left Germany for good in 1940, reached the USA a year later and penned a scathing critique of her mother and her Nazi associates.

Having portrayed Ilse as a 'plump, inelegant blonde with a deep voice' who scorned 'powder and make-up', Friedelind recalled how Ilse offered the guests some of 'Hitler's favourite candies' to keep them occupied while waiting for him to appear. Unfortunately, Hitler was in a foul mood; sitting next to Ilse at lunch, he fumed silently as Friedelind, her mother and the rest of the ensemble endured an unappetising bowl of noodle soup before retiring for coffee. No longer able to contain himself, Hitler flew into the next room and subjected one of his underlings to a ten-minute ear-bashing, screaming at full volume; Ilse and company heard every word of his blistering tirade. Mortified and paralysed by embarrassment, Ilse finally 'found the courage to tell him that his guests were leaving'.[9]

Ilse never felt at home in the perpetual whirl of the Berlin social scene; Bella Fromm noted that she rarely made an appearance. Despite the fact her husband's responsibilities obliged him to be in the capital more often, she visited as little as possible; Ilse's reluctance to embrace life in Berlin stemmed from its reputation as a citadel of sin, a toxic environment that sapped the moral fibre of anybody who stayed there too long. In Munich, she could remain true to the values that had animated her since her student days and uphold her and her husband's self-appointed mission; they would be the keepers of the Nazi flame. Years later, Ilse reminded Hess of their vow to 'never sell our birthright as idealists for the sake of external things'.[10]

While others enriched themselves at the party's expense, she and Hess led a frugal, typically bourgeois lifestyle. Their villa in a wealthy Munich suburb – with a large garden and several annexes – was a relatively modest abode compared to other prominent Nazi homes; the nearest they got to a country estate was a small lodge in the mountains that they used as a base for their hiking and camping holidays in the summer and skiing in the winter, cross-country rather than downhill. Hess's one indulgence was expensive motor cars; Mercedes was his brand of choice, and he liked nothing better than letting rip on the open road. Nevertheless, once he'd used up his monthly allowance of subsidised petrol, Hess paid for every extra drop of fuel out of his own pocket.

Because of Hess's honesty and disinterest in accumulating material wealth, he was dubbed 'the conscience of the party'; which was quite a label to live up to given the open criminality of the regime. After the Night of the Long Knives, in June 1934, when Hitler decapitated the leadership of the SA and settled a number of old scores – and the body count mounted in an orgy of violence – Hess had to clean up the mess caused when an innocent civilian was killed by mistake.

The intended target was a certain Dr Will Schmitt; instead the perpetrators butchered a respected music critic, Dr Wilhelm Schmidt. His widow described how four SS men came and took her husband away while he was practising the cello and she was preparing dinner. She heard nothing of his fate until his corpse appeared in a sealed coffin and the SS offered her financial compensation, which she angrily refused. Fed up with the SS men's repeated attempts to get her to accept the money, she marched over to the Brownhouse – the party's huge headquarters in Munich – and made a complaint.

The response was swift. On 31 July, Hess appeared at her door. This unfortunate sequence of events had come to his attention and he was there to make amends. Hess assured her that those responsible would be punished; as she recalled it, Hess then advised her to 'think of my husband's death as the death of a martyr for the great cause'.[11] Convinced that Hess's apology was sincere, she agreed to his offer of a monthly pension equivalent to her murdered husband's salary.

On a more personal level, Hess intervened on behalf of his and Ilse's close friend Professor Haushofer. The professor's wife was half-Jewish and he feared for her safety, his reputation and his son Albrecht's career prospects. Hess made Professor Haushofer head of two organisations designed to cater for the needs of the 20 million Germans living abroad. Hess also secured a post for Albrecht, a talented academic working in his father's field, at the Berlin High School for Politics. As Professor Haushofer remarked years later, Hess 'protected me and my family from bad experiences with the party'.[12]

Ilse also got in on the act; in late 1933, she wrote to Himmler complaining about the Gestapo's heavy-handed tactics and intrusive surveillance; her specific bugbear was its tendency to tap everybody's phones, no matter who they were, and she demanded to know why Himmler's agents kept tabs on loyal members of the regime. Unfazed, Himmler let Hess know about Ilse's letter. Hess blew his top at Ilse and ordered her not to raise her voice in protest again.

However, it's important not to read too much into Ilse's gesture of defiance; she was objecting to the Gestapo's methods, not the motives behind them. Neither she nor her husband made a fuss about the concentration camps and the torture chambers. Hess never questioned the raft of prohibitive measures that required his signature. He may have helped Professor Haushofer but he had no qualms about the Nuremberg Laws. Passed in 1935, the legislation formally separated Jews from the rest of the population; they effectively ceased to be German citizens. With a few minor exceptions, Jews were prohibited from entering into marriages or sexual relationships with non-Jews.

As it was, Hess and Ilse's fanaticism was undiminished, and she never failed to take her place in the front few rows on the podium during the

Nuremberg party rally every September, a week-long homage to Hitler that grew more elaborate and extravagant with every passing year. A more cultural, if no less mandatory event was the Bayreuth Festival; Ilse had remained friends with Bayreuth's curator and patron Winifred Wagner and enjoyed any chance to catch up with her, while carefully avoiding getting dragged into the controversies and running battles about which of the maestro's operas should be performed and who should conduct them.

Other members of the elite were not as keen to attend the Wagner jamboree and were only there reluctantly. The general public was even less interested and tickets proved difficult to shift. As Bayreuth's finances were in a poor state, these shortfalls were potentially ruinous. However, Hitler would always bail out Winifred and made sure the auditoriums were full and the seats filled. Bulk bookings were made by the SA, the National Socialist Teacher's Association, and the Nazis' women's organisations; from 1934, Goebbels's Propaganda Ministry covered a third of the festival's budget.

From her home base, Ilse diligently maintained a wide-ranging correspondence with the Nazi faithful, dispensing advice and dealing with a multitude of requests and queries. Though she liked to think of herself as a kind of honest broker, Ilse managed to rub people up the wrong way. Responding to a family member's request for a spare ticket to the 1935 Nuremberg rally, Ilse adopted a self-righteous tone, reminding her relative that they were 'not among the long-standing party faithful' so could hardly expect special treatment when tickets were in 'such short supply that even old comrades-in-arms in the movement are having to stay away'.[13]

Ilse's tendency to meddle in other people's private lives got her in hot water with Bormann when she involved herself in his younger brother Albert's marriage plans. Albert was the polar opposite to his brother; well-mannered, sophisticated and naturally conservative, he was a university graduate with a background in banking. Bormann plugged Albert into the party in 1931, landing him a job in Hitler's Private Chancellery, a purely administrative office that mostly dealt with Hitler's huge mailbag. The two men maintained a civil working relationship until Albert decided to marry a woman Bormann disapproved of because she wasn't Nordic enough.

But Ilse, who liked both Albert and his bride-to-be, encouraged them to take the plunge, which they did in 1933. Bormann was outraged and never spoke to his brother again; Christa Schroeder remembered how the two of them went to inordinate lengths to ignore each other; if either Bormann or his brother 'told a funny story', the other one would 'keep a straight face',[14] even if everyone else was laughing. As for Ilse, though Bormann was cordial in public, he bore a grudge against her from that moment on.

Ilse's behaviour also grated with Hitler, and by the mid 1930s he'd lost patience with her. Dr Karl Brandt – who was Hitler's personal physician for many years and a member of his inner circle – said that Hitler would frequently criticise Ilse because of 'her ambition', and complain about the way she would try 'to dominate men and therefore almost lose her own femininity'.[15] Ilse's unapologetic intellectualism clashed with Hitler's archaic view that women should not hold political opinions, and even if they did, they should keep their mouths shut.

On 13 June 1936, Gerda had her fifth child, a son named Heinrich after his godfather Himmler – Bormann had forged an uneasy alliance with the SS supremo – who gave the boy a teddy bear on his first birthday. That year, the family acquired two new properties, a larger house in the same exclusive Munich suburb as the Hesses, which was ready by mid September, though extensive renovations and refurbishments continued for another year, and a three-storey cottage in Obersalzburg.

Bormann purchased their place in the Bavarian Alps, sitting on a plateau that sloped away to trees below and was surrounded by towering mountain peaks, and began converting it; while he opted to retain some of the exterior features and outer walls, the interior was thoroughly remodelled and significantly enlarged. In autumn 1937, Gerda and her clan moved into what would be their almost permanent residence. A visiting journalist was bowled over by what he saw: 'From the cellar to the attic there was nothing but luxury and the best of everything.'[16]

Gerda's nearest neighbour in Obersalzburg was Hitler; he'd taken possession of a castle in the sky, the Berghof, which became an alternative command centre during his stays there. The Berghof emerged out of the cottage that Hitler had been renting since 1927 and subsequently bought in June 1933. Rather than raze it to the ground, a new structure grew upwards and outwards from its central core. Construction began in March 1936 and proceeded at lightning speed; by 8 July it was ready for occupation.

Money for both the Bormanns' and Hitler's new dwellings came from the Adolf Hitler Industrial Fund. The fund was the brainchild of a steel baron who convinced his fellow captains of industry to take a portion of their employees' wages and donate it to Hitler. From its inception, Bormann was in control of the treasure chest, making him Hitler's personal accountant and paymaster. Between 1933 and 1945, 350 million RM passed across his desk.

Though deliberately isolated, the Berghof complex was well connected to the outside world – it had a wireless station, three telephone exchanges and a post office – while the nearby market town of Berchtesgaden had a railway station and an airstrip for Hitler's personal use. Bormann arranged tight security. A 6ft-high electrified fence ran round the area, every one of the residents and staff carried ID and there was a barracks for a company of elite SS men.

At the Berghof, Hitler held court, relaxed, and pondered crucial decisions and questions of strategy. It was also where Bormann consolidated his place at Hitler's right hand, the executor of his every whim and idle request, and ultimately the gatekeeper of Hitler's domain. Over the years, under Bormann's management, it grew into a vast private estate for the Nazi elite with its own school and functioning farm: to give the many labourers who were employed on all the building work something to do other than drink and fight, there was a theatre and a brothel – with around twenty French and Italian prostitutes – in a barracks about 4 miles from Obersalzburg.

Initially, Bormann concentrated on removing more than 400 locals from their homes. Paying considerably more than the going rate, Bormann acquired their chalets and farms for modification or demolition.

On one occasion, Hitler pointed out a particular building that bothered him because it didn't blend in with the surroundings. Bormann promptly bought it, kicked out the inhabitants, had it torn down, and re-turfed the land on which it stood. The next time Hitler looked in that direction, he saw cows grazing in a field.

Hitler also had issues with the mobs of tourists who gathered outside the Berghof every day hoping to catch a glimpse of him; he would wander out and let them see their glorious leader as they paraded by. The process often took over an hour and in summer Hitler was forced to stand there in the blazing sun, which made him feel ill. In July 1937, Hitler casually mentioned this to Bormann. Immediately, his faithful servant got busy. Within twenty-four hours, Bormann had the head gardener and his team uproot a large lime tree and replant it in a spot where it could provide Hitler with the shade he needed.

Bormann also modified his personal habits to fall in line with Hitler's; a chain-smoker, Bormann refrained from lighting up in his master's presence – Hitler despised smoking – and complied with his vegetarian diet, though Heinrich Hoffmann observed that Bormann, having 'consumed raw carrots and leaves', would 'retire to the privacy of his room' and help himself to pork chops.[17]

In this new setting, Gerda slowly and tentatively began to emerge from her shell and gain a degree of independence, primarily because of her good relationship with Eva Braun. After Eva's 1935 suicide attempt, Hitler went out of his way to accommodate her; in August of that year, he rented a three-bedroom apartment for Eva and her sister; the following March, Hitler bought her a two-storey villa and a new car. More importantly for Eva, she was given the room adjoining Hitler's at the Berghof. It took her a while, and there were continued restrictions on her freedom of movement, but at the Berghof she came into her own.

Eva and Gerda were only three years apart in age, and Gerda's unthreatening demeanour went down well with Eva, whose main regret was that Gerda had so little free time because of her regular pregnancies and responsibilities as a housewife. Eva certainly knew that she had no reason to be jealous of Gerda. Hitler's abiding affection for her stayed within the bounds of his 'Uncle Adolf' persona; every year, he gave

Gerda a bouquet of red roses on her birthday. But Hitler also appreciated that Gerda was a model of German motherhood; according to a Berghof regular, he 'treated her with special respect'.[18]

Eva was less keen on Gerda's husband, and Bormann didn't care for her either. Yet they both recognised their mutual dependence on Hitler and the significance they both held for him and developed a marriage of convenience, presenting a united front where he was concerned, confining their rivalry to the minutiae of daily life; as time went on and Hitler was there less often, the power struggle between them for mastery of the Berghof bubbled up to the surface.

As Hitler made Bayreuth the home of opera, he wanted Munich to be the beating heart of German art. On 15 October 1933, at a ceremony broadcast on the radio and filmed by newsreel camera crews, Hitler laid the foundation stone for a new museum, the House of German Art. Three years later, the neo-classical building was complete. On 18 July 1937, Hitler opened its galleries with a speech that compared the new spirit in German art, which expressed 'the joy of life', with the 'deformed cripples and cretins' who practised modernism.[19] To commemorate this auspicious moment, the Nazis staged a massive parade in honour of 2,000 years of German culture and history. The chronologically themed procession was 6 miles long, took three hours and featured a Saxon warship, floats bearing medieval knights, mythological scenes, tributes to famous kings and military leaders, and tributes to cultural heavyweights like Wagner.

At the same time, in a hastily converted warehouse, the Degenerate Art Exhibition, which featured the work of prohibited artists, opened its doors and proved far more popular with the public than the House of German Art. Its collection of paintings of peasants, nude sculptures and heroic depictions of combat was no match for the degenerate alternative that included 730 artworks by German and foreign artists like Picasso, Matisse and van Gogh. Over 2 million people visited it at an average of 20,000 a day: the House of German Art only attracted around 3,000 a day.

Ilse and her husband liked to think of themselves as patrons of the art scene and aspired to turn their home into a sort of salon; one of their chosen artists was the modernist Georg Schrimpf. Munich based, Schrimpf's early Expressionist paintings reflected his left-wing attitudes, but by the late 1920s he'd moved to the right both stylistically and politically. This switch in style and viewpoint meant that Schrimpf escaped censure and in 1933 he became professor of the Royal School of Art in Berlin. Then, in 1937, the wind changed; Schrimpf was sacked and banned from showing his art, which was then removed from galleries and museums to join the others on display at the Degenerate Art Exhibition.

But the Hesses had his paintings hanging on their walls, and Hitler – who'd always hated Schrimpf's work – was disturbed to see these abominations when he visited Ilse and her husband in 1934. Up to that point, Hess seemed the logical choice to succeed Hitler; he was head of the party and had been at Hitler's side for over a decade. But after that evening, Hitler changed his mind. He told his press secretary that he couldn't possibly allow somebody with 'such a lack of feeling for art and culture' to be his second-in-command.[20] Shortly after this conversation, Hitler made Goering heir to the throne.

Hitler wasn't the only prominent Nazi who objected to an evening with the Hesses; Magda claimed that 'parties at the Hess home' were 'so boring that most people refused invitations'. Nobody was allowed to smoke. Instead of alcohol, Ilse served 'fruit juice and peppermint tea', and 'the conversation was as thin and dull as the drinks'; the guests were just thankful that Hess 'regularly broke up the party at midnight' so they could make an early getaway.[21]

Ilse did her best to compensate for her husband's reluctance to have fun, but it was an uphill struggle; when the director Leni Riefensthal dropped by for tea she remembered that Ilse 'chatted ... vivaciously' while 'her husband stayed silent'.[22] However, Hess did occasionally enjoy himself. In late October 1937, he and Ilse entertained the Duke and Duchess of Windsor. They were on a short trip to Germany and had spent the afternoon at the Berghof – where Magda played hostess – before dropping in on the Hesses.

The duke had briefly been King Edward VIII. He had acceded to the throne in January 1936 after the death of George V, but his love affair with the American socialite Wallis Simpson – who was on her third marriage at the time – led to his abdication eleven months later. With Simpson's divorce finalised, the couple got married in June 1937.

Ilse thought that the duke would have made an 'exceptionally clever king' and the duchess 'a fine' queen. During the course of a pleasant evening, Hess and the duke disappeared upstairs. After they had been gone an hour, Ilse went looking and 'found them in one of the attic rooms, where my husband had a large table with a collection of model ships from the German and English fleets of World War One'; the duke and Hess had arranged the models in formation and were 'excitedly' recreating one of its most dramatic sea battles.[23]

As for Munich's night-life, Ilse and her husband rarely ventured out except to go to classical concerts to hear music by their favourite composers, Mozart, Bach and Brahms. They studiously avoided the wild party crowd that inhabited Munich's sleazy underbelly and revelled in hedonistic excess.

Unity Mitford was part of this group; with Hitler rarely available to see her and her sister Diana mostly absent after her marriage to Mosley, she fell in with this fast-living Nazi clique as it ran around town, her energy and zeal never flagging. In fact, Unity was showing signs of becoming increasingly mentally unstable; she took poor care of herself, barely ate anything substantial and almost never slept. A string of unsuitable lovers and failed relationships didn't help matters. If anything, Unity would have benefited from Ilse's steadying hand on her shoulder, providing reassurance and guidance. It's not as if Ilse didn't have a reputation for looking out for the welfare of troubled young women, but Ilse and her husband viewed Unity as an interloper with no sense of decorum and no moral compass.

In the end, Ilse and Hess's quiet lifestyle suited them, with one notable exception. Hess had not completely lost his thirst for adventure and physical danger; drawing on his First World War training, he took up flying again, competing in an annual race to reach the peak of the Zugspitze, Germany's highest mountain. In 1932, he came in second. Two years later, he won the challenge cup and received a telegram of congratulations from the famous American aviator – and Nazi supporter – Charles Lindbergh.

No doubt Ilse was proud of her husband's achievement; if she'd known where his airborne antics would eventually take him, she might not have been so supportive. Hitler, on the other hand, was alarmed at the risks involved and promptly grounded Hess. For the time being, Hess only performed feats of death-defying speed when he was behind the wheel of his car; his adjutant remembered how Hess drove the Mercedes 'as if he were flying an aeroplane. At any moment one had the feeling that he was about to take off.'[24]

For all the apparent respect and hard-won status that Eva had gained at the Berghof, she was still operating within strict limits. On a regular basis, she was banished to her room, or back to her Munich villa, or told to disappear off-site for a few hours, often staying the night with Gerda. Her forced departures coincided with the arrivals of VIP guests and foreign statesmen at the Berghof. The same rules applied when Hitler was engaged in high-level political meetings with the senior Nazi leaders and officials such as Goering and Goebbels.

Eva usually took part in the social rituals of birthdays and seasonal holidays where the wives and children of the leading personalities joined their husbands at Hitler's table, but she kept a low profile when Magda stayed at the Berghof without her family in tow. These solo visits only occurred a handful of times and never for very long; when they did, Magda was seeking escape from her rocky marriage and a morale boost from her beloved Hitler.

Yet Magda never became part of the Berghof community; she and Goebbels didn't even have a property in the area. This was partly due to Eva; though Magda tried to assert her authority, Eva now felt secure enough to hold her ground. One story about them illustrates this shift in power; while having a chat, a heavily pregnant Magda asked Eva if she wouldn't mind tying her shoelace as she found it difficult to bend over; unfazed by this request to kneel before her superior, Eva calmly rang a bell and got her maid to do it.

Emmy and her husband did have a substantial home in the complex but were not Berghof insiders. Given that they had Carinhall, they weren't down south very often. However, there was also the Eva factor. For some reason – which is hard to pin down since Emmy was clearly not a competitor for Hitler's attention like Unity and Magda – Eva deliberately avoided her: perhaps she sensed Hitler's discomfort around Emmy; perhaps she objected to Emmy's pompous, regal manner; maybe she felt intimidated by her; maybe it was a generational conflict; or maybe she simply didn't like her.

Whatever the cause, Eva turned her back on Emmy. Evidence for this comes from a number of the Berghof staff who were privy to an incident that occurred while both Hitler and Goering were elsewhere. What seems to have happened is that Emmy, in an effort to break the ice, invited Eva – and her ladies-in-waiting – to tea one afternoon. But Eva and her little gang didn't turn up, and Emmy never received an apology or an explanation. Having been so rudely snubbed, Emmy didn't bother to extend the hand of friendship again.

Ilse, on the other hand, was always welcome; Eva regarded her as a long-term friend and potential confidante. However, Ilse – perhaps sensing that Hitler no longer appreciated her company – only visited the Berghof when she was obliged to. Instead, she often looked after Eva when she was exiled from the Berghof; Ilse recalled that the two of them 'would go on a walking tour in the mountains or something'.[25]

Eva valued Ilse's companionship; Ilse understood the difficulty of Eva's situation and treated her with kindness and sympathy. Yet no matter how complimentary Ilse was about Eva – praising her looks and sweet nature – she couldn't help comparing her to Geli, Hitler's one true love: Ilse thought Eva was a perfectly acceptable replacement, just not as good as the original.

When Hess stayed overnight at the Berghof – which he did every now and then – he occupied the Untersberg Room, which was rarely used except by him. On the top floor, the suite had a large wood-panelled living area with a desk, a bathroom and bedroom, and a balcony that offered stunning views across the mountains that stretched as far as

Salzburg. While this sleeping arrangement appeared to flatter Hess and confirm his elevated position in the movement, it also reflected his growing estrangement and detachment from the Nazi elite, including Hitler: to many, he was the eccentric weirdo in the attic, lost in his own world.

With Bormann dealing with the vast bulk of the administrative workload, Hess had more free time to indulge his esoteric interests. As an awkward adolescent, Hess was enthralled by astrology and in 1907 he was inspired by Daniel's Comet, the most brilliant to appear in the northern hemisphere for twenty-five years, which was visible at dawn from mid July until the end of August. Hess later recalled his first sighting of the comet: 'The tail shimmered swiftly across what was about a third of the sky. Every night I got up to observe its rapid flight and changing form. From that moment I never lost interest in the stars.'[26]

In 1933, Ilse introduced Hess to Ernst Schultz-Strathaus, whom she had first met in the early 1920s when she was working in the antiquarian bookshop. Strathaus was a literary scholar who had run several journals for bibliophiles; he was also an expert on the occult. Knowing Hess's fascination with the stars of the zodiac, Ilse brought the two of them together. In 1934, Hess secured Strathaus a position on his staff as an advisor on cultural affairs. At the same time, Strathaus acted as Hess's personal astrologer, providing him with a daily horoscope. Though Ilse was not quite as immersed in the occult as her husband, she endorsed his mystical outlook and believed, like him, that supernatural forces shaped human destiny. She once observed that 'in moments of extreme spiritual tension there comes to us, from regions lying outside the field of reason, knowledge that will not let us be deceived'.[27]

The regime's attitude to astrology was ambiguous. Officially, it was considered to be an alternative belief system and therefore a threat, not least because it was hugely popular with the general public. As a result, soothsayers suffered sudden waves of persecution. In 1937, the German Astrological Society was abolished and its periodicals banned.

Yet Hess – who was often singled out for his reliance on Strathaus's charts – was not alone. At various points, Himmler consulted astrologers, and there was speculation that Hitler saw a clairvoyant, a wizened old gypsy who was said to have the magic touch. But Hess was considered the main offender and there were rumours he dabbled in mesmerism and employed psychics to manipulate solid objects like metal.

Another of Hess's pet subjects was alternative medicine, which sprung from his own persistent health problems; the first sign of stress-related illness was a severe outbreak of boils during the tense autumn of 1932 that put him in hospital. From then on, he was afflicted by a range of problems: bloating, kidney pain, heart palpitations, rotten guts and insomnia. To combat these complaints, Hess adopted a macrobiotic diet. Both he and Ilse turned vegetarian when Hitler did – so even their digestive tracts could be in synch with his – but Hess was even more fastidious than Hitler when it came to his meals. At first, Ilse went to great lengths to prepare appropriate food for her husband, but eventually Hess hired a special cook who accompanied him everywhere. On a trip to Vienna, Henriette Hoffmann – who was living in the Austrian capital with her husband Baldur von Schirach – remembered that Hess 'carried with him a little pot of spinach with mysterious ingredients'.[28]

His stubborn refusal to ingest any other food – no matter what – was a bone of contention with Hitler: when Hess ate at the Reich Chancellery, he would spurn the vegetarian option chosen by Hitler in favour of the nourishment he'd brought with him; a lunch guest remembered how an annoyed Hitler offered to have his 'first-class cook' prepare whatever Hess liked. Hess declined, explaining that 'the components of his meals had to be of a special bio-dynamic origin'.[29] Hitler took Hess's refusal personally, suggested that he eat at home in future and rarely invited him again.

Hess's rigid regime was not just a personal quirk. With Ilse's backing, he devoted considerable time and energy to the promotion, study and development of alternative therapies and treatments. In 1934, Hess lobbied successfully for the incorporation of a wide range of associations – such as the German Natural Healer's Association, the Society for Spas and Climatic Science, and the League of Hydro-therapists – into the Nazis' official organisation for health professionals. Next, he set up the Rudolf Hess Hospital in Dresden as a centre for naturopathic medicine; run by a cancer specialist who admired the theories of the renowned psychotherapist Carl Jung – as did other senior staff members – its patients were treated to water cures, a variety of diets and periods of fasting.

In 1937, Hess hosted the World Conference of Homeopathy in Berlin; he began his opening speech with a plea to the medical profession to 'consider even previously excluded therapies with an open mind', then declared that homeopathy was the most appropriate 'form of science' for treating 'living creatures', confidently stated that the 'demand for holism' was getting 'stronger and stronger',[30] and assured his audience that political conditions in Nazi Germany provided an opportunity to make great strides forward.

As with astrology, Hess was unfairly victimised for being a sucker, duped by cranks and their irrational mumbo jumbo. Asides from Himmler, whose interest in herbal medicine was hardly a secret, the regime sought to harness the power of natural healing. Its war on cancer was an overriding priority: it involved research into whether a plant-based diet could ward off the disease, and identified the use of chemicals in food and everyday household products as a potential cause.

At the root of Hess's experiments in organic medicines – and his reliance on mystical prophecies – was his and Ilse's failure to conceive a child. Given their self-image as the torch-bearers of the movement, it felt shameful not to have added one of their own to the Nazis' ranks. Together, they went to extreme lengths to make amends; Hess worked hard to overcome his aversion to sex. Though their efforts were fruitless, Ilse refused to give up hope; Magda told one of Goebbels's staff that Ilse 'assured her five or six times over a number of years that she was at last going to have a child – generally because some fortune-teller had said she would'.[31]

Desperate, Hess abandoned his principles and went in search of a pharmaceutical pick-me-up. In Munich, there was a chemist directly opposite Heinrich Hoffmann's studio. Every day, witnesses observed Hess enter the pharmacy and come out with a life-enhancing potion designed to boost his virility.

This wonder cure was probably one of the wide range of hormone-based anti-impotence pills available without a prescription. The biggest seller was Titus Pearls, created by Magnus Hirschfeld, the noted sexologist whose Institute for Sexual Science was shut down by the Nazis. However, the product containing his formula stayed on the shelves. The firm that manufactured it also made a breast enlargement drug for women; the sales pitch boasted that it would transform their figures 'from the inside out'.[32]

Around the same time Hess was taking his supplement, the advertisements for Titus Pearls were targeted specifically at men like him; jaded middle-aged executives looking to spice up their love lives. The marketing campaign's underlying message – which implied that a sexually inactive man was not a useful member of the community because of his failure to reproduce – applied directly to Hess; the general assumption was that Hess was the one with the problem, not Ilse, and the pressure was on him to rectify matters.

Whether it was the drugs, or the alignment of the stars, or the miraculous properties of his diet, Ilse finally became pregnant in early 1937. The couple were thrilled; now all Ilse had to do was deliver an all-important boy and their work would be done. Hess searched for favourable omens. According to folklore, if a larger than average number of wasps appeared during the summer, you could expect a higher percentage of male births; Hess kept careful count of the wasps buzzing round his and Ilse's garden by trapping them in honey jars.

The signs were good, and on 18 November, Ilse had a son – their only child – named Wolf Rüdiger Hess. Hitler was the godfather, and 'Wolf' was a nickname he'd used back in the early days. Ilse and her husband had become proud parents; but in doing so, Hess lost what was left of his credibility.

According to Magda and her husband, when Wolf was born, Hess 'danced with joy' in a manner that resembled 'South American Indians'. Hess then issued an order to all the regional party bosses asking them to send 'bags of German soil' to 'spread under a specially built cradle' so that his son could begin life 'symbolically on German soil'. Goebbels found the request highly amusing, considered sending a 'Berlin pavement stone'[33] to reflect his urban constituency, but in the end opted for a sealed package of manure taken from his garden.

8

SS WIVES' CLUB

Margaret Himmler and Lina Heydrich were not part of the Berghof clique. Margaret made no more than a couple of appearances at formal events; Lina never got past the front door. Despite their husbands' expanding empire they were not in the same league as Magda and Emmy – neither Lina nor Margaret had a public profile to speak of – or as established in Hitler's entourage as Gerda and Ilse.

Their secondary status annoyed them both. They expected to be treated with greater respect given their husbands' achievements, and granted the seniority due to them. Both complained incessantly that Himmler and Heydrich were not appreciated enough by Hitler or rewarded with the same generosity as other senior figures; the fact that her husband 'did not get enough recognition'[1] was a constant refrain in Margaret's diary.

However, rather than join forces and work together – as their husbands so successfully did – they were constantly at loggerheads. Margaret resented Lina's obvious ambition to be the most influential SS wife; Lina couldn't bear playing second fiddle to a woman for whom she had nothing but contempt. Lina thought Margaret was inferior to her in every way and never missed an opportunity to ruthlessly put her down. She mocked Margaret's more than full figure – '50 size knickers, that's all there was to her' – and called her a 'narrow minded, humourless blonde female', who was 'always worrying about protocol'.[2]

Lina wasn't alone in having such a negative view of Margaret; Heinriette Hoffmann thought she was 'a small bad-tempered woman who seemed born to be unhappy'. Many agreed with Lina that Margaret 'ruled her husband and twisted him round her little finger'.[3] The Nazi in-crowd refused to take her seriously, even Unity Mitford would 'laugh openly about Frau Himmler'.

Word of Unity's insults got back to Margaret and she complained to a mutual friend about that 'good-for-nothing Unity'; the acquaintance apologised on her behalf, then warned Unity to watch her mouth. This kindly woman – who'd been round the movement for years – expressed sympathy towards Margaret, 'a poor wretch who'd been through the First World War as a nurse', and had given her all; as a result, 'nothing was left of her'.[4] Others echoed this assessment, arguing that Margaret was the way she was because she'd suffered shell-shock, a piece of idle speculation that could be cruel or kind depending on the context.

Margaret was well aware of Lina's open hostility and raised the matter with her husband. Himmler already disapproved of Lina's tendency to speak her mind and interfere in SS business, which also got on Heydrich's nerves. Himmler asked another SS wife, Frieda Wolff – she knew both Margaret and Lina well and her husband was Himmler's personal adjutant – to have a quiet word with Lina, which Frieda did at a naval regatta. Lina didn't take kindly to being told she was out of order – 'I was accused of the most impossible things, my husband was accused of not being able to keep me within my limits' – and angrily rebuffed Frieda.

Having failed with this indirect approach Margaret allegedly persuaded Himmler to order Heydrich to either divorce Lina or quit the SS. Heydrich must have told Lina because she claimed she had a showdown with Himmler at one of Goering's garden parties when they were seated at the same table. Rather than being her usual voluble and assertive self, Lina kept quiet throughout; 'I put on my most mournful expression and sat stock still'. This unnerved Himmler, and he asked Lina if she was all right. She shrugged off his question and then they danced, which Himmler did 'badly'. And that apparently was that. Himmler told her everything was fine and never mentioned it again. Lina concluded that the whole incident was 'typical Himmler, on paper he ordered us to divorce, but when face to face with me, his courage left him'.[5]

In the end, regardless of what Margaret wanted, Himmler had no desire to jeopardise the excellent working relationship he had with Heydrich. The two made a formidable team. Heydrich never challenged the authority of his superior and did everything he could to fulfil his wishes; he might argue a point or grumble behind Himmler's back, but Heydrich's loyalty never wavered. Himmler was in awe of his subordinate's organisational capabilities and his 'absolutely amazing' ability to tell if someone was lying and judge whether somebody was a 'friend or foe'.[6] Their strengths and weaknesses complemented each other. Himmler was better in social situations; when Heydrich walked into a room the temperature dropped. Heydrich's thought processes were logical and linear; Himmler's were more abstract and convoluted.

For all the energy Margaret and Lina expended on doing each other down, they suffered from almost exactly the same problems in their marriages; a feeling of neglect and abandonment. Their husbands had no time for them or their children, only for their work.

On 23 December 1934 Lina gave birth to her second child, a son named Heider. Now she had two boys, and although there were servants to lighten her load, there was a lack of family support; her parents were a long way off on the Baltic island of Fehmarn, while Heydrich had virtually cut all ties with his parents and siblings.

Margaret, meanwhile, was having serious trouble with her adopted son Gerhard; he stole, he lied, he played truant. Punishing the boy made no difference, even though Himmler beat him with a riding crop. As far as Margaret was concerned, Gerhard was 'criminal by nature'. At her wits' end, Margaret tried to return Gerhard to his real mother but she wanted a big pay-off, so he was sent away to boarding school where he was ruthlessly bullied by the other pupils. Their daughter, Gudrun, on the other hand, was 'sweet and nice', yet she was still subjected to the same severe discipline and expected to meet Margaret's high standards.

Himmler's family were around to give her support but Margaret never got on with them. Her own parents had never approved of the marriage and stayed away, though from 1934 her younger sister, a trained seamstress, was a permanent resident and available to lend a hand, along with the servants, the cook and the gardener. However, Margaret was always clashing with her domestic staff. After firing one impertinent and 'lazy' couple, she remarked that 'people like that should be locked away and forced to work until they die'.[7]

Over Christmas and New Year 1934–35, Margaret and her husband had house guests: Walther Darré – head of the SS's Race and Settlement Office and Reich Minister for Food and Agriculture – and his wife Charlotte, the elegant well-educated daughter of an aristocratic landowner with right-wing anti-Semitic views. Having joined the SS in 1930, Darré, who'd served in the artillery during the First World War, worked as a farm manager and written extensively about animal breeding, quickly became friends with Himmler; Darré shared Himmler's vision of a racially pure peasant utopia and had coined the phrase 'blood and soil'.

Darré had hired Charlotte as his secretary in 1929 and they were married three years later. Charlotte and Margaret had a fair amount in common; they were roughly the same age and had both grown up on large farms. As a wedding present, Margaret and Himmler gave Darré and Charlotte two silver pots and a massive biography of Genghis Khan.

The families were enjoying the Himmler family's first Christmas at their new lakeside property in Tegernsee, which was not far from Munich. Bought from a singer, the substantial chalet-style house had a separate command post manned by four SS men, a private dock, land for livestock – sheep, ponies, pigs and deer – a fishpond, a greenhouse and a meadow used for croquet in summer and ice skating in winter.

That holiday season there was much for Himmler and Darré to celebrate; 1934 was a critically important year for their organisation as it expanded its power at the expense of Röhm's SA, which had become an obstacle to Hitler's plans to prepare Germany for war; he needed stability at home and abroad, and the full cooperation of the army. The SA, however, wanted to supplant the armed forces as the main source of military power and clean out the surviving remnants of the old order. In the meantime, Röhm refused to curb the street violence, vandalism and intimidation for which his men were infamous.

By spring 1934, the tension had built to a point where some kind of reckoning seemed inevitable. The question was who would strike first. This was Himmler's moment. In exchange for using the SS to suppress the SA, Goering agreed to give his police powers in Prussia to Himmler – who'd already assumed them in all the other regions – and control over the Gestapo.

During the night of 30 June–1 July, Himmler's hit squads struck. Anywhere between 83 and 200 people – including the unfortunate Dr Schmidt – were assassinated on the Night of the Long Knives. Röhm survived a few hours longer as Hitler and his cronies debated his fate; in the end he was gunned down in his cell. The fact that Röhm had befriended Lina and her husband, and was godfather to their first child, made no difference in the cutthroat world of Nazi politics; neither she nor Heydrich expressed any remorse. Hitler, meanwhile, was delighted: 'In view of the great services rendered by the SS ... I hereby promote the SS to the status of independent organisation.'[8]

For all the goodwill flowing that yuletide, Christmas was a not a straightforward matter for the Nazi elite. The holiday was a muted affair at the Berghof due to the depression that always dogged Hitler at that time of year, brought on by the memory of his mother's death, which occurred on 21 December 1907 and still haunted him. Usually Hitler would spend Christmas Day alone in Munich; one Christmas Eve, he hired a taxi to drive him aimlessly round the city, killing time.

On a less personal level, Christmas was a key battleground in the Nazis' struggle to detach the German people from Christianity. Hitler considered it to be a religion that worshipped weakness and blunted the nation's fighting spirit. Though Hitler remained agnostic, most of his cohorts abandoned the faith of their childhoods and adopted paganism, reconnecting with the symbols and rituals of the old gods.

Himmler and Darré were practising pagans. So were the Hesses. Both Lina and Gerda's husbands despised Christians and did everything in their power to make life uncomfortable for them. Magda and Goebbels endorsed the anti-Church campaign; only Emmy and Goering main-tained a notional commitment to its traditions.

Given Christmas's significance for Christians, the Nazis did their best to appropriate the holiday. There were Nazi-themed carols, Christmas cards emblazoned with swastikas, tree decorations bearing Nazi party insignia, and chocolate SA men. Mothers were encouraged to bake bis-cuits in the shape of runic symbols. Though Himmler tried to reintroduce a pagan holiday called the Feast of Midsummer, which he hoped would eventually be more popular than Christmas, he also pushed the SS brand every December – you could buy advent calendars with pictures of SS personnel and special yule candlesticks with the SS logo on them – and promoted the idea that Santa Claus was based on the Norse god Odin.

Himmler left no stone unturned in his efforts to discredit the Church. He commissioned a detailed investigation into the witch-hunts of the sixteenth and seventeenth centuries. Researchers collected a vast archive of material – amounting to nearly 34,000 pages – to prove that the so-called 'witches' were in fact good pagans who provided a hugely ben-eficial service to their communities because they knew how to exploit the magical properties of herbs and plants; by demonising and burning these wise and spiritually gifted women, the Christian authorities had committed an awful crime.

Himmler's 'Special Witch Project' was only one of a bewildering range of pseudo-academic initiatives that he launched, the majority of which were undertaken by his unique creation, the *Ahnenerbe*. This sprawling organisation employed ideologically sympathetic archaeolo-gists, anthropologists and scientists who operated on the margins of their disciplines and were charged with uncovering the ancient and prehis-toric lineage of the Aryan race and its crucial role in the development of the human species; there was even an attempt to prove that the very first *Homo sapiens* were of Aryan origin. Teams of experts visited potential sites of interest in North Africa, the Middle East and as far away as Tibet.

Quite what Margaret made of her husband's ideological obsessions is hard to gauge. She did continue to absorb the reading material that Himmler regularly gave her – from history books recounting the exploits of tribal chieftains who took on the mighty Roman Empire to archaeo-logical papers analysing skulls. She would dutifully plough through these texts and referred to them in her diary and in her letters to Himmler. She usually expressed an interest without offering much in the way of comment or feedback. Clearly Himmler wanted Margaret to share his passions, or at the very least approve of them. On 25 May 1935 he took her to Wewelsburg to see the castle he was going to renovate and restore to its former medieval glory and use as a gathering place for his elite SS knights, like King Arthur's Camelot. When Margaret visited, it was still a ruin.

Perhaps Margaret tolerated Himmler's bizarre enthusiasms in the same way that countless wives put up with their partner's pet projects, encouraging them while keeping their real feelings to themselves. In the end, the time Himmler spent on his castle and myriad other schemes was time he wasn't spending with her and Gudrun. Throughout the whole of 1935, Himmler only managed to fit in six weeks at their Tegernsee home.

Lina said that she and Heydrich found Himmler's eccentricities amusing – 'we laughed about his hobbies' – but essentially harmless; 'my husband and I just had a well-meaning smile for them', she remembered, and they listened 'without emotion to his theories about pagan stones'.

Even so, Heydrich was not totally disinterested in Himmler's 'mysticism'.[9] On the summer solstice 1935, he was being shown round Fehmarn – the island where Lina grew up – by a local historian who led him to a well-known eighteenth-century farmhouse that stood on the site of a much older building that had ancient stone graves beside it. Given Himmler's interest in early Scandinavian cultures – the *Ahnenerbe* explored Denmark, Sweden, Norway, Iceland and Finland – Heydrich proposed establishing a big museum there and a foundation to pay for it. Fehmarn was also where Lina and her husband had their holiday home; work on it was finished the day Heydrich made his archaeological discovery. With money borrowed from the son of a rich industrialist who'd inherited his father's fortune, they bought a good-sized plot of land by a beach overlooking the Baltic and erected a traditional timber-framed house with a thatched roof. Lina loved it and the family spent most of their summers there.

One of the results of the SS's elevation after the Night of the Long Knives was that Lina and Margaret acquired apartments in Berlin. A new world of possibilities was opening up for them. In Munich, Lina always felt out on a limb, excluded from the upper echelons of Nazi society; now, in Berlin, she was determined to mix with suitably distinguished and influential people.

Coming to her aid was the 25-year-old Walter Schellenberg. Handsome and intelligent, Schellenberg was a student at Bonn University who'd done two years of medicine before switching to law; he enrolled in the SS in 1933 and entered the SD after being recruited by two of his professors. Soon he was socialising with Heydrich and Lina. According to Schellenberg, Lina 'was glad to find … someone who could satisfy her hunger for the better things in life, her longing for more intelligent and cultivated society in the world of literature and art.' He took the couple 'to concerts and the theatre' and they 'began to frequent the best circles in Berlin society'.[10]

Entertaining was made easier for Lina in February 1937 when the family moved to a new nine-room house – each one with its own alarm – spread over three floors with two extra rooms for the servants, SS guards at the front gate, and a large garden where Lina installed a playground and a hen-house.

Lina was hampered in her endeavours by her husband; not only was Heydrich thoroughly bored by polite society – he preferred trawling the bars and nightclubs accompanied by his SS comrades – he also had little interest in making friends. Lina observed that he never had 'any personal friends' and 'tried to avoid any social contact between neighbours and fellow workers'.[11]

Nevertheless, there were exceptions. Herbert Backe and his wife Ursula, together with their children – who were roughly the same age as Lina's boys – were regular guests in the Heydrich home, spending weekends and evenings with them. Backe, who'd joined the SS in 1933, was an agricultural expert and protégé of Darré. Backe then got Darré's job after Himmler ditched him and ended their friendship. Like Lina, Ursula was a wholehearted Nazi and acted as her husband's unofficial secretary, PA and archivist combined; her diary was essentially a forensic record of Backe's activities.

Yet the relationships Lina did manage to foster were fragile, subject to the machinations of Nazi politics and the rivalries in which her husband was constantly engaged. A case in point is the Heydrichs' relationship with Wilhelm Canaris and his wife Erika. Canaris was a war hero who'd joined the navy in 1905 aged 18, commanded a brutal *Freikorps* regiment, and by 1923 was an officer aboard the same ship as the young trainee Heydrich. Erika was a cerebral, cultured woman with a passion for music. A capable violinist, she held tea parties where she'd perform with a string quartet. When one of them dropped out, Canaris suggested Heydrich as a replacement; Erika was delighted by his sublime violin playing and Heydrich became a permanent member.

The friendship was short-lived and Canaris and Heydrich went in separate directions. By 1933, Canaris's career was stalled, but with the ascension of the Nazis his fortunes changed and on 1 January 1935 he became head of the *Abwehr*, the army's espionage section. Not long after, Lina and Heydrich ran into Canaris and Erika as they were out walking with their children and discovered they were neighbours.

Lina appreciated Erika's refined character while Heydrich and Canaris seemed pleased to renew their acquaintance. They went riding in the nearby Grunewald forest, played croquet in the afternoon, and held a weekly music evening with Heydrich on first violin, Erika second, his younger brother on cello and a friend on viola. Canaris, who was a keen cook, provided fine food; his specialities were wild boar in a red wine sauce and herring salad served with brandy and caviar.

However, despite Lina's claims that the professional rivalry between Canaris and her husband 'did not touch our private and social life',[12] tension between them was never far from the surface. The *Abwehr* and the SD were natural opponents, especially as Heydrich wanted to control every aspect of intelligence work both at home and abroad. Though the two of them hammered out a deal – known as the Ten Commandments – that defined and clarified their areas of responsibility, they never trusted each other. When Heydrich noticed one of Erika's daughters taking an interest in the desk in his study, he accused her of spying, while in his diary Canaris referred to Heydrich as a 'brutal fanatic with whom it will be difficult to have open and friendly cooperation'.[13] They may have maintained a civilised exterior, but the two men were locked in a deadly struggle for dominance.

Once settled in Berlin, Margaret became immersed in the world of a First Lady of the Reich. She was now part of the diplomatic party circuit and faithfully recorded her reactions to each event in her diary: she thought the French Ambassador was 'the funniest, most amusing person I have ever met'; at the Argentinian embassy she saw 'many people I know'; the Egyptian embassy was 'very nice'; a soiree hosted by Hitler at the Reich Chancellery for 200 people featured 'gorgeous flowers everywhere, just marvellous'; and five days later, she was at the Ministry of Propaganda, which was 'very boring, we left early'.[14]

Aside from getting on well with the odd countess and being intrigued by the Japanese ambassador's German wife – who told her 'many intimate and interesting things' – Margaret struggled to fit in with the crowd and was clearly out of her comfort zone in high society: 'New invitations are starting again. If only I didn't need so much sleep.' A good night out for Margaret was a trip to the theatre – she preferred comedies like the farce *All Lies*, which she found 'very funny'[15] – and sometimes the cinema. Otherwise, she was perfectly happy having a quiet evening in, playing bridge and retiring early with a good book.

Despite her social awkwardness, Margaret wanted to be seen as an important figure, worthy of respect. Every Wednesday, she hosted a tea party in her new fourteen-room villa for the leading SS wives. Normally anywhere between six and ten women showed up. Margaret's guests were all from middle- and upper-class families, like Frieda Wolff, whose aristocratic father had worked for the Grand Duke of Hesse, run a district court and owned shares in a paper company. Frieda's husband, and the spouses of the other wives in the club, had similar professional backgrounds – lawyers, economists, political scientists and businessmen – that reflected Himmler and Heydrich's recruitment strategy.

Lina was dead against Margaret's initiative and set about sabotaging it. Her first move was to bring the wives into her orbit. With the help of one of them, an ex-dancer, Lina staged a one-off musical performance that began with the SS ladies singing folk songs and ended with them doing the cancan. Next, Lina organised a fitness class; scheduled to clash with Margaret's tea parties, it combined gymnastics and calisthenics, and was run by an instructor provided by Heydrich.

After their first gruelling session, Lina's exercise group were all hot and sweaty, but they were embarrassed about using the gym's communal showers. To encourage them to overcome their shyness, Lina stripped off and stood naked in full view of them, which was enough to get her fellow SS wives to shed their inhibitions and their clothes. Overall, the class was a success; at the end, eight of the ladies won a gold sports badge, while another twenty got silver.

In 1936, sport offered Lina another chance to get one up on Margaret. Her husband was on the German Olympic Committee and during the games Lina and Heydrich were given much better seats than Margaret and Himmler – an arrangement that delighted Lina because it 'did not suit Himmler. He was used to my husband being second to him'[16] – and they were invited to all the gala events. They even sat at a top table during the International Olympic Committee ball, a six-course feast of the finest food at the magnificent White Hall in Berlin Castle held the night before the opening ceremony. Lina and Heydrich were also awarded VIP status at the Winter Olympics earlier that year and had their own fleets of cars and a private plane at their disposal.

Of all the sports Heydrich excelled at, fencing was the most important to him. He practised with the best and competed at a high level; at the SS Fencing Master's tournament in November 1936, Heydrich was fifth in the rapier class and third in the sabre class. This was a more than creditable performance, but Heydrich hated losing, often ignored fencing etiquette, and challenged the referee's decisions.

Himmler's sport was tennis, and he was a keen player. For a time, Margaret took up the game; aside from needing the exercise – she was in her forties and had problems with her weight – it was one activity she could share with her husband. The effort obviously proved too much for her and she soon stopped taking to the court with racquet in hand. Himmler, however, kept up his tennis on a regular basis.

Himmler's genuine interest in the sport did not mean he was prepared to compromise his principles. The aristocratic Gottfried von Cramm – twice winner of the French Open and twice runner-up at Wimbledon – was the undisputed no. 1 German tennis player. Though von Cramm had gone through the necessary motions and married in 1930, his preference was for men, and before the Nazi era he was relatively open about his sexuality, taking advantage of the liberated atmosphere of Weimar Berlin. Himmler deeply feared and hated homosexuality; in a 1937 speech, he declared that it was the reason why 'the male state is in the process of destroying itself'.[17] Initially, the Nazis continued using the Weimar law on homosexuality that made it illegal for two men over the age of 21 to have penetrative sex. Under its provisions, 4,000 men were convicted between 1933 and 1935. Then the scope of the law was widened to include any 'indecent activity between men'.[18] This change produced a dramatic escalation in convictions; from 1935 to 1939, 30,000 men were sent to prison or concentration camps.

After being denounced by a hustler, von Cramm was picked up in April 1937 by two Gestapo agents, grilled for several hours and released. He was spared jail because he was about to contend the inter-zonal final of the Davis Cup, a competition Germany had never won despite getting close in recent years.

The decisive match, played on the Centre Court at Wimbledon, against Don Budge from the US team, has gone down in tennis history as a classic; millions in Germany, including Hitler – who'd called von Cramm just before the match to wish him luck – tuned in to hear ball-by-ball radio commentary, willing von Cramm on to victory. With the stakes incredibly high, he came close but was beaten in five nail-biting sets.

Had von Cramm won, his fate might have been different. But defeat left him totally exposed and, worse still, his wife divorced him. Himmler seized the chance to put him behind bars; in May 1938 he was sentenced to a year's imprisonment for a relationship with a young Jewish actor, but was paroled after six months. In 1939, von Cramm tried to make a comeback but was stopped in his tracks when the All England Club – using his criminal record as an excuse – prevented him from playing at Wimbledon.

By 1936, Lina was convinced that Heydrich was cheating on her; in a brutally honest statement about her husband, she said that 'he was keen on anything in a skirt'.[19] Lina didn't have any clear idea about who the women concerned might be, but she was sure she wasn't imagining things; why else would her husband stay out all night – which he frequently did – returning at dawn reeking of booze and perfume? Lina repeatedly confronted Heydrich about it and hurled accusations at him, but he denied everything.

Her fears on that front were unfounded; Heydrich was not having affairs or keeping any mistresses hidden away. Several of his SS colleagues, however, testified that he regularly visited prostitutes and gained a reputation for treating them badly. One SS officer claimed that after being with Heydrich 'even the most pitiful whore would not want him a second time'.[20] The same man recounted a visit to a brothel in Naples where Heydrich emptied a purse of gold coins on the floor and watched the prostitutes and the madam fight over them.

Taking into account the questionable reliability of the witnesses who had every reason to make their boss appear as twisted and depraved as possible – thereby making themselves appear less appalling – there is definite pattern to Heydrich's sexual behaviour. In May 1926, he was on a naval exercise that included a spell in Barcelona. One of his fellow officer cadets remembered that Heydrich went in search of a brothel the second he disembarked. The former cadet also recalled an unsavoury incident during a function at the German Club; Heydrich took 'a young lady of impeccable social background' for a stroll in the garden and 'behaved in such a manner that the girl slapped him in the face'.[21] Soon after, Heydrich caused a scene at a dinner dance when he repeatedly asked the wives of some English officers to dance. Then there are the circumstances surrounding his dismissal from the navy and the distressed girlfriend he dumped for Lina.

These actions – added to the revelations of his fellow SS men – are strong indications that Heydrich's treatment of prostitutes wasn't merely malicious gossip; they offer further confirmation of his sociopathic tendencies. Emotionally stunted and lacking empathy, Heydrich viewed other people as objects, things that could be manipulated to serve his own needs. He also loved the thrill of pushing boundaries and proving to himself that he was untouchable; if his nocturnal habits had become public knowledge, Heydrich would have been ruined.

Fearing the spread of sexually transmitted diseases, the Nazi regime was extremely tough on street-walkers – during 1933 thousands were arrested – but it was more flexible when it came to brothels. Having been closed down in the Weimar era, brothels began to open for business again, especially in the big cities. In 1937, it became legal for a prostitute to rent a room in a building as long as there were no children under 18 living there. However, that same year, prostitutes were caught up in mass arrests of 'anti-social' elements. They were also subject to regular health tests; if a prostitute showed any signs of VD, she was sterilised.

Regardless of the severe punishments inflicted on those in the sex trade, Heydrich decided to become a brothel owner. According to Schellenberg, Heydrich wanted an 'establishment where important visitors from other countries could be "entertained" in a discreet atmosphere where they would be offered seductive feminine company' and hopefully 'reveal some useful information'.

For this purpose, an elegant house in a fashionable quarter of the capital was requisitioned, a leading architect chose the furnishings and decor, and there were double walls with microphones in them, connected by 'automatic transmission to tape recorders which would record every word spoken throughout the house'. Three technical experts – 'bound by an oath' – ran the apparatus. An experienced madam, known as 'Kitty', was put in charge of sixteen carefully selected high-class prostitutes, who all spoke a number of foreign languages.

Salon Kitty did a roaring trade; everybody from foreign dignitaries to high-ranking Nazis and government ministers, military men and figures from showbusiness, uttered the password – 'Rothenburg' – and went through its doors. Schellenberg said the collected pillow talk yielded a plentiful haul of 'diplomatic secrets'.[22]

Though Lina remained ignorant of her husband's night-time pursuits, she was nevertheless convinced that Heydrich was playing around. However, Lina was not the type of woman to let anybody take advantage of her. She was attractive, still only in her twenties, and had needs and desires that were not being satisfied by her workaholic husband; the evidence is circumstantial, but it does appear that Lina sought out the company of other men.

One of Lina's alleged trysts was with Walter Schellenberg. In Schellenberg's version of events, he deflects any suggestion that he was actually engaged in a relationship with Lina by focusing on Heydrich's paranoia. Suspicions alerted by what was probably no more than a harmless flirtation, Heydrich tried to catch Schellenberg and Lina in the act. Schellenberg had been at the Heydrichs' island retreat attending an SS conference with other senior personnel and stayed on an extra day after his boss flew back to Berlin, during which he and Lina visited a lake, had coffee together, and according to Schellenberg 'talked about art, literature and concerts'.

Four days later, and back in the capital, Heydrich asked Schellenberg to join him and the head of the Gestapo, Heinrich Mueller, for a night on the town. Following their meal, they went to an obscure bar and ordered drinks. Once Schellenberg had taken a few swigs, Mueller – a veteran policeman – switched into interrogation mode. Had Schellenberg enjoyed his little outing with Lina? Didn't he realise he was being watched all the time? Rattled, Schellenberg insisted nothing untoward was going on. Then Heydrich coolly informed Schellenberg that his drink was poisoned; if he swore on his honour that he was telling the truth, Heydrich would give him the antidote. Having insisted that he was, Schellenberg was immediately handed a dry Martini, which he thought tasted a bit odd; it 'certainly seemed to have an added dash of bitters'.[23] After that, nothing more was said and the three of them caroused the night away.

It's possible that Schellenberg's story was exactly that; he was not above spinning an elaborate yarn to conceal the truth and preserve his reputation. But whether or not Heydrich set the honey trap, it seems unlikely that Schellenberg, who was fixated on advancing his own career, would have risked incurring Heydrich's wrath in order to sleep with Lina.

The other potential contender was Wolfgang Willrich, painter, poet, art critic and polemicist whose views were extreme even by the standards of the SS. His paintings were pure propaganda, all rosy cheeked farm girls and young SS recruits, with titles like *Guardians of the Race*. Willrich's articles and essays divided opinion and he was a controversial choice as one of the six-man panel responsible for selecting the artists for the Degenerate Art Exhibition, an appointment that inspired Willrich to write a book, *The Cleansing of the Temple of Art* (1937).

Heydrich made the mistake of asking Willrich to paint Lina's portrait. It's not hard to imagine Lina being drawn to Willrich's dynamic character during the long hours she spent posing for him, aroused by the strange intimacy that develops between an artist and their subject. Heydrich was obviously worried, and seized on an opportunity to intimidate Willrich.

In March 1937, a magazine called *People and Race* put the finished portrait of Lina on its front cover. Rather than confront Willrich directly, Heydrich had Frieda Wolff's husband write a stiff letter to the editors demanding that they cease publishing Willrich's work. Though Willrich was barely affected by this ban, it was warning enough, and if there was an affair between him and Lina it ended around this time.

Shortly after, in an effort to save their marriage, Lina and her husband decided to go on holiday together, just the two of them, hoping that a few weeks away from everything would revitalise their relationship. They went on a Mediterranean cruise – as regular tourists – and stopped off in Italy, Greece, Tripoli, Tunisia and Carthage. After this welcome break, their marriage seemed to stabilise, for a while at least, and the following summer Lina became pregnant for the third time. But the underlying factors that fuelled her discontent were not so easily resolved. Lina continued to play a secondary role in her husband's life, which was about to get even busier. Heydrich and his partner in crime were planning to conquer new territory.

On 12 March 1938, within a few hours of German troops marching unopposed into Austria, Margaret and Lina's husbands arrived in Vienna. They'd been preparing for months. At their disposal was the data they'd been accumulating about potential Nazi opponents; the remnants of the left; prominent Austrians who might dare to resist; intellectuals, writers and artists with suspect CVs; and the large Jewish community – concentrated in Vienna – and especially its richest members and their businesses.

From the moment Heydrich formed his intelligence service, he recognised the value of information. Almost immediately, he began compiling a library of colour-coded index cards containing precise details about individuals of interest. This filing system that Heydrich had once stored in boxes in his and Lina's apartment in Munich had swollen in size and now included thousands of people. By the time Heydrich and Himmler landed in the Austrian capital all the relevant cards had been sorted and they were ready to put all their knowledge to work.

In the first few days after their arrival, between 20,000 and 70,000 people were seized and given a taste of Nazi justice. On his way home, Himmler stopped off at Mauthausen near the Danube and decided it was the perfect location for a new concentration camp. In her diary entry for 27 March , Margaret wrote that her husband 'returned from his performance in Austria with great satisfaction, almost jubilant'.[24]

The unification of Germany and Austria – the *Anschluss* – had always been a high priority for Hitler, and he was committed to bringing his homeland and the Reich together. The Nazis had been chipping away at Austrian independence for years. A failed coup attempt in 1934, launched by the Austrian Nazi party and approved by Hitler, resulted in a more cautious approach, but by 1938 he was intent on overthrowing the Austrian government, whose chancellor made himself a hostage to fortune when he announced a plebiscite to decide whether his people wanted to be part of Germany or not. Fearing a 'no' vote would derail his plans, Hitler went on the offensive. He issued an ultimatum backed up by Goering's threat to unleash the Luftwaffe, and the Austrian chancellor caved in to Hitler's demands.

Six weeks later, on 2 May, Hitler and a large retinue set off on a state visit to Italy. His alliance with Mussolini had been further strengthened by *Il Duce*'s last-minute decision to grant Hitler a free hand in Austria – whose territorial integrity he'd previously guaranteed – and the five-day tour was meant to demonstrate the harmony between them. For Margaret, this was the one and only occasion when she truly experienced First Lady of the Reich treatment.

Margaret had been on a semi-official whirlwind tour of Italy six months earlier. In Rome, she loved the food, went to the hairdressers, visited the Colosseum and the Forum, and had a drive round the Vatican garden thanks to 'the accommodating policies of the police, and the SS flag on our car'. Next up was Naples, then Pompeii and Herculaneum, where she was affected by the sight of 'people surprised by sudden death'. While viewing the ancient Roman ruins at Catania, Margaret came to the conclusion that 'countries are so poor nowadays' because 'there are no slaves any more'.[25]

The state visit to Italy, however, was on a different order of magnitude, especially since both Emmy and Magda were about to give birth and stayed at home, and although Eva was allowed to tag along, she was not permitted to join the main party. Once in Rome, Eva did some sightseeing, filmed the big public events with her new camera and went shopping; she visited the premises of her favourite shoemaker, who thought she was an actress and remembered that Eva 'had good, normal feet and anything would fit her'.[26]

In the absence of Emmy and Magda, Margaret, Ilse and Anneliese von Ribbentrop got top billing: Anneliese was the wife of the Nazis' foreign minister and a good friend of Margaret's. Together, the wives did not exactly impress their hosts, whose fears were realised when Ilse and Margaret went against protocol and refused to curtsey before Queen Elena, the wife of King Victor Emmanuel who technically remained head of state. Their actions affronted the Italian dignitaries but gained approval from their own side. Hitler was ill at ease with all the bowing and scraping and resented the king's attempt to overshadow Mussolini.

Despite this shaky start, the trip passed off without further difficulties. Though Ilse tried to boss the wives around – Margaret noted that 'Mrs Hess wanted to lecture Mrs Ribbentrop' – the women got on reasonably well. Margaret was in fine spirits. She enjoyed the huge naval display in Naples and thought a sports demonstration given by fascist youth groups at the Mussolini Stadium was 'fantastic'.[27]

After all the years of sacrifice, of feeling alone and undervalued, Margaret finally had something to show for it. But her good mood didn't last: from then on, life was only going to get more difficult.

9

A LEAP IN THE DARK

On the evening of 20 April 1938 – Hitler's forty-ninth birthday – the Nazi elite joined him and the cream of the movie business for the premiere of the director Leni Riefensthal's *Olympia*, her film about the 1936 games. Leni's propaganda masterpiece of the previous year, *Triumph of the Will*, had gone down very well with Hitler, and even Goebbels, who still resented Leni for rejecting his amorous advances, had to admit that her work was touched by genius. With her star in the ascendant, Leni was commissioned to produce a film about the Olympics.

During the two weeks of competition, Leni's massive camera crew were everywhere, using innovative techniques to shoot trackside and capture the action close up. At the end, she had miles of footage and would spend the next year or so locked in an editing room trying to make sense of it all. By the time Leni's movie was ready to screen, *Olympia* had gone hugely over budget and schedule, much to Goebbels's annoyance. However, the film was ecstatically received and gained widespread critical acclaim, including first prize at the Venice International Film Festival.

In the audience for opening night was the Czech actress Lida Baarova, whose affair with Goebbels had become progressively more serious. While Goebbels had quickly tired of other actresses and tossed them to one side, he couldn't get enough of Baarova, and she was beginning to believe that she might soon to be more than just his mistress. Perpetually worried that Magda would grasp the true extent of his feelings for Baarova, and concerned that his own phone was not secure enough, Goebbels went out on limb and asked for Emmy's help; could he use her phone to make a few calls? Emmy agreed, but when she realised Goebbels 'had begun to use our private telephone to maintain contact with Frau Baarova'[1] she had to remind Goebbels that the Gestapo tapped everybody's lines, including hers.

Pregnant again, Magda had been weighed down by health issues – like her long-standing heart problem – that always afflicted her when she was expecting a child and continued to bother her after she gave birth to another daughter, Hedda, on 5 May. Once this hurdle was negotiated, the seriousness of her husband's infatuation with Baarova was brought home to her by Goebbels's private assistant, Karl Hanke.

A diligent man, with a fondness for all things military, Hanke was nevertheless something of a nonentity, and was working as an instructor at a technical high school when he entered the Nazi party in 1928 as part of the SA. After Hanke lost his job in 1931 due to his Nazi affiliations, he worked full time as a secretary in Goebbels's office, and within a year was permanently at the propaganda minister's side. Hanke had been nursing a crush on Magda for some time and had compiled a scrupulously precise dossier detailing Goebbels's infidelities and his relationship with Baarova, which he showed to Magda. Shocked, Magda could no longer deny what was right before her eyes.

These revelations coincided with a period of doubt and disillusionment for Magda. In conversations with her only confidante, Ello Quandt, her ex-husband's younger sister, Magda expressed her doubts about the direction Nazism was taking – she objected to the militarisation of German society, which was robbing it of its 'culture', its 'mirth' and its 'joy' and replacing them with 'blind obedience, regulations' and 'commands' – and she questioned Hitler's judgement, especially the way he let the regime treat women as second-class citizens when they deserved 'to receive more consideration'.[2]

Matters came to a head at the beginning of August when Goebbels – who could no longer cope with his double life – confessed all to Magda and begged her to consider the possibility that the three of them could find a way to co-exist. Confused and disorientated by this sudden and unexpected suggestion, Magda agreed and grimly sat through tea with Baarova and Goebbels. He took Magda's stoic silence as a positive sign and arranged a weekend on his yacht. The sight of Baarova sunning herself on the deck and acting as if she'd already won the battle was too much for Magda to bear and she abandoned ship. Soon after, in an unusually intimate conversation with Emmy, Magda called her husband a 'devil in human form'.[3]

Magda had survived one divorce and was prepared to go through another. As it happened, recent changes in the marriage laws had made it easier for couples to separate. Though the Nazis vigorously promoted marriage, the divorce rate steadily increased from 1933 onwards, and the regime did little to reverse this trend; ultimately, it wanted productive unions not failed ones. Alongside the other grounds for divorce – like adultery or biological or racial unsuitability – the new law, introduced on 6 July, added 'irretrievable breakdown' to the list. This meant that Magda would not have to prove in court that her husband was unfaithful.

But before Magda could take such a serious step, she had to consult Hitler. Divorce would break the unique bond between them. It was weaker than it had been, but was still strong, and Hitler did not hesitate to answer her distress call. At first, Hitler didn't want to believe Magda, but when Hanke verified her account Hitler turned his anger on Goebbels, mad at him for betraying Magda. Then he brought them together and laid down the law. Divorce was out of the question. They would have to try and mend their marriage and Goebbels would have to dump Baarova. But this was easier said than done, and neither Magda nor her husband left the Berghof with much hope that their relationship would survive the test.

That summer, Hitler had every right to rest on his laurels and relax at the Berghof. He'd restored Germany's status as a major European power and gone a long way to delivering on his promise to dismantle the hated

Treaty of Versailles. At home, though some of the early gloss had worn off his regime and the return of economic hardship and uncertainty was beginning to erode support, his personal popularity was unaffected and the *Anschluss* had given it a huge boost. But he was restless and in a hurry to achieve his vision of empire and a brave new world. Hitler's greatest fear was dying before he'd completed his historic mission and fulfilled his destiny, and he was increasingly preoccupied with his own mortality. Earlier that year, on 2 May, he'd drawn up a will: Eva was the first beneficiary named and would receive a decent monthly income for the rest of her life. With his affairs in order, Hitler was contemplating how to subdue his next victim. The amalgamation of Czechoslovakia with the Reich appealed to Hitler; he was keen to get his hands on its raw materials, including coal, and one of Europe's largest armaments manufacturers – Skoda.

Also within the Czech borders was the Sudeten region, which had been carved out of Germany under the Treaty of Versailles and contained a substantial German population. Detaching the Sudetenland, as a prelude to the full absorption of the rest of the country, was Hitler's immediate focus as nervous European leaders scrambled to prevent him from moving forward, but Hitler would not yield an inch and began mobilising his army.

The possibility that Britain might feel obliged to use force to resist Hitler's plans was weighing heavily on Unity Mitford. With her hair bleached to 'a more Nordic gold', Unity had followed Hitler's triumphal trip to Austria after the *Anschluss* and toured the Czech-German border in May; she continued to fully support everything Hitler did. Yet, Britain was still Unity's homeland and as the stakes got higher she seemed determined to destroy herself. When she contracted bronchitis she refused to take it seriously. According to Friedelind Wagner, Unity defied her doctor by 'pouring her medicine out of the window, standing there in a thin night-gown' and 'courting pneumonia'.[4] Inevitably, Unity deteriorated and had to be transferred to a clinic, where all the bills were covered by Hitler.

The escalating threat of outright war over Czechoslovakia wasn't just affecting Unity; there was a fraught and strained atmosphere backstage at the party rally in Nuremberg, which spilled over into a head-to-head confrontation between Margaret and Lina. Since her grand state visit to Italy, Margaret had been dealing with the same old domestic problems, Himmler's absences – 'he is never here any more' – and clashes with the domestic staff; she had to fire yet another 'shameless maid'.[5]

However, Margaret was looking forward to the rally and she'd drawn up a timetable of events and meetings for the other SS wives to follow. Lina balked at the idea of being micro-managed by Margaret and convinced Frieda Wolff that Margaret was deliberately preventing them from having a good time. Together, they ignored Margaret's schedule, did their own thing, and revelled in the late-night party scene that existed on the fringes of the rally.

Incensed at their blatant disregard for her authority, Margaret confronted Lina and Frieda and gave them a good telling off. They promptly went straight to their husbands to complain about Margaret's overbearing behaviour and Heydrich and Wolff felt obliged to report what had happened to Himmler, who neither defended nor condemned Margaret for losing her cool. Instead, he merely shrugged helplessly and suggested they forget the whole thing.

The tension that had pervaded the rally evaporated at the end of September because of the Munich conference, during which Hitler, Mussolini, Neville Chamberlain and Léon Blum haggled over the future of Czechoslovakia. In exchange for promises of peace and an end to further territorial expansion, Hitler was granted control of the Sudetenland. The Czech government was not invited to the talks and had little choice but to accept the deal, and on 3 October the Nazis claimed their prize.

Mission accomplished, Hitler had time to show off his latest toy, the Eagle's Nest, a guesthouse perched on top of a mountain, the Kehlstein, which was visible from the Berghof. For months, the silence that normally reigned over the peaks at Obersalzburg had been shattered by an almighty din; Hitler's press secretary observed that the local oxen had been usurped by 'gigantic trucks and diggers' and 'the rumble of dynamite detonations'.[6] A small army of construction workers was labouring round the clock to complete the building, which Bormann hoped to able to present to Hitler on his fiftieth birthday the following April.

As it was, Bormann pushed his workers so hard – several died during avalanches and torrential rains – that the construction was complete seven months early. Hitler's housekeeper called the finished structure 'a true masterpiece of architecture, engineering and workmanship'.[7]

Throughout October, Hitler took a steady stream of foreign dignitaries up the Kehlstein: the first phase of the journey was by car along a 4-mile road that had been carved out of the rockface and led to a car park over a mile above sea level, next to a tunnel whose entrance was guarded by a massive brass gate; the tunnel ran deep into the mountain itself and ended at a copper hall with a lift big enough to hold forty people, which took guests another 400ft upwards in less than a minute and deposited them directly into the Eagle's Nest, with its bedrooms, reception room, dining room, conference room, kitchen, basement, guardroom, balcony and panoramic circular picture window.

Among the early visitors to the Eagle's Nest were Magda and Unity, who were treated to a tour of Hitler's penthouse in the sky on 21 October. Spirits lifted by the Munich Agreement, Unity had recovered her strength and irrepressible exuberance, while Magda was in Obersalzburg to resume her discussions with Hitler about the crisis in her marriage. Magda was still bent on a divorce but Hitler remained dead against the idea. Two days later, they were joined by Goebbels – who had failed to shake off Baarova – and he and Magda agreed to a three-month trial separation during which Goebbels would have to behave himself or risk losing everything: if he failed to keep his end of the bargain, Hitler would accept that a divorce was unavoidable and Goebbels would have to resign.

With a measure of calm restored, Emmy and her husband felt free to go ahead with the christening of their daughter Edda, who'd been born on 2 June. The delighted parents – Emmy recalled that her husband 'claimed with absolute conviction that it was the most beautiful child he had ever seen'[8] – received 628,000 telegrams of congratulations, while their baby daughter was given two paintings by the German Renaissance painter

Lucas Cranach the Elder, one of which, *Madonna and Child*, was a gift from the city of Cologne.

Edda's christening took place at Carinhall on 4 November, and the ceremony was performed by Reich Bishop Mueller, the most senior figure in the German Protestant Church and a convinced Nazi and anti-Semite. Despite Hitler's aversion to Christianity, he showed up to give the baby his blessing. Also present were photographers from *Life* magazine, who captured an image of Hitler cradling the baby in his arms.

Five days later, as an affirmation of their pagan beliefs and rejection of Christianity, Ilse and her husband held a ceremony to mark their son Wolf's entry into the world. The rites performed involved the soil that Hess had ordered delivered from all over the Reich a year earlier, which was arranged in piles round Wolf as he lay in his crib. The ritual coincided with a deeply significant day in the Nazi calendar; 9 November was the anniversary of the 1923 Beer Hall Putsch and every year the survivors of that botched coup gathered for a series of ceremonies that commemorated the fourteen Nazis who'd died during it. Each year, the celebrations grew more elaborate and pompous as Hitler - and Goering, who'd taken a bullet that day consecrated the memory of the fallen heroes, laying a wreath in a temple surrounded by flaming torches.

That November, the atmosphere in the city was even more charged than usual, seething with violent undercurrents. Two days earlier, a German diplomat in Paris had been shot by a young currently stateless Polish Jew. Since then, as the official fought for his life in hospital, Goebbels had been ramping up the anti-Semitic rhetoric and promising bloody revenge if he failed to recover from his wounds.

Wolf's pagan baptism went ahead anyway on the early afternoon of 9 November. Hitler was in attendance along with a few close friends including Professor Haushofer. Once the ritual was over, Haushofer and Hitler disappeared into a side room and the professor proceeded to give Hitler a lecture on the current European situation and the importance of maintaining good relations with the British, which only served to put Hitler in a bad mood: he never sought Professor Haushofer's advice again.

By the time Hitler had left Ilse and her husband, and was on his way to give a speech to the old fighters at the infamous beer hall, the diplomat had passed away. News of his death reached Hitler at around 9 p.m. when he was having dinner with his comrades. After a brief meeting with Goebbels, Hitler authorised a pogrom that was carried out by his SA thugs and quickly became known as *Kristallnacht*, the Night of Broken Glass.

According to Lina, the action took her husband by surprise; apparently Heydrich only realised what was going on when he looked out of his hotel window and saw a synagogue in flames. Both Heydrich and Himmler were alarmed by the wanton violence and unsupervised mayhem; it went against the methodical persecution they favoured, what they liked to think of as a 'scientific' approach. Lina said her husband thought the Jewish question was a 'medical problem' not a 'political' one, and compared the Jewish community to a parasite that 'clung like leeches to the body of another nation'. Yet Heydrich's view of himself as a surgeon clinically removing a poisonous growth was underpinned by an almost existential revulsion, which Lina shared; the Jews were 'unbearable to him and to me in the soul and in the psyche'. The only solution as far as they were concerned was 'that the Jews should be forced to emigrate from Germany'.[9]

At 1.20 a.m. on 10 November, as the pogrom raged and SA men ran riot, Heydrich attempted to impose some order on proceedings and issued instructions to all Gestapo and SS units: no attacks on foreigners; no looting of wrecked Jewish homes; and with the overall total of 20,000 'healthy men' in mind, the arrest of 'as many Jews, especially rich ones' that could be 'accommodated in the existing jails'.[10] The following morning, Heydrich sat down and calculated the overall loss of property and life, but his figures fell well short of the real number. In the end, 267 synagogues were destroyed, 7,500 businesses vandalised and 91 Jews killed, while hundreds more committed suicide or died in detention.

On 12 November, Heydrich was present at a major conference with a host of ministers, plus Goering – who was fretting about the potential blow to the economy from all the *Kristallnacht* destruction – and Goebbels, who was supremely satisfied by his handiwork. Together they proceeded to draft a series of decrees that accelerated the absolute segregation of Germany's Jews and their exclusion from society, forced them to pay for the damage done during the pogrom and stripped them of their remaining assets.

With everything that had been going on, the Christmas break offered a momentary respite for the Nazi elite. At the Berghof, the New Year's Eve party – attended by Gerda, her husband, Eva and the rest of the Berghof in-crowd – was a livelier gathering than usual and there was a buzz about the place as the guests prepared for the evening's entertainment. Eva's sister, Gretl – who was slowly edging her way into the Berghof world – noted that 'the hairdressers are under siege by the women, and the gentleman are fondly looking forward to their tuxedos'.[11] After dinner, there was a firework display, then everybody moved into the great hall for traditional toasts and the countdown to 1939. Normally teetotal, Hitler forced himself to have a drink of champagne before retiring just after midnight, signalling that it was time to start winding things down.

The kind of parties with drinking and dancing until dawn were never a feature of life at the Berghof, at least when Hitler was there. Most evenings culminated in either a screening of a movie, or one of Hitler's endless fireside chats where he spun out his thoughts into the early hours while his audience struggled to stay awake. Gerda was usually there – a Berghof regular observed that she would sit 'by the fireplace among the wives of Hitler's closest staff, not saying a word all evening'[12] – but she was spared the late nights. Bormann had imposed a 10 p.m. curfew on her, because it was inappropriate for a mother like her (she had another new infant to contend with, a five-month year old girl she'd named Eva) to be out too late; Gerda needed her rest if she was going to keep their household in order.

So once the evening movie had finished or the clock struck the appointed hour in the room where Hitler held court, Gerda was sent home. Hitler's valet remembered that even when Bormann 'threw his own seasonal parties', where the guests were 'principally film actresses who interested him personally', Gerda was 'not permitted to circulate' despite the fact she had to 'do all the arranging and the chores'.[13]

Five days after the New Year's Eve bash, Goebbels arrived in Obersalzburg. He'd had a miserable couple of months, contracted an ulcer and was taking heavy-duty sleeping pills to fend off bouts of insomnia. But after twelve days rest and less fraught discussions with Hitler, his batteries were recharged and he was ready to face Magda in Berlin. Her health had also been poor and though she was not yet prepared to forgive her husband, she consented to an official statement of intent regarding their marriage.

A lawyer was brought in to draw up a contract – which the couple signed on 22 January 1939 – that postponed a final decision for a year, enough time for Goebbels to demonstrate that he was truly a reformed character. In the wake of this, Baarova – who'd been waiting patiently in the wings – was exiled back to Czechoslovakia, and not allowed to return, while all her films were removed from circulation; as far as the viewing public were concerned, she had ceased to exist.

Margaret spent her New Year's Eve in bed suffering with a stomach ailment that had blighted her Christmas and exacerbated her usual worries: 'The maid situation is catastrophic. What I have to put up with is unbearable. I don't feel well.' Yet only a few weeks earlier Margaret had been enjoying a vacation in Salzburg with her husband that was almost perfect – 'we spent beautiful days together and talked a lot' – and left her feeling contented and fulfilled: 'Today I am firmly convinced that I have earned my place in the sun, and love and happiness.'[14]

Little did she know that Himmler had fallen in love with his 26-year-old secretary, Hedwig Potthast. Born on 6 February 1912 to middle-class parents who put her through a *Gymnasium* and finishing school, where she picked up a smattering of English, Hedwig subsequently got her degree at the Economics Institute for Interpreters in Mannheim. Graduating in 1932, at the height of the Depression, she ended up getting a job as a clerk in a post office. Bored and seeking a challenge, Hedwig applied for a position with the Gestapo's press department in autumn 1935; this was still not enough to satisfy her ambitions and in January 1936 she became Himmler's personal secretary.

Hedwig was friendly and upbeat – her friends nicknamed her 'Bunny' – and she enjoyed gymnastics and rowing. She was popular with her colleagues; in October 1937, she joined other members of staff for Himmler's birthday at Lake Tegernsee and was welcomed into the SS family. As they worked in close proximity, Hedwig and Himmler's relationship snowballed and sometime over Christmas 1938 – perhaps at the equivalent of the SS office party – they admitted their feelings for each other, as Hedwig explained to her sister: 'We had a frank conversation during which we confessed that we were hopelessly in love.'[15]

Though the couple kept their affair under the radar as much as possible – according to Hedwig they were trying to find an 'honourable way … to be together'[16] – those in the know included Lina, who liked and respected Hedwig, whom she considered 'an intelligent woman characterised by warm-heartedness'. Unlike Margaret, Hedwig wasn't 'a narrow minded petit-bourgeois', nor was she 'an eccentric', or 'one of the SS sophisticates'. As far as Lina was concerned, Hedwig was a genuine, well-meaning person who helped Himmler 'achieve true stature'.[17]

Margaret apparently had no idea what was going on. As it was, her poor health continued into January, and she went into the Hohenlychen clinic, a former sanatorium for tuberculosis just north of Berlin. Himmler had converted this turn-of-the-century building with Gothic spires into a centre for orthopaedic care and a health spa for the SS elite; it had a large swimming pool with a retractable roof, a state-of-the-art operating theatre, and rooms fitted out with all kinds of exercise equipment. The facility was run by Professor Karl Gebhardt, an old schoolfriend of Himmler's who'd qualified as a surgeon in 1932. An expert in sports medicine, Gebhardt did pioneering work with disabled patients improving their strength and coordination. Having joined the SS in 1935, Gebhardt gained considerable recognition after successfully treating a number of athletes during the 1936 Olympics.

Margaret stayed at Hohenlychen for a couple of weeks and apart from the fact that her only visitor was Himmler and the only person who bothered to call her was Anneliese von Ribbentrop, she enjoyed the peace and quiet and the chance to catch up on some reading. But back in Berlin, Margaret struggled with the demands of the hectic diplomatic social scene, her energy flagging: 'Many invitations. I am terribly tired again.' Even Margaret's regular trips to see stage plays – which included the classic comedy *The Concert* that Emmy had previously starred in, and a production of *Hamlet* – were not giving her the same pleasure as before; in her opinion, the theatre was 'getting worse and worse'.[18]

Margaret could at least feel pleased by her husband's contribution to the next phase of Hitler's plan to reshape the map of Europe. In early March, he increased the pressure on the Czech president and hurled a barrage of threats at him as German troops massed on the border and Goering pledged to obliterate Prague if the Czechs refused to go quietly. With no sign of either Britain or France coming to the rescue, the Czech president gave way. On 15 March, Margaret's husband was in Prague with Hitler. As with the *Anschluss*, Himmler and Heydrich had accumulated a database of people to be arrested and quickly put in place what was needed to execute the round-ups and crush any dissent.

A few weeks later, on 9 April, Lina gave birth to a little girl called Silke, her first daughter. Though pleased about the new addition to his family, Heydrich was barely at home to see her grow. He was engaged in a major reorganisation of the SS and the Gestapo, consolidating all their various functions into one agency – the RHSA – divided into six departments. Aside from this, Heydrich had also been ordered by Goering to assume responsibility for the 'emigration and evacuation'[19] of all the Jews in the Reich. Nevertheless, despite his bulging in-tray, Heydrich did manage to squeeze in some holiday time with Lina and his children at their beach house in Fehmarn.

By the time Magda arrived at the Bayreuth Festival on 25 July 1939, she was on the verge of a breakdown. Even though she'd signed the contract with Goebbels, Magda had not made up her mind about whether or not to take him back and was torn between his pleading and bullying and her ardent admirer Hanke; having driven the wedge between

Magda and her husband – and convinced her to sleep with him – Hanke believed that she would eventually be his. The strain affected her health and in the spring she retired to her preferred clinic in Dresden, which was becoming like a second home to her. To add to her agony, Hitler was keeping his distance; perhaps he didn't want to be seen playing favourites, or perhaps he'd been disappointed by her conduct.

At the same time, Hitler was also giving Goebbels the cold shoulder. Goebbels knew full well that his only hope of restoring Hitler's confidence in him was to save his marriage, and he went all out to persuade Magda to forgive and forget, except she was blowing hot and cold; on 17 March, Goebbels noted in his diary that Magda had been 'so sweet', but on 30 May, she was seeing everything 'in a false, distorted light'.[20]

Crushed by pressure from all sides, Magda escaped for a few weeks' holiday in Sicily and southern Italy with Dr Karl Brandt, Hitler's chief physician; Albert Speer, Hitler's pet architect; Arno Breker, Hitler's favourite sculptor, and their wives. Away from the madness, Magda was more like her usual self, comfortable in her own skin. The return to Berlin shattered any equilibrium she'd regained; Hanke, who had nothing to lose since he'd quit working for Goebbels and joined the army, was pushing her to make a commitment to him and Goebbels was threatening to take the children away from her if she did.

At Bayreuth, it all caught up with her during a production of the tragic love story *Tristan and Isolde*. Sharing a box with her husband, Hitler, Winifred Wagner and Speer, Magda 'cried silently throughout the whole performance' and spent the interval 'racked with incessant sobs in the corner of one of the drawing rooms'. According to Speer, Hitler was appalled by such a publicly embarrassing scene, and after the opera finished he told Goebbels that 'it would be better if he left Bayreuth immediately with his wife' and 'dismissed' him without shaking hands or waiting for a reply.[21]

By the end of July, Margaret was back at Lake Tegernsee after a holiday at a Baltic resort with her daughter, but not with her husband, who was otherwise engaged. Margaret had a reasonable time without Himmler – 'peaceful days and the weather quite good' – but expressed concern about Gudrun; she was doing poorly at school and her reading was 'really quite bad'.[22] On 14 August, Margaret noted in her diary that Himmler was with Hitler at the Berghof awaiting news of von Ribbentrop's trip to Moscow. Hitler was seeking an alliance with Stalin that would keep them from each others' throats for the time being and ensured they both got a piece of Poland, and had dispatched his foreign minister to thrash out a deal.

In between consultations with Hitler, Himmler was packing in lots of games of tennis – between mid July and mid August he played thirteen times – a trend that continued when he returned to Berlin at the end of the summer. No doubt Himmler was trying to burn off the anxiety and stress that was accumulating inside him and caused his chronic stomach problems; that year, his condition got so bad that he hired a Swedish healer to give him massages on an almost daily basis.

His apprehension was mixed with excitement; Himmler had Poland in his sights. It promised to be a land of opportunity for the SS. Not only were he and Heydrich expected to decapitate the Polish intelligentsia, the aristocracy, political and Church leaders and any representative of Polish nationalism, there was its huge Jewish population to deal with and the prospect of launching the great *Lebensraum* experiment of colonisation in the East.

To accomplish the SS's primary task of murderous suppression, Heydrich established eight special task forces – the Einsatzgruppen – which would accompany the German army once the invasion began. Heydrich himself planned to be there in the thick of things and hoped to see some action one way or another.

Before the campaign began, Heydrich wrote to Lina a letter to be opened in the event of his death. In it he adopted a formal, almost bureaucratic tone as he instructed Lina to educate their children to be 'true to the ideas of the Nazi movement', asked her to 'remember our life together with respect and fondness', and gave her permission, 'once time has healed the wounds', to find a new father for their children, as long as he was like 'the kind of man I aspired to be'.[23]

Margaret was also preparing to serve her country by putting her First World War nursing experience to good use: 'If there is a war I have to work with the Red Cross.' After the Nazi-Soviet pact was signed on 23 August, and the way was clear for the invasion of Poland, Margaret told Gudrun about her decision, which would mean them being apart for long periods; 'she, of course, cried a lot and cannot calm down'.

When it came to the moment when Margaret had to leave Lake Tegernsee for Berlin and her new duties, Gudrun saw that her mother was weeping and tried to put on a brave face; Gudrun 'heroically laughed' even though 'tears kept streaming down her face'. Yet despite this traumatic parting, Margaret was 'glad' she could 'participate' and believed that 'the war will be over soon'.[24]

The day before Hitler's armies steamrollered into Poland, Emmy and her husband went for a walk after breakfast at Carinhall. Goering's mood was sober and he confessed to Emmy that the war was 'going to be appalling, more terrible than we can yet imagine'. The only hope of avoiding a protracted bloodbath was to keep Britain out of it and Goering asked Emmy to 'pray that I can bring peace'. That night, as Hitler's tanks rolled into action and Goering's planes took off from their airstrips to pummel the enemy, Emmy was consumed by premonitions of doom: 'The future rose up ... like a high wall, sinister and threatening.'[25]

For all his boasting about the devastating strength of the Luftwaffe, Goering knew that it wasn't as powerful as he pretended, and he was well aware of the difficulties the economy would face if it needed to sustain a long war, particularly one fought on two fronts. The memory of defeat in the First World War loomed large; during that conflict Britain's navy was able to blockade Germany's coastlines – which contributed massively to the slow starvation of the civilian population – and maintain a steady flow of men and material from its empire.

Goering feared a repeat performance. And he wasn't the only one. Hess, another First World War veteran, was equally wary of taking on the British and getting mired in a two-front conflict, especially as Hess understood better than most that Hitler would never abandon his cherished dream of laying waste to the Soviet Union; the truce with Stalin was only temporary. Ilse remembered that her husband thought 'a new war would be a disaster for Europe and the whole world'.[26]

However, Hess was no longer able to influence Hitler's decisions. He was still an important figure in the public eye, performing his many duties and speaking engagements, but behind the scenes Hess was yesterday's man, isolated from power. Ilse was also out of the loop for much of 1939 and focused on domestic life. She was devoted to their son Wolf and engaged in supervising major extensions to their Munich home. Ilse wanted a telephone exchange installed, extra accommodation for more staff and enough garage space for up to ten cars. When Ilse's mother heard about these expensive additions, she wrote her daughter a stern letter condemning her extravagance. Sensitive to any suggestion that she was letting herself be corrupted, Ilse rejected the accusation that she and her husband were over-indulging themselves: 'We're not suffering from megalomania Mama: we haven't got any more cars ... we haven't even got a new one.'[27]

In the midst of all this, and the worsening international situation, Ilse and Hess managed to have their annual hiking holiday in the mountains, which he recalled with great fondness. On their return, Hess set about trying to forge a clandestine link to members of the British government through Professor Haushofer's son Albrecht, who was a firm opponent of the Nazi regime. Albrecht Haushofer's academic position as a foreign policy expert – which had been secured by Hess – allowed him to travel and in the autumn Albrecht began seeking out potential contacts in Switzerland and Spain. But beyond a tentative and cautious exchange of communications nothing much was achieved.

Goering's peace efforts also came to nothing. Several of his Swedish business associates agreed to help and managed to set up a meeting at a remote farmhouse with Goering and half a dozen British industrialists but the discussions went nowhere, which was a disappointment to the British ambassador in Berlin; having visited Carinhall numerous times and gone hunting with Goering, the ambassador thought he was a thoroughly decent chap and Emmy a fine woman. On their last night together, Goering and the ambassador contemplated the coming war and Goering promised that if one of his Luftwaffe bombers happened to kill the ambassador during a raid, he would personally fly over to London and drop a wreath on his grave.

The first casualty of this failure to find an agreement was Unity Mitford. When Britain and France reacted to Hitler's annexation of Czechoslovakia by announcing their readiness to defend Poland if necessary, Unity found herself looking into the abyss; all her efforts to exploit her celebrity to convince her countrymen that Britain and Hitler's Germany were natural allies had come to nothing, and she started telling people she'd kill herself if they came to blows. Her sister was with her during the Bayreuth Festival, and after a meal with Hitler, Diana remembered that Unity 'said once again that she would not live to see the impending tragedy'. For Diana, her sister's sombre words made that evening's performance of *Twilight of the Gods* even more poignant: 'Never had the glorious music seemed so doom laden.'[28]

On Sunday, 3 September, after Britain declared war, Unity wrote a series of farewell letters and headed over to the HQ of the regional party leader, left an envelope containing her prized signed portrait of Hitler and gold Nazi party badge with instructions to have them buried with her in Munich if anything happened to her, then drove to a park, sat on a bench, took a pistol from her handbag, fired one round into the ground to make sure it was working and shot herself in the right temple.

Unity was found slumped unconscious by the police a few hours later and whisked straight to a top private clinic; a doctor who examined her said she looked 'very white and corpse like'.[29] The bullet was jammed into the left side of her brain and could not be removed. It had caused severe and irreparable neurological damage; Unity could barely speak or move. Hitler was shocked when he heard the news: Heinrich Hoffmann said that 'Unity's attempted suicide made a profound impression' on him[30]; Hitler paid for her treatment, sent her flowers every day and made one brief visit, during which Unity simply stared into space.

Hitler knew that with the war now in progress, Unity couldn't stay in Germany, so he had her possessions put in storage and arranged for her to be taken in a reserved train carriage – accompanied by a doctor, a nurse and a nun – to a Swiss clinic, and from there back to Britain. An invalid, Unity died in 1948, at the age of 33. Reflecting on Unity's involvement with Nazism, Diana wrote that her sister had 'adopted' their 'creed … including their anti-Semitism, with uncritical enthusiasm'.[31] Unity had sacrificed everything on the altar of Hitler's obsessions; she'd wasted her young life on a toxic fantasy that was about to send millions more to their deaths.

Carin Goering stares thoughtfully into the distance. (AKG)

Hermann Goering in the courtyard of Carinhall – his country estate – inspecting a parade of Japanese recruits. (Wikimedia Commons)

Emmy Goering and her husband on their wedding day standing on the steps of Berlin Cathedral saluting the crowds of well-wishers. (Bundesarchiv)

Emmy Goering modelling one of her many fur coats. (Wikimedia Commons)

Emmy Goering and her husband attend a concert in Berlin. (Bundesarchiv)

Emmy Goering cuddles her pet lion cub while her husband and Mussolini look on. (AKG)

New Year's Eve at the Berghof 1939: Eva Braun by Hitler in the front row, Gerda Bormann two rows back. (AKG)

Gerda Bormann on her wedding day sitting between her husband and father – Walter Buch – with Hitler in the front passenger seat. (AKG)

Ilse Hess looks relieved that her husband has survived the Zugspitze Mountain Flying Race, coming in first place. (AKG)

Ilse Hess and her husband follow the action at the Olympic Games 1936. (AKG)

Magda Goebbels, the 'First Lady of the Reich'. (Bundesarchiv)

A family portrait – staged for propaganda purposes – featuring Magda Goebbels, her husband, their six children, and Magda's son from her first marriage, Harald, – wearing his uniform. (AKG)

Magda Goebbels and her husband are greeted by the faithful at Berchtesgaden railway station. (USHMM)

The triumvirate; Hitler next to Magda Goebbels, her husband and three of their children. (AKG)

Lina Heydrich, her husband and their young son Klaus enjoying some fresh air. (Bundesarchiv)

Lina Heydrich accompanies her husband through the corridors of the Wallenstein Palace in Prague on their way to watch a classical music concert. (Bundesarchiv)

The young Margaret Boden a decade before she met Himmler. (Bundesarchiv)

The newly wed Margaret Himmler and her husband outside their farm near Munich. (USHMM)

Margaret Himmler does her best to enjoy the great outdoors. (USHMM)

Eva Braun and Hitler pose with their beloved dogs on the Berghof terrace. (Bundesarchiv)

Geli Raubel and Hitler relaxing on a summer's day. (AKG)

The main entrance to the Oberzalzburg complex. (Bundesarchiv)

One of the many vast drawing rooms at the Berghof. (Bundesarchiv)

PART THREE

A LONG WAY DOWN

10

WAR AND PEACE

B y the end of 1939, Magda and her husband were at peace. Despite all the quarrelling and emotional turmoil, the terms of the marriage contract they'd signed at the beginning of the year had been fulfilled and the couple reconciled. Their reunion met with Hitler's approval and on 30 October he invited them for tea at the Reich Chancellery, then on 15 January 1940 he paid them a visit at their country house – bringing a puppet theatre for the children – and was back again on 1 February. Hitler and Magda and her husband reminisced about the time when the three of them were inseparable; according to Goebbels, they 'revived old memories'.[1] Soon after, Magda discovered she was pregnant again; the First Family of the Reich were back in business.

On 29 December, Goebbels had attended the premiere of the film *Mother Love*, which traced the different stages of a widow's life, from youth to old age, as she raises her four children while running a laundry business to keep food on the table, sacrificing her own happiness as she battles against the odds to turn her troubled children – one son gets involved with a married woman, another impregnates one of her employees, another loses his eyesight, while her daughter becomes a dancer – into useful members of the community. Publicity for the film claimed that it aimed 'to represent the image of the mother, to reveal her unending love and kindness, and by doing so erect a monument of fidelity and thanks to all mothers'.[2] Goebbels sobbed during the screening and in his diary wrote that it was 'a victory for German cinema'.[3]

Margaret Himmler was equally moved when she saw *Mother Love* shortly after it came out. She thought it was 'a beautiful movie',[4] which was high praise from her; she rarely expressed such strong feelings about a film, except when she didn't like it. Perhaps Margaret identified with its message and themes, the lone protagonist giving her all and receiving very little in return, ground down by the burdens of motherhood, yet always doing her best.

Margaret's worries about her own family were more acute now she was doing her bit for the war effort. In the first few months of the conflict, she'd been based at a Berlin hospital and was 'looking forward to surgical work',[5] but she kept clashing with the senior doctors and staff, who weren't keen on having Himmler's bossy wife breathing down their necks. Frustrated, she quit and on 3 December 1939 she took up a supervisory position for the German Red Cross, monitoring its field hospitals and the treatment facilities near the main railway hubs that cared for injured and wounded soldiers in transit.

By the mid 1930s, the German Red Cross had fallen into the hands of the SS. Its titular head was Charles Edward von Saxe-Coburg-Gotha – who went from the *Freikorps* to the SA and then onto the SS – but real authority was wielded by the SS physician Ernst-Robert Grawitz, a favourite of Margaret's husband and her overall boss.

From the end of 1937, all 9,000 German Red Cross units were merged into one organisation under the control of the Ministry of the Interior. Once nurses had been vetted for their political and racial fitness, they had to join the party and swear an oath of allegiance to Hitler. As war approached, the German Red Cross stopped treating civilians and began preparing for military casualties; the number of emergency staff swelled from 13,500 in 1933 to 142,000 in 1938, ready to be deployed in reserve hospitals on the home front, or field hospitals in the war zone, situated 15 miles behind the frontline with 200–1,000 beds. A network of soldiers' homes were established for those who required long-term rehabilitation or were permanently disabled.

Margaret's separation from 10-year-old Gudrun hit her daughter hard – she was having trouble sleeping and wept down the phone – and her distress was compounded by the fact that she hardly ever saw her father. Not that Margaret fared any better; as she glumly noted in her dairy. Himmler was 'almost never home evenings although he is in Berlin'.[6] That year, Margaret would face a reckoning in her marriage. Himmler and his mistress Hedwig had decided that they wanted to have children, and as a result felt they had to tell Margaret the truth about their affair.

On 12 September 1939, fifteen days before Poland capitulated, Heydrich took to the skies in a Heinkel plane as a turret gunner, risking death to fire on retreating Polish soldiers. Lina's husband had begun his quest to see action in 1935 when he trained as a sports pilot, becoming skilful enough to participate in aerobatics shows. During the summer of 1939, he completed a course that qualified him to fly a fighter plane and had an airstrip marked out in a field near the family's Fehmarn villa so he could fly from Berlin to the house at the weekends; Heydrich would gun his engine to announce his imminent arrival and Lina would get the dinner on. Lina, who viewed his new hobby with some alarm, went up with him once and they flew round the island; Lina loathed it and never got in his plane again.

Once Poland was occupied, Heydrich made a number of trips there to check on the brutal progress of his Einsatzgruppen death squads and begin herding the local Jewish population into ghettos. To make his absences more bearable, Lina had acquired some new editions to her small Berlin social circle, including Walter Schellenberg's new wife, Irene. Her mother was Polish, which would cause problems getting an SS marriage certificate, but Heydrich helped Schellenberg out and per-suaded Himmler to allow the couple to wed. Lina and Irene got on exceptionally well; they hung out, shopped, had lunch and dinner, and went to the movies.

The other couple brightening her days were Max de Crinis and his wife Lilli, a former actress. Lina met de Crinis and Lilli in 1939 when he was made professor of psychiatry at the world-renowned Berlin University teaching hospital, Le Charité. De Crinis was about to become a key figure in the regime's euthanasia programme – known as T4 – and on 10 August he attended a meeting with around a dozen other psychiatrists to select technical staff capable of implementing its mandate, which was endorsed by Hitler, and stated that 'patients who … are considered incurable can be granted mercy death after a critical evaluation of their health'.[7]

De Crinis's involvement with T4 was based on both his professional and ideological credentials. The son of a doctor, de Crinis was born in Austria in 1889. By 1924, he'd become an associate professor of neurology and from then until 1934 he was very active in the Austrian Nazi party. That year, he took up a chair at Cologne University. In 1936, he joined the SS and the SD. His personnel file described him as 'a well-known pioneer in the anti-Semitic realm'.[8]

De Crinis was an enthusiastic advocate of the sterilisation programme that had paved the way for the regime's adoption of euthanasia. The 'Law for the Prevention of Hereditarily Diseased Offspring' was drafted on 14 July 1933, and supplemented by the 'Law Against Habitual Criminals', which enforced the castration of anyone over 21 who had done more than six months in jail for a second offence. Four of the nine conditions named in the legislation covered mental health: manic depression, schizophrenia, 'congenital feeblemindedness' – which included those with criminal records, prostitutes, the unemployed and the homeless – and 'anyone suffering from chronic alcoholism'.[9]

Potential victims were selected by psychiatrists like de Crinis – who had done studies on both epilepsy and alcoholism – and appeared before one of the 220 local health courts, where their fate was decided. By 1939, 345,000 people had been sterilised: 200,000 'feeble-minded', 73,000 schizophrenics, 37,000 epileptics and 30,000 alcoholics.

Though the first to die were children, the T4 programme focused on adults. In mid January 1940, the decision was made to use carbon monoxide gas; at the beginning of February, de Crinis was on a panel recruiting suitable doctors and forms went out to health officials at asylums and sanatoriums for registering potential 'patients'. During a conference in March, de Crinis discussed T4 with psychiatrists from state mental hospitals. Killings were initially carried out at four different locations; around twenty 'patients' were gassed at a time in a room designed to look like a communal shower. All the deceased had their gold teeth removed.

In August 1941, T4 was halted after protests from the Catholic Church; by then 70,000 had been murdered. De Crinis was one of prime movers behind the reintroduction of the programme in the autumn of 1943, and it continued until the end of the war. In 1939, there were between 300,000 and 320,000 people in German mental health institutions; by 1946, there were only 40,000.

Schellenberg regarded de Crinis as his best friend, a fine man with a 'most pleasant and cultivated household'.[10] Heydrich thought he was 'a very nice fellow'.[11] Lina and her husband would often go riding with de Crinis and his wife in the early morning, galloping round the Grunewald forest on horses from a Berlin stables. Afterwards, they would go back to de Crinis's villa on Lake Wansee for a champagne breakfast.

During April 1940, Heydrich spent four weeks in Norway with a fighter squadron, strafing the enemy, drinking in the officers' mess and playing cards. His participation in this short campaign ended on 13 April when his Messerschmitt 109 overshot the runway on take-off and crashed; the plane was wrecked and Heydrich broke his arm. The next day he was back behind his desk in Berlin with an Iron Cross Second Class.

After the rapid conquest of Poland, there followed several months of stasis as Hitler waited to see if Britain or France – particularly Britain – were prepared to rethink their decision to go to war. With no clear sign that either of them were going to back off, Hitler resumed hostilities and attacked Norway in order to secure vital sea routes.

Job done, Hitler turned his attention westwards towards the old enemy France; he craved revenge and redemption for the defeat of 1918, a chance to erase that shame and humiliation from the pages of history. What he didn't have was the means to wage a long campaign. Out of this necessity arose the infamous Blitzkrieg strategy: the concentration of force to achieve a rapid breakthrough, punching a hole through the enemy's defences with a combination of tanks and aircraft, racing through the gap and deep into its territory, leaving those left behind vulnerable to encirclement. The results were nothing short of spectacular. On 10 May, the attack was launched; on 17 June, six weeks later, the French surrendered.

Soon after, Emmy – who was wearing the latest Parisian fashions – and her husband had a special dinner to celebrate this stunning victory and the Luftwaffe's role in it. Goering had brought some pâté de foie gras from Paris to accompany different coloured vodkas from Poland, and they also consumed 'roast salmon done in the Danzig style with Moselle ... and then a tiny very light Viennese torte'[12] with white wine. The meal was provided by Otto Horcher, Emmy and her husband's personal chef and caterer, who ran Horcher's restaurant in Berlin. Opened in 1904 by his father Gustav, it served solid German fare, dishes such as smoked eel with horseradish sauce, lentil soup with frankfurter, and potato salad with Pommery mustard and poached egg. Goering had started going there in the late 1920s to wine and dine aristocrats and industrialists. Otto catered all the Goerings' big parties, including the Olympics banquets, as well as receptions and private dinners at Carinhall.

The Horcher brand benefited from Nazi expansion. After the *Anschluss*, Otto took over the top restaurant in Vienna. When the war began, Goering made sure all of Otto's waiters and cooks were exempt from military service. In Norway, Otto set up exclusive Luftwaffe Clubs serving food and drink to officers and opened two for the public in Oslo. After the fall of France, Otto acquired the legendary Maxim's in Paris so his patron would have somewhere to eat on his frequent trips to the city, as he orchestrated one of the greatest art thefts in history.

In early March 1940, Margaret arrived in Poland for an inspection tour of German Red Cross sites. She visited Posen – which had a school and boarding house for nurses – Lodz, which was the centre of German Red Cross activity in Poland, and finally Warsaw. Like many of her colleagues, Margaret complained about the primitive living conditions and poor hygiene in the hospitals and transport trains, what she called 'indescribable filth'. She was also offended by the appearance of the local inhabitants: 'This Jew trash, these Pollacks, most of them don't even look like human beings.'[13]

Prejudices confirmed, Margaret returned to Berlin, where, at some point, Himmler told her about Hedwig. However much this must have hurt her, Margaret never contemplated divorce. For her, it would have amounted to a shameful humiliation. Then there was Gudrun to think of; Himmler was devoted to her and she idolised him. Given she was already struggling to cope with both her parents away most of the time – according to her mother, she was 'very nervous and doing poorly at school'[14] – neither of them wanted to disrupt Gudrun's life any further. Himmler continued to put in appearances at Lake Tegernsee, tried to call every day and wrote regular letters. Himmler's willingness to maintain appearances was not simply because he wanted to spare Margaret and Gudrun unnecessary pain. He was dead set against divorce; 77 per cent of the SS leadership cadre were married, as opposed to around 44 per cent of the general population, and any SS man who wanted to leave his wife had to get Himmler's permission; if they defied him, they were expelled from the SS.

An example of Himmler's uncompromising attitude was the way he treated his old comrade, Karl Wolff, who wanted to split from Frieda and marry his long-term mistress, a widowed countess with whom he'd been conducting an affair since 1934; she had borne his child in 1937 and was housed in a love nest in Budapest with ten rooms and a bath house. But Himmler refused to let Wolff dump Frieda. In the end, Wolff appealed over Himmler's head to Hitler, who gave him the go-ahead to divorce.

Throughout this drawn out process, Frieda – who had written to Himmler to say that she did not want to stand in the way of Karl's happiness – stayed at their Lake Tegernsee home with her children. Though she and Margaret were neighbours who'd known each other for nearly a decade and their daughters were good friends, the bitter quarrel between their husbands impacted on their relationship. Once it became clear that Karl was defying Himmler's orders, Margaret distanced herself from Frieda, abandoning her in her hour of need.

Perhaps Frieda's experience was too close for comfort; Margaret's unhappiness, her sense of loss and abandonment, began appearing in her diary. On 9 June 1940, she wrote that 'so much sadness makes it hard to be alone … so in the evenings I mostly play Solitaire and read a little'. On 4 January 1941, she reflected that 'the old year has gone by. It took a lot of courage to go through it.' A month later, she bemoaned the fact that 'every young girl craves a man' without realising 'how bitter life is' and hoped that she would be able to 'protect my daughter from the worst'.[15]

One of the pieces of art proudly displayed in the Bormanns' Munich household was a bronze bust of Gerda done by the regime's most visible and lauded sculptor, Arno Breker. Breker was known for his monumental, classically themed works – with names like *Prometheus*, *Torchbearer* and *Sacrifice* – featuring naked men in dynamic and heroic poses. Breker's portraits in bronze were mostly private commissions; he did busts of Hitler, Goebbels, Magda's son Harald Quandt, and Edda Goering.

Born in 1900, the son of a stonemason, Breker spent time in Paris in the 1920s after qualifying from the Dusseldorf School of Arts. He was in Rome in 1932 when Goebbels tracked him down and tried to persuade him to return to Germany, which he did in 1934. Two years later he entered two sculptures into the Olympic arts competition, won silver, met Hitler at the reception and was very impressed. The feeling was mutual; in 1940 Hitler awarded Breker the golden badge of the Nazi party.

Breker was also the richest Nazi artist, earning a fortune from state commissions, prizes and his own factory, which used slave labour to mass-produce versions of popular works like his portrait of Hitler. Gerda sat for Breker in 1940 and after the bronze of her was complete, she befriended Breker and his wife, the glamorous Demetra Messala, an ex-model who'd sat for Picasso in Paris; by the time she joined Breker in Germany, she was a successful art dealer. They married in 1937 and had five children.

That Gerda felt comfortable in such sophisticated company is indicative of her rising status as a Nazi wife. Gerda was an integral part of life at the Berghof, which had settled into a fixed daily routine revolving round Hitler's habits. He slept late, appearing around noon; lunch was taken a few hours later and then most days at around 4 p.m. Hitler, Eva and their guests would take a twenty-minute stroll downhill to the Little Tea House instead of scaling the heights to reach the Eagle's Nest: aside from the fact it was often very cold up there, the thin air at that altitude made Hitler queasy.

The Little Tea House was much cosier. According to Hitler's faithful secretary Christa Schroeder, Hitler and Eva always had cocoa rather than tea or coffee, and though the 'selection of cakes and pastries was very tempting', Hitler 'always had apple pie, its pastry breath thin, low in calories, with slices of baked apple'. In this relaxed atmosphere, 'Hitler would love to hear amusing stories, and people who could tell them were very welcome.'[16] Sometimes, if the company was not stimulating enough, Hitler would fall asleep in his chair.

The evenings were monopolised by Hitler's monologues, whether delivered over dinner or at the fireside. On 5 July 1941, a member of Bormann's staff began work on an ambitious project to record all of Hitler's pearls of wisdom. The end result – known as *Hitler's Table Talk* – covered every meal at the Berghof up to mid March 1942; after that, the entries were intermittent, with large gaps between sessions.

Until recently, historians believed that the final text, which ran for hundreds of pages, was a verbatim reproduction of Hitler's speeches, but recent research suggests that Bormann's assistants transcribed the material from memory each morning and then handed their notes over to Bormann for shaping and editing. Bormann took the whole process of capturing his master's voice very seriously, performing the role of a faithful disciple and curator of Hitler's thoughts, preserving them for future generations.

That summer at the Berghof, Hitler was pondering a dilemma. Despite the subjugation of France in record time, Britain refused to fold. Invasion was an option and plans were assembled, but it was a risky prospect. Then Goering stepped forward and offered to resolve the problem by using the Luftwaffe to bring Britain to its knees. Goering's solution appealed to Hitler and for six months, beginning in August, his air force tried to do just that, initially attacking the RAF and its infrastructure and then switching to bombing London and other economically significant cities.

However, for all the destruction and mayhem caused, it was clear by the end of February 1941 that Goering was not going to keep his promise to Hitler: the Luftwaffe was losing planes and experienced pilots at a fearsome rate, while Goering's poorly managed, institutionally corrupt, wasteful and inefficient Four-Year Plan office had become a sprawling behemoth incapable of producing enough aircraft to subdue a whole nation, especially one fighting so tenaciously while manufacturing its own planes at a faster rate and in greater numbers.

Throughout this critical period, the most challenging of his Nazi career, Goering dedicated a lot of time and energy to his art collection, which he'd begun building seriously in 1936 after setting up a private fund for purchasing art. The main contributor was the cigarette manufacturer, Philip Reemstama, who accounted for 75 per cent of the market. Goering did him a number of favours, fending off the competition, getting him out of legal scrapes and winning him army contracts that amounted to billions of cigarettes. The tobacco king was understandably grateful and every three months he donated 250,000 RM to Goering's fund.

Goering bought through a number of dealers and sought out work by sixteenth- and seventeenth-century German artists, the Dutch masters, and Italian Renaissance painters, sometimes paying above the odds, sometimes below. Otherwise, he shamelessly stole from Jewish owners and galleries, and by 1940 he had acquired 200 pieces.

After the war started, his agents scoured Poland, coming back with thirty-one drawings by Albrecht Durer, which Goering gave to Hitler, and ransacked the art market in Amsterdam, buying whole collections of paintings from big private owners, including a fake Vermeer. At the same time, Goering used degenerate art as collateral. He exchanged paintings by Cezanne, Van Gogh and Munch for hard cash, and on 3 March 1941, he swapped eleven works – including one by Degas, two by Matisse, two by Picasso, a Braque and a Renoir – for a Titian. A month later, in a similar deal, he got a Rembrandt and two tapestries for twenty-five degenerate paintings. Once France fell, however, the real bonanza began. In Paris, a massive warehouse was filled to the brim with art confiscated from the city's Jewish community. Between 3 November 1940 and 27 November 1942, Goering made twenty-five visits to the warehouse and removed 700 items, mostly paintings but also tapestries and sculptures.

All these treasures were transported by rail to Carinhall, where Emmy could enjoy them. Like her husband, she claimed they had no intention of keeping the art for themselves; they were its custodians, keeping it safe and secure. Once the war was over, Emmy said her husband would open the Hermann Goering Museum and put it all on public display.

Magda spent much of 1940 in and out of hospital, her heart condition aggravated, as always, by her pregnancy. In August, she was fit enough to return home, but by early October she was – according to her husband – 'suffering badly with her heart'. On the 10th, she was 'nervous and irritable' and towards the end of the month, as delivery day beckoned, Magda faced 'her critical time' with 'great courage'. On the 29th, her ordeal was over and she gave birth to their sixth child, another daughter.

The following day there was a party for her husband's forty-third birthday. Magda and her children – with some professional assistance – had put together a special present for Goebbels, a short home movie featuring them walking in a forest, playing with a toy castle and hunting rabbits. Once Goebbels had been treated to a private screening, the film appeared in the cinemas as a piece of morale-boosting propaganda. Goebbels was delighted by this celluloid gift, inspiring 'laughter and tears' because it was 'so beautiful'.[17] In return, he laid on 'a small party for Magda's birthday' on 12 November. Pleased that she was 'dazzlingly beautiful again', Goebbels was also thrilled that Hitler decided to drop by: 'The Führer arrives towards ten in the evening, and stays until four in the morning. He is absolutely confident and relaxed, just as in pre-war times.' The trio discussed 'vegetarianism', the 'coming religion', and Goebbels proudly noted that with them Hitler could be 'a proper human being again'.[18]

But such scenes of domestic tranquillity were repeated less and less during 1941. That year, Magda and Goebbels were increasingly apart and leading separate lives. This was due to Magda's persistent health issues – a minor heart attack in February, bronchitis in March – Goebbels's packed schedule, which included a fair amount of foreign travel, and the potential threat of British bombers over Berlin, which encouraged them to send their children down south; for a time they stayed at Obersalzburg and other locations in Bavaria. Later, they were shipped off to the Upper Danube region.

During all this, relations between Magda and her husband remained cordial, with plenty of goodwill on either side. Yet they were drifting away from each other, the gulf between them steadily growing. Soon, the familiar problems that had dogged their marriage from the outset would make a mockery of the contract they signed.

During late October 1940, Margaret was in the Balkans for a couple of weeks on German Red Cross business, accompanied by Professor Gebhardt, who ran her favourite health spa, the Hohenlychen clinic. They travelled to Romania via Budapest – where they were entertained by 'gypsy music' in their hotel – had a quick stopover in Belgrade and went to see a 'German resettlement' in the Bessarabia region of northern Romania. This area had been ceded to the Soviets as part of the 1939 Hitler-Stalin pact; it was subsequently reclaimed by the Romanian army, who descended like locusts on its Jewish population, killing around 8,000, and dumping 250,000 in concentration camps.

As a result, whole villages and towns were emptied and a large amount of land was made available, which prompted Margaret's husband to include the region in his plans to resettle ethnic Germans in places where they could establish model farming communities. Margaret and Professor Gebhardt were given a tour of one of these so-called *Volksdeutsches* villages, and she was impressed by how 'clean' it was.[19]

Back in Berlin, Margaret's social life had dwindled to almost nothing; the diplomatic soirees were over for her and she saw very few people.

One of them was Anneliese von Ribbentrop. Out of all the leading Nazi wives, Anneliese was Margaret's closest friend. Strong-willed, ambitious, intelligent and stylish, Anneliese was roughly the same age as Margaret and came from the Henkel family, who had grown wealthy selling their unique brand of sparkling wine. She married Ribbentrop in 1920 after meeting him at a tennis tournament, and together they had an enviable lifestyle. Their elegant Berlin villa had its own tennis court while their country estate boasted a nine-hole golf course. After inviting Hitler to dinner in 1932, Anneliese converted to Nazism and pushed her husband into his inner circle.

Unfortunately for Margaret, their friendship was abruptly terminated because their husbands fell out with each other. The two men had become close after Ribbentrop joined the SS in 1934, bonding over their shared love of tennis. However, once Ribbentrop had been made foreign minister, they squabbled over their respective spheres of influence in Allied and neutral countries. Matters came to a head in 1941. Angered by the SD's support for a failed coup against the Nazi-friendly government in Romania, Ribbentrop forced Himmler to sign an agreement that underlined his authority over foreign affairs.

On 8 May 1941, Margaret noted in her diary that 'the relationship' between her husband 'and Herr von Ribbentrop has ended' because 'Ribbentrop had too many pretensions'.[20] At the same time, Margaret ended her association with Anneliese; without her for company, Margaret's isolation in Berlin was complete.

During the winter of 1940–41, Ilse Hess suspected that her husband was planning something out of the ordinary, as 'he was extremely busy with all sorts of activities and his state of tension was visible'. Hess was flying again, using the airfield at Augsburg so often that Ilse found it hard to believe he was simply seeking some 'distraction from the cares of office'.

The mystery deepened when 'a large brand new radio apparatus appeared in the work room of our home … and was used behind closed double doors'. She investigated it and discovered that it was tuned to receive reports from a weather signals station. Most curious of all was 'the astonishing amount of time – and in the middle of a war – that my husband spent with our son'.

On Saturday, 10 May 1941, Hess had scheduled an early lunch with an old comrade, Alfred Rosenberg, but Ilse was feeling unwell and didn't join them. After Rosenberg left, Hess popped upstairs to see Ilse and asked her to take tea with him at the 'usual hour'. When he appeared at 2.30 p.m., Ilse was surprised that he was 'wearing bluish-grey breeches and high airman's boots' and 'even more astonished to see he had on a light blue shirt with a dark blue tie, a colour combination I had so often advocated without the slightest effect'. When Ilse questioned him about his attire, Hess replied that he was trying to please her. Ilse was not convinced. Later she realised that her husband had been sporting a Luftwaffe officer's uniform.

After tea, Ilse remembered that 'he kissed my hand and stood at the door of the nursery, grown suddenly very grave, with the air of one in deep thought'. Hess bade his sleeping son farewell and left for the airfield at Augsburg, where he took off in his Messerschmitt plane, embarking on a mission to bring about peace between Britain and Germany.

Ilse started to worry when he didn't return home that night: 'The next two days, Sunday and Monday … we knew absolutely nothing of what had happened.' On Monday evening, the 12th, Ilse had 'arranged for a show in our little cinema at home' for Hess's staff, the chauffeur and the servants. During the film, Hess's youngest adjutant appeared in a terrible state; he'd just heard on the radio that Hess had crashed in the North Sea, having suffered a 'mental aberration'.

Ilse immediately rang the Berghof, fully intending 'to speak to the Führer and give him a piece of my mind', but she was connected to Bormann instead, who said he knew nothing, which at that moment was true. Ilse did not believe him and 'expressed' her 'indignation with an emphasis and rhetoric I had never employed before or since'. Bormann – who had everything to gain from Hess's disappearance – promised her that a ministry official would bring her more news as soon as possible, but when the official arrived long after midnight he had nothing meaningful to say.

The next morning, the 13th, Hess's old friend and mentor, Professor Haushofer, dropped by; he was 'deeply shaken and filled with despair' because he thought Hess was dead. Once Haushofer had limped off, Ilse, who was overcome with exhaustion, took her son and went to bed, falling instantly 'into a deep sleep'. When she awoke, her prayers were answered; her husband had landed safely in Scotland.[21]

Before she had time to digest the news, Ilse was summoned to her husband's Berlin apartment to find Bormann waiting for her. After giving her a thorough grilling, Bormann asked to her to list what items in the flat belonged to the state – which would be seized – and what belonged to Hess, which she could keep. As it turned out, only the carpets were hers, while the rest of the fixtures and fittings were government property. Having set her this deliberately degrading task, Bormann added insult to injury; if Ilse wanted to buy the bedroom furniture, he'd give her a 50 per cent discount.

Ultimately, Ilse's fate depended on Hitler. He was at the Berghof the morning after the flight when Hess's adjutant arrived with a letter from his boss. Having read it, Hitler reacted with a mixture of rage and incomprehension that only increased as more details emerged. Some close to Hitler – including his valet – thought he knew what Hess was going to do and had given his approval; his enraged response was nothing more than a performance from a gifted actor. But Ilse categorically denied this: 'I have certain knowledge that my husband desired to make a personal sacrifice without being ordered to do so, without any knowledge of this act as far as Hitler was concerned.'[22]

Hitler immediately had all of Hess's private staff arrested; some of them languished in camps until 1944. Hess's brothers were also picked up then released after being given the fright of their lives. Professor Haushofer was already a marked man – Hitler referred to him as 'the Jewish tainted professor'[23] – and he was held in custody by the Gestapo for four months. His son Albrecht was dragged before Hitler and asked to account for himself.

Albrecht wrote a report about his contacts with the Duke of Hamilton – whom Hess had briefly met at the Olympics – and the letter he wrote to the British peer on Hess's behalf that outlined proposals for peace between the two countries. As a result of this confession, Albrecht was imprisoned for two months at Gestapo HQ in Berlin and fired from his job. Fearing further harassment, Albrecht took refuge in the Bavarian mountains.

Hess's own version of events did not mention Albrecht Haushofer or his father. In an official statement Hess made to his British captors, he explained his reasons for taking such precipitous action: 'After the end of the war in France, Hitler made an offer to reach an understanding with England; but this was turned down. This served to make me more sure than ever that my plan must be put into practice' to prevent 'an endless line of children's coffins with weeping mothers behind them, both English and German; and another line of coffins of mothers with mourning children.'[24]

Hess's concern for the lives of the innocent did not extend to Soviet civilians; he was fully aware that Hitler was about to launch the long-awaited invasion of the Soviet Union – scheduled for that summer – and realised that the campaign would be waged with unprecedented savagery. By attempting to convince the British to lay down their weapons, thereby removing the threat of a two-front war, Hess was doing what he could to help Hitler annihilate his Bolshevik enemies. In his letter to Hitler, Hess acknowledged that his 'project' had only 'a very small chance of success' and was likely to end 'in failure'. If so, Hess thought the best way for Hitler to avoid any 'detrimental results' and 'deny all responsibility' was to heap the blame on him and tell the world that he 'was *crazy*'.[25]

Whether it was down to Hess's suggestion or not, this was the explanation given by the regime as it attempted to neutralise speculation about what had happened, downplay its significance and minimise the effect of the propaganda being produced by the British media. Goebbels was in charge of getting the message out there, and he had no doubts about who was responsible for the fiasco: 'Professor Haushofer and Hess's wife were the evil geniuses in this affair … the whole thing can be traced back to his mystic obsession with healthy living and all that nonsense about eating grass … I'd like to give a good thrashing to that wife of his!'

On 14 May, the main Nazi newspaper – under Goebbels's direction – referred to Hess's 'delusions' and criticised his reliance on 'magnetic healers' and 'astrologists'. This was bad news for Hess's personal astrologer Ernst Schulte-Strathaus, who was arrested that afternoon. Allegedly, Strathaus had made a series of positive predictions about Hess's mission, one in January, one in March, and one the day before Hess flew off. Strathaus was interrogated for two weeks, then moved to Gestapo HQ in Berlin where he was placed in solitary confinement for eleven months before being transferred to Sachsenhausen concentration camp; he was released after two miserable years there.

On 16 May, Goebbels observed that 'the Hess affair is still a big talking point' but 'the rumours are cancelling themselves out'. The following day, he was pleased to note that 'the public is slowly calming down and already jokes about it are doing the rounds'.[26] But the jokes showed how confused and bewildered the German people were; Hess had always been the reliable stalwart, the dependable man at Hitler's side. After all, he gave the Christmas radio address every year and now they were meant to believe he'd gone mad. One joke ran: Two friends meet in a concentration camp, and one asks the other 'Why are you here'? Answer: 'Because on May 5th I said to someone that Hess was crazy. And why are you here?' Answer: 'Because on the 15th I said he wasn't crazy.'[27]

Hess was definitely not a well man. He was suffering from severe hypochondria. After he landed in Scotland, the British Medical Research Council analysed the twenty-eight different sorts of medicine Hess had brought with him. There was an elixir for his gall bladder, opium derivatives for pain, aspirin for headaches, atropine for colic, barbiturates to stay awake, amphetamines for fatigue and a saline mixture for constipation. In addition, there were 'mixtures of unknown products made up along homeopathic lines' that were 'so diluted it's impossible to say what they are'.[28]

11

CASUALTIES

At around 4 p.m. on 10 June 1941, twelve days before the largest invasion force ever assembled – 3 million German soldiers plus another half a million foreign troops – rolled like a tidal wave into the Soviet Union, a terrifying storm hit the Berghof. According to the housekeeper, it had been 'an unbelievably hot day' with 'a heavy storm brewing in the north' when 'all of a sudden it started getting dark everywhere, as if it were a real solar eclipse' and there was 'an incredible crack' accompanied by 'a deafening explosion'. A bolt of lightning had obliterated the 33ft-long pole – adorned with a huge swastika flag – which jutted proudly out of the Berghof, leaving 'thousands of wood splinters' the size of 'match-sticks' scattered everywhere.[1]

Stunned, the housekeeper was frantically trying to figure out what to do when a call came in from Bormann; he'd seen the lightning strike from his house down the hill. Bormann instructed the housekeeper to remove the identical flagpole that stood in the car park and use it as a replacement and warned him not to breathe a word to anybody in case this freakish accident was interpreted as a bad omen, a warning of imminent disaster.

Dealing with this minor emergency was but one of the many tasks Bormann performed in his role as the Obersalzburg estate manager. His pride and joy was the 200-acre Manor Farm. Though the poor quality of soil on the lower slopes made it difficult to grow crops, the farm's cattle and pigs provided the Obersalzburg residents with meat and dairy products, the chickens laid eggs, and an apple orchard produced cider. There was also a greenhouse for fruit and vegetables and mushrooms sprouting in the Berghof cellars.

Yet both Bormann and his master were increasingly absent. After the invasion of the Soviet Union, Hitler moved to a series of Führer HQs; first, he based himself at the Wolf's Lair, then the following year he moved to Werewolf; both were massive concrete bunkers buried deep in thick forests populated by swarms of mosquitoes. According to Christa Schroeder, Hitler's long-term secretary, those at the Wolf's Lair were at their worst in July, while Werewolf was blighted by 'the dangerous Anopheles strain whose bites can give you malaria'.[2] Bormann spent a lot of his time at both complexes, shuffling back and forth from Berlin.

With the two dominant males away from Obersalzburg, the Berghof increasingly became Eva's domain. With a select group of women to keep her company, Eva indulged her love of photography and shot hours of footage with her film camera, sunbathed on the terrace, and frequently went swimming in Lake Königsee, which was only 5 miles away. Aside from her own friends with whom she would run around Munich and invite to tea at the Berghof, two women who were part of the Nazi elite – Anna Brandt and Margarete Speer – were the most constant members of her little gang.

Anna Brandt caught the dictator's attention in the 1920s when she was a champion swimmer. Her speciality was backstroke; between 1924 and 1928 she won five national titles, broke seven German records and took part in the Amsterdam Olympics. Her achievements made her a celebrity and she graced the covers of newspapers and magazines. Anna was introduced to Hitler at his cottage in Obersalzburg and she joined the Nazi party before her husband did. Karl Brandt was made one of Hitler's personal doctors in the mid 1930s, had considerable influence over the regime's health policies and was overall head of the T4 euthanasia programme.

Margarete Speer was not a world-class athlete but she and her husband Albert enjoyed outdoor activities like hiking and camping; on their honeymoon they went canoeing. At the same time, they were fans of the theatre, literature and classical music. Speer's father was a successful architect while Margarete's was a master joiner with his own small firm, and the young couple had to overcome his parents' misgivings about their son marrying beneath him. Speer, who'd taken up his father's profession, first heard Hitler speak at his university. Intrigued, he joined the party. Initially, Goebbels was his patron, but then Hitler adopted him and came to treat Speer like a long-lost son.

With much of her time occupied by her offspring, Gerda was on the fringes of Eva's group. Though her eldest son was now at an exclusive and extremely strict boarding school – the National Socialist Education Institution – her most recent child had been born in October 1940 and she had another son in March 1942, followed by one more in September 1943. As her other six kids got older, Gerda, the qualified kindergarten teacher, took a serious interest in their education, recording their progress in letters to her husband as if she was completing an end of term report.

A sign of Eva's growing assertiveness was the offer of help she extended to Ilse not long after Hess's flight; 'I like you and your husband best of all. Please tell me if things become unbearable, because I can speak to the Führer without Bormann knowing anything about it.'3

Allegedly, Eva intervened with Hitler to stop Bormann from having Ilse arrested, ended his surveillance of her and demanded she receive a monthly pension. Though Eva insisted Ilse was treated with dignity and respect, Bormann did everything he could to make Ilse's life difficult. He blocked and delayed the payments due to her, tried unsuccessfully to have her Munich home confiscated and haggled with her over the furniture in the Berlin residence, charging her twice what it was worth. Ilse may have been shielded from worse treatment than this, but she was still an internal exile, a pariah with an uncertain future, her destiny out of her hands.

Her husband was also at the mercy of forces beyond his control. He'd put his case to a number of dignitaries, including the Duke of Hamilton, but his pleas fell on stony ground. The British government had no intention of coming to terms with Hitler. Hess had made a fundamental error of judgement. Like others in the Nazi elite, he believed that Britain was ruled by its aristocracy; as long as you secured the backing of a few important lords, you were bound to get what you asked for.

Demoralised and dejected, Hess attempted suicide. At around midnight on 15 June 1941, Hess distracted his guard by asking for a whisky to help him sleep. Dressed in his Luftwaffe uniform and polished leather boots, he slipped out of his room, crept onto the landing, and threw himself over the bannister. He dropped 25ft and broke his leg on impact. In July, after observing Hess for eighteen days, one of his psychiatrists wrote that Hess believed 'poison of a subtle kind' was being added to 'his food and medicine' that affected 'his brains and nerves' with the 'intention of driving him insane'. On the basis of his 'bizarre ideas of persecution and torture', the psychiatrist concluded that Hess was paranoid.[4]

Ilse had no idea about what her husband was going through. A glimmer of hope appeared on the horizon that summer when Hitler agreed to let her write to Hess, although this gesture was not entirely benevolent. The Nazi leadership were anxious to have some way of monitoring Hess's situation and Schellenberg was put in charge of handling the correspondence: 'I had to organise measures for him and his wife to write to each other. After a time, the British allowed him to correspond, within limits, by the way of the International Red Cross in Switzerland, and it fell to me to supervise the arrangement.'[5] But as it took up to eight months for Ilse's letters to reach her husband, it would be some time before she got a reply.

The final phase of retribution for Hess's actions was set in motion by Heydrich in early June 1941 and targeted the purveyors of 'occult doctrines and so-called occult science'. Lina's husband relished this particularly assignment. Himmler's affection for mystics and prophets irritated him; Heydrich thought they were misguided fools who exerted a malign influence on society. On his hit list were 'astrologers,

occultists, spiritualists, supporters of occult radiation theories, soothsayers' and 'faith healers'.[6] Hundreds were arrested by the Gestapo.
Thousands of books, magazines and pamphlets were seized. Goebbels,
who supported the clampdown, couldn't resist making a joke at their
expense; in his diary he noted that 'not a single clairvoyant predicted
that he would be arrested. A poor advertisement for their profession!'[7]
However, most of those detained were released after a short stay in a
camp, having been beaten and humiliated, while *Aktion Hess*, as it was
known, failed to undermine their popularity: in 1943 there were an estimated 3,000 tarot card readers in Berlin.

Much as Heydrich enjoyed locking up astrologists, his main concern at the time was preparing for the invasion of the Soviet Union.
On 17 June, he assembled the leaders of four Einsatzgruppen task forces
and gave them unambiguous instructions for the coming campaign: they
were to act with 'unprecedented severity'; all Jews in the service of the
Communist Party were to be 'eliminated', plus all other Soviet officials
and 'radical elements'.[8]

Heydrich's orders dovetailed neatly with the responsibility he was
given by Goering on the 31st to find 'a total solution of the Jewish
question in the German sphere of influence in Europe'. By the end
of 1941, Heydrich's Einsatzgruppen had butchered 500,000–800,000
people, most of whom were Jewish. Dispatching their victims with
bullets and blunt objects, the killings took a heavy toll on the perpetrators, quite a number of whom went insane or committed suicide.
As a result, Heydrich and his boss began considering a less hands-on
approach to mass murder and looked to the euthanasia programme
for inspiration.

On 20 July, Heydrich re-joined his fighter squadron – without
Himmler's authorisation – which was operating over the Soviet Union.
Two days later, just after 2 p.m., his plane was hit by flak, his engine
malfunctioned and he was forced to make an emergency landing behind
enemy lines. Forty-eight hours passed before he was found by members of an Einsatzgruppen death squad who'd killed forty-five Jews and
thirty other hostages on the day they found him. Lina remembered that
her husband arrived home 'dirty, unshaven and very upset'.[9]

After this adventure, Heydrich was grounded and took no further part in the campaign, which was making giant inroads into Soviet territory, seizing the Baltic states, Belorussia, and driving deep into Ukraine. By the autumn, the Germans had captured over 3 million Soviet soldiers and had reached the outskirts of Moscow before grinding to a halt.

In the midst of all this, Heydrich managed to find time for fencing, an hour every morning and more at weekends. Earlier that year he'd become president of the International Fencing Federation after out-manoeuvring his rivals. In June and July, while he was in the Soviet Union with Himmler, he was training for the German National Championship; he came fifth. During September, he was preparing for a sabre-fencing match with Hungary, the reigning champions, and won his three bouts. This packed agenda was guaranteed to make Lina miserable: 'It was terrible for me. He was never, never at home.'[10] Even when her husband was in Berlin, he continued to go out on the town at night, trawling the bars and clubs. On one occasion, Heydrich kept the happily married Schellenberg up until 5 a.m., hopping from one venue to another, engaging 'in stupid conversations' with the bar staff, who all 'knew him and feared him, while pretending devotion'.[11]

During March 1941, Margaret went on a two-week tour of German Red Cross facilities in France and Belgium. Travelling alongside Emmy's sister-in-law, Margaret covered a lot of ground and visited various soldiers' homes – the largest of which was at Amiens – a number of field hospitals and several railway stations that handled incoming wounded. Along the way, Margaret was also able to take in regular tourist attractions; chateaus in the Loire, the cathedral at Chartres, the palace at Versailles, and a day of shopping and sightseeing in Paris, where she stayed at the Hotel Ritz and was wined and dined by the local SS chieftains. Overall, Margaret was 'very pleased', and thought 'the trip was very harmonious'.[12]

Not long after, on 22 July 1941, Himmler treated her and Gudrun to a tour of the vast herb and spice garden for homeopathic medicines he'd established at Dachau. Work had begun in 1938 to drain 200 acres of marshy land near the camp. Some 1,000 prisoners toiled and sweated to lay garden soil, mixed soil and sand. Using only natural manure and compost – fertilisers and pesticides were forbidden by Himmler – the garden, which the camp inmates called the 'plantation', produced thyme, basil, estragon, rosemary, peppermint, caraway, marjoram, sage, and gladioli for its vitamin C.

On 23 January 1939, the plantation came under the management of the German Research Institute for Nutrition and Food Provision (one of the many SS businesses) with the aim of supplying herbal medicines to domestic and foreign markets, carrying out experimental research and maintaining laboratories, and selling livestock, honey from its bee colony and fruit and vegetables – potatoes, leeks, tomatoes, cucumbers, swedes, and onions – from its greenhouses.

Gudrun wrote to her father after their visit and told him she'd seen 'the large nursery, the mill, the bees' and 'how all the herbs were processed', gushing about how 'magnificent' and 'lovely' it all was.[13] For Margaret, the plantation was the end result of the plans she and her husband had nurtured in the early days of their relationship, the homeopathic nurse and the agriculture student who wanted their own small herb garden. To see their dream realised on such a grand scale must have been deeply gratifying. Not once did she stop to consider what it cost in human suffering: the back-breaking work, long hours, poor food rations, severe cold and outbreaks of deadly diseases.

Margaret's enjoyment of the day was probably undermined by the fact she was still suffering the after-effects of a domestic accident a month earlier:

The water heater exploded while I sat in the bath tub and the porcelain shattered all over me. Had to get stitches that night at the hospital in Tegernsee. I bled like a pig and had to be bandaged in six places; they spent two hours on my right arm and on the left side of my abdomen there is a big wound, which got infected and often hurt terribly.

On 19 July, Professor Gebhardt made a house call to see how she was doing and was satisfied with her condition; a few weeks later he wrote her a 'very calming letter'. By then, she was 'doing much better', and thought things were 'gradually getting back to normal'.[14]

However, this meant dealing with her errant stepson – 'terrible things are happening continuously' – and with her worries about Gudrun, who'd had her appendix out in March, who was 'doing very poorly at school',[15] and who was missing her father terribly; though she had a party for her birthday with nine guests and loads of presents, Himmler couldn't make it. Instead, he sent her photos of him playing tennis in Berlin.

Reading the correspondence he exchanged with Margaret that autumn, it's hard to find any sign that their marriage was irretrievably broken. In one letter, Margaret told 'her good husband' that she and Gudrun were waiting for him 'with so much longing';[16] for Margaret's birthday, he sent her coffee and roses. But at the same time, Himmler's mistress, Hedwig, was expecting their first child and he was busy plotting their future together.

Hedwig described these plans in a letter to her sister: 'As soon as the war is over he wants to buy us a house in the country on a piece of land', that could be made 'profitable' by planting 'a small tree nursery' or 'breeding small animals' or 'cultivating berries'. Enchanting as this was, Hedwig was an urban creature and had her doubts: 'The idea is not bad. I have not quite decided about it yet. It would certainly be a huge adjustment, and I would have to learn so much.'[17]

On 13 February 1942, Hedwig gave birth to a son named Helge at the Hohenlychen clinic. Professor Gebhardt was present at the birth and became the child's godfather. It was now a matter of some urgency to find Hedwig a secure and appropriate home in which to raise her child, especially as her parents had disowned her. Himmler found her a cosy woodman's lodge in the Mecklenburg forest, about 50 miles north of Berlin, with lakes dotted around it and a tiny village nearby.

Hedwig's new residence was 5 miles away from Ravensbrück concentration camp, the first SS facility solely for women prisoners. Opened in May 1939, by August 1940 there were 3,200 inmates lodged in crowded barracks with around fifty female guards watching over them and high-voltage electric fences to deter any thoughts of escape.

Also 5 miles away, but in the opposite direction, was the Hohenlychen clinic. That Christmas, Professor Gebhardt wrote Hedwig a fawning letter:

> When I think back to the hour of the birth of your little son, my god-child, and on all the responsibility and joy that we felt at the time, then I am at a loss for words to express myself … I can only give you the assurance that I will endeavour to be an absolutely faithful follower of Himmler.[18]

Did Margaret know about her husband's love child? A few weeks after the birth, Himmler spent three days at Lake Tegernsee. Whether he told her then or not, Margaret did eventually become aware of what had transpired: 'Sometimes I cannot believe what I live through each day. We poor women.' A later diary entry was even more explicit: 'Surrounded by lies and betrayal. I can't bear it any more … I am always alone.'[19]

One evening in mid September, Lina went to the cinema with Schellenberg's wife Irene and returned home to find him and her husband breaking open the champagne to toast Heydrich's new appointment as the 'Protector of Bohemia and Moravia', the Nazi-run chunk of the former Czechoslovakia. The Protectorate's armaments industry was crucial for the war effort but production was down due to sabotage. Heydrich's mission was to get the assembly lines back on track, something he achieved with a mixture of the carrot and the stick; he arrested and executed hundreds of subversives, real and imagined, while increasing food and beer rations for key workers.

Though this was a significant career move for her husband, Lina was less than happy when he departed on 27 September 1941, particularly when she realised she was pregnant again. Her mood improved, however, after it was decided that she and the children could join him in Prague. Three months later, Lina arrived at her new home, the imposing Prague Castle, and felt overwhelmed by the majesty of it all: 'I am standing at a window in the castle and looking down over the gleaming, golden city. I am seized by sublime feelings. I feel that I am no longer an ordinary human being. I am a princess in a fairy tale land.'[20]

Her initial euphoria wore off. The castle was too much like a museum for her tastes and she found the weight of its accumulated history oppressive. She longed for a space she could make her own for her family and husband to enjoy. Meanwhile, Heydrich was commuting back to Berlin two or three times a week. On one of these visits, he chaired the notorious Wansee Conference, during which representatives of various government and state departments were informed about the Final Solution and discussed the logistics and timetable for the eradication of all Europe's Jews.

Lina's desire for a more suitable domestic arrangement was finally answered and the family moved to a neo-classical manor house that had been seized from its Jewish owner by Heydrich's predecessor. Situated 12 miles north of Prague, a mere half an hour's drive away, the house had thirty refurbished and redecorated rooms with central heating, a 7-hectare garden and 125 hectares of forests. Concentration camp labour was drafted in to build a swimming pool.

As the family settled in, Lina was the happiest she'd been since the early days of her marriage. When he wasn't in Berlin, Heydrich was home every evening at a decent hour to be with her and play with the children. At weekends, Lina and her husband went riding; the kids had a pony; the boys got fencing lessons. Lina started collecting antique German porcelain. Some evenings, she helped Heydrich prepare his speeches, giving him advice and stern criticism. There were music evenings. The couple often had guests, including Heydrich's old friend Canaris and his wife Erika; Lina remembered their stay with some affection; 'they were happy days'. Otherwise, Heydrich 'liked being able to be less formal ... he stretched out on the sofa and read, often into the small hours'.[21]

There were also public events to attend. On 15 May 1942, Heydrich opened the city's first 'cultural festival' with works by Bruckner, Mozart and Dvorak, performed by the German Philharmonic Orchestra of Prague. In his programme notes, Heydrich stated that 'music' was 'the everlasting manifestation of the cultural workings of the German race'.[22]

On 21 February 1942, a British psychiatrist noted that Hess was displaying 'a distinct loss of memory'.[23] On the 27th, Major Foley – an officer from military intelligence who was familiar with Hess – observed similar symptoms and wondered if they were 'genuine or simulated'. Neither Major Foley nor the nurses believed that Hess was 'such a consummate actor that he is able to consistently pretend he has forgotten things which should have impressed themselves strongly on his memory'.[24] Hess's amnesia was a transitory phenomenon; his memory would slip in and out of place, his ability to recall events came and went from one day to the next. In his first letter to Ilse, dated 20 May 1942, he discussed the Nazis' war on cancer, reflected on the fact that his son Wolf was about to start school – 'it is almost impossible to think of him as a schoolboy, confronted for the first time with the serious side of life' – and made an unambiguous reference to the period before his flight, remembering Wolf as 'the tiny wide-eyed child who was sitting' in his nursery 'when I last saw him'.[25]

By then, Hess had been moved to a former mental hospital near Abergavenny in Wales that was being used to accommodate wounded soldiers. Hess had a whole wing to himself and was guarded by thirty men. He read a lot of Goethe, jotted down notes for an autobiography, and was sometimes allowed to take a walk after lunch. Hess found the 'colours of the landscape ... unusual and attractive' and relished witnessing the change of seasons as 'the red earth, lying between meadows and fields of green' turned 'yellowish ... when ripe'.[26]

Despite this apparently relaxed routine, Hess remained convinced the British were trying to poison him. He kept a secret record of what he believed was a systematic attempt by his captors to ruin his digestion and prevent his bowels from functioning properly with the overall aim of 'destroying his memory';[27] according to Hess there was caustic acid mixed in with his food, which was so salty that he got kidney infections, and poisons in his water that affected his ability to urinate. He was plagued by insomnia and had become hypersensitive to noise. Yet in his letters to Ilse, Hess never ranted or raved about his situation. His tone was always measured and thoughtful, even philosophical: 'The world is out of joint in every respect. But one day the joints will be fitted together again – and we too shall be reunited.'[28]

During 1942, Magda did her best to live up to her image as the First Lady of the Reich and performed a number of public duties. She visited a military hospital where 'the head physician was not able to handle the wounded right, and their morale is pretty low', and delivered a speech to 'a thousand Berlin women on Mother's Day'.[29] There was also a sequel to the home movie made for Goebbels's birthday two years earlier. The 1942 version was a much more professional effort and had been carefully planned; there was a classroom scene, humorous antics, the kids playing games and wearing Mickey Mouse masks, and a sequence showing the war hero Rommel – who was giving the British a pounding in North Africa – visiting the family at home. Unlike its predecessor, the film was pure propaganda.

Perhaps it was inevitable, but the truce between Magda and her husband did not last; slowly but surely the cracks reappeared. Magda was in her forties and all the years of sickness and ill health had taken their toll on her looks; Goebbels no longer desired her like he used to. He regarded her with affection, respected her intelligence and strength of character and probably loved her in his own utterly selfish and possessive way, but the erotic spark was gone, so he started cheating again. As Magda wearily conceded to her confidante Ello Quandt, 'I'm getting old. I often feel exhausted and I can't change matters. Those girls are twenty years younger than me and have not brought seven children into the world.'[30]

Goebbels began seeing his secretary. One night in February, Magda spotted her climbing from the garden into his study. Enraged, she threatened him with divorce and went to see her lawyer. However, Goebbels was able to talk her down. There was no repeat of the intense battle of wills that occurred over Lida Baarova; neither of them had the energy for that again, and Hitler had made it brutally clear what the consequences would be if they divorced. So Magda withdrew her challenge and didn't protest when the secretary came to their home for meals and private parties. In the end, the secretary dumped Goebbels because she was worried her fiancé would find out about the affair.

Unable to prevent her husband from sleeping around, Magda amused herself by playing tricks on his girlfriends. One of them used a special key to enter a passageway where the door was usually closed, so Magda had the locks changed. She prank-called another, informing her that Goebbels would send a car to meet her at a crossroads in the Grunewald forest at 11 p.m. Magda let her wait there for an hour before telling Goebbels what she'd done.

On 27 May 1942, the Heydrich household was moving at a more leisurely pace than usual; the previous night Lina and her husband had been the guests of honour at a special event held at the Wallenstein Palace as part of the Prague cultural festival. That evening, alongside an opera, the programme featured a violin concerto written by Heydrich's late father and played by a quartet of his ex-students from Halle. Afterwards, a reception was held for guests and performers at the swish Hotel Avalon. Lina remembered that Heydrich was in his element, 'a master of etiquette, entertaining, interested in everyone, a charming conversationalist'.[31]

After a late breakfast, Heydrich strolled the grounds with Lina and played with his kids. At 10 a.m. he climbed into his dark green Mercedes and his SS chauffeur set off for the capital. At a crossroads on the outskirts of Prague, Heydrich's car was ambushed by two members of the Czech resistance, who'd been parachuted in from Britain some months earlier. One had a gun, but it jammed; the other threw a bomb that landed on the back seat and exploded, tearing holes in Heydrich's midriff. Bleeding heavily, Heydrich fired a couple of shots at the fleeing assassins, collapsed, and was rushed to hospital in a baker's van.

Two Czech doctors immediately extracted a small piece of metal from the wound in his back and sent him for an X-ray, which revealed puncture wounds, damage to the pancreas, and signs of a foreign body – possibly a bomb splinter or a piece of the car's upholstery – in the spleen area, which would require another operation. Heydrich wanted it performed by a German surgeon, so his Czech carers tracked down a suitable candidate and he got to work at around midday. A steel fragment, 8cm x 8cm, was removed from his spleen, but bits of leather and horse-hair were still embedded in Heydrich's guts. Nevertheless, he seemed fit enough and they stitched him up and put him to bed. Lina arrived soon after. Hitler phoned the hospital at 12.30 p.m. Professor Gebhardt flew in that night. On the morning of 31 May, Himmler showed up. Lina brought her husband home-cooked meals. Heydrich seemed to be on the mend.

But on 2 June his temperature soared to 102°F (39°C). At this point, one of Hitler's personal doctors – who'd arrived on the scene to give his verdict on Heydrich's recovery – suggested they use the drug sulphona-mide to fight the infection. Professor Gebhardt rejected this suggestion and on the 3rd he phoned Himmler to tell him the fever was receding and the wound was draining freely. After lunch, however, Heydrich lost consciousness. Lina rushed to his bedside. In the early hours of the 4th, he came round and deliriously uttered his last words to Lina: 'Go back to Fehmarn.'[32] Distraught and overwhelmed, Lina took a sedative. By the time she awoke, he was dead. Heydrich passed away at 4.30 a.m., killed by septicaemia.

When Hitler heard the news he couldn't contain his anger. Why had Heydrich ignored protocol? Driving about with his car roof down with no bodyguards or SS escorts? All the top Nazis had bulletproof vehicles and their own protection squads. How could he have been so irrespon-sible? Reflecting on her husband's casual attitude to his own safety, Lina was convinced he'd harboured a death wish: 'It seemed to me he had long embraced the idea of dying soon … I know it sounds trite, but I believe he wanted to sacrifice himself.'[33]

For two days, his coffin sat in the courtyard at Prague Castle. Tens of thousands of ethnic Germans and Czechs filed past to take a final peek at their 'Protector'; no doubt some of them were just making sure that he was dead. On 9 June, the coffin went by train to Berlin for a ceremony that began in the Mosaic Room at the Reich Chancellery with Wagner's 'Twilight of the Gods' playing in the background.

Himmler spoke first and praised his colleague's steely determination and unflinching dedication to his work: 'I know what it cost this man to be so hard and severe despite the softness of his heart: to make tough decisions in order to act in accordance with the law of the SS.'[34] Hitler went next. Visibly moved, he kept it brief; Heydrich was 'one of the best National Socialists' and 'one of the greatest opponents of all the enemies of the Empire' who'd 'died a martyr for the preservation and protection of the Reich'.[35]

His oration finished, Hitler passed by Heydrich's two sons – who were in the front row next to Professor Gebhardt – and patted them on the cheek. The coffin was then taken away to the strains of Beethoven's *Eroica*, and a carriage drawn by six black horses ferried Heydrich's corpse to the Invalides cemetery where a swastika was draped over the coffin, there was a three-gun salute, and all the senior SS officers and police leaders solemnly gathered at the graveside for a final tribute.

Lina was not in any condition to attend the funeral. Her nerves were shattered and she had the health of her unborn child to consider; on 23 July, she gave birth to her second daughter, Marte. In Heydrich's old stomping ground, eighteen Czech towns were renamed in his honour, along with dozens of streets in the capital. A year later, a bronze bust of him was erected at the spot where the attack took place.

The retribution dished out by Heydrich's successor, Kurt Daluege – a hard-headed, crude and violent SS man – was comprehensive. The assassins and their team were cornered and eventually killed in a church crypt in the city centre; 3,188 Czech civilians were arrested and 1,327 of them sentenced to death; 4,000 others were deposited in camps. The most shocking atrocity occurred at the village of Lidice: all the adult male inhabitants were executed, the children were farmed out to SS orphanages and the women were transported to Ravensbrück.

At the Hohenlychen clinic, not far from the Lidice women's final destination, Professor Gebhardt was also facing the consequences of

Heydrich's death; Gebhardt had refused to use the drug sulphonamide to combat the infection that killed him and now he feared that he might get the blame.

In order to demonstrate that his judgement had been correct, Gebhardt organised a series of experiments at Ravensbrück. Trials began at the end of July. The first victims were male prisoners from Sachsenhausen concentration camp. Their legs were fractured and infected with virulent bacteria; half of them were given sulphonamide, the other half nothing at all. The results were mixed, so Gebhardt selected around seventy Polish women from Ravensbrück – known as 'the rabbits' – and subjected them to horrific treatment: large incisions were made in their legs, and dirt, small pieces of wood, fragments of glass and, in one case, a curved surgical needle, were inserted in the gaping wounds.

Margaret's boss at the German Red Cross, Ernst-Robert Grawitz, even suggested shooting the women with bullets in order to reproduce battlefield injuries, but Gebhardt decided to stick with severe tissue damage. In the end, Gebhardt got what he wanted; five of the women who'd taken the sulphonamide died, confirming his claim that the drug was ineffective. Gebhardt presented his findings to over 200 army doctors at the Third Working Conference of Advisory Physicians, 24–26 May 1943, and his assistant gave a lecture on 'Special Experiments with Sulphonamides'.

During July and August 1942, Margaret spent four weeks in Latvia at the town of Mitau, 20 miles from Riga, for the anniversary of its liberation from the Soviets. Though she found the trip 'interesting and instructive'[36] and she visited a SS-run field hospital, she came down with smallpox and was in bed most of the time.

Back at Lake Tegernsee, and recovering from her illness, Margaret was on the receiving end of care packages sent by Himmler that were stuffed with basic household goods and domestic products that were in extremely short supply and beyond the reach of the majority of the population: tissues, wax paper, toilet paper, two little lamps, two wash cloths, a wooden tray and a wooden bowl, a laundry bag for travelling, scouring powder and an old toothbrush for polishing shoes. He also sent her so much caviar that she didn't know what to do with it; should she give it away?

In September, Margaret returned to Berlin to resume her German Red Cross duties, which was good for her morale: 'Without any work outside the house, I could not live through the war.'[37] That month, she wrote to her husband about Gudrun and the difficulties she was having finding anybody at school who was prepared to be her friend. In the evenings, Margaret filled the lonely empty hours sewing, reading and making preserves.

Every Christmas, Emmy hosted two parties. One was at the Goering's official residence in Berlin, where 300–400 guests mingled beneath coloured decorations hanging from chandeliers, stood next to walls covered with the branches of pine trees and listened to Emmy's friends from the Berlin Opera singing carols. The other was at Carinhall, a more intimate affair for family – which included Carin's son Thomas and her sister – and the staff. A well-known actor from the State Opera dressed up as Santa Claus, there was a ballet performance, and on Christmas Eve a professional organist played 'Silent Night' before everyone opened their presents.

That year, the festivities were overshadowed by the unfolding disaster at Stalingrad. The German spring and summer offensives had pushed its armies even further into the Soviet Union and a thrust to take this industrial city on the Volga began in the autumn; the whole Sixth Army was sucked into an urban quagmire, bitterly contesting every inch of the ruined city, reduced to rubble by Goering's Luftwaffe. As the Germans battled away, the Soviets counterattacked, rolling back their lightly defended flanks and trapping them in Stalingrad.

All the while, Goering had assured Hitler that his planes could continue to supply the beleaguered troops with what they needed to survive and fight on as winter asserted its fearsome grip. However, Goering's mission of mercy was doomed from the start. It would take 300 flights a day to fulfil the soldiers' needs, but the weather made that impossible; in freezing temperatures aircraft couldn't start their engines, there was ice on the wings, zero visibility and heavy snow meant planes had to be dug out before take-off. To make matters worse, the airfields were in range of Soviet guns and planes. In the effort to feed the troops, 488 transport planes were lost and 1,000 aircrew killed.

As a consequence, the surrounded army starved and eventually its commander defied Hitler's no surrender order and capitulated on 31 January 1943. This was Hitler's first major defeat of the war, one from which he would never recover; the momentum that had taken him so far had gone.

12

UNDER PRESSURE

On 18 February 1943, Magda was in the huge Berlin crowd gathered to witness her husband give a speech – also broadcast on the radio – in which he called for total war; the absolute mobilisation of every facet of German society for the titanic struggle ahead. Anything that wasn't useful, any economic or social activity that didn't contribute directly to the war effort, or diverted resources away from it, was to be terminated.

Goebbels directed some of his invective at women and urged them to 'devote all their energy to waging war, by filling jobs wherever possible to free men for action!'[1] By that point, over 50 per cent of the workforce was female but Goebbels and other leading figures were keen to maximise any untapped potential. Compulsory labour conscription was introduced for women aged 17–45, although the recruitment drive was hampered by the exceptions available for those with poor health or difficult domestic situations. By the end of June, 3.1 million women had registered at employment offices but only 1,235,000 were suitable for work, and half of those only part-time. The shortfall was filled by hundreds of thousands of labourers imported from across Europe, many of them women, who endured unspeakable living conditions and inhumanly long hours.

Inspired by her husband's words, Magda was determined to make a contribution: Goebbels noted that she was 'absolutely uncompromising and radical on the question of total war'.[2] Magda found herself a position at a local factory – owned by Telefunken, a major communications company –

and commuted there by tram. The demands of the job were immediately too much for her, and by 1 March she was back in the Dresden clinic again.

On 18 March Goebbels noted that Magda was 'having a hard time recovering from her illness … the war depresses her not only physically but psychologically'.[3] Her heavy mood was not improved by the fact that her husband had told her about what was going on in the East. A year earlier, Goebbels had met with Hitler and got a clear indication of what the answer to the Jewish question would be: 'The Führer was as uncompromising as ever. The Jews must be got out of Europe, if necessary by applying the most brutal methods.'[4]

Himmler had assumed full control of the Final Solution after Heydrich's assassination; on 19 July 1942, Himmler launched *Aktion Reinhard* – named in honour of his fallen comrade – to exterminate Poland's Jews. The first transports to Treblinka death camp, which was equipped with gas chambers and crematoriums, began three days later. Two other killing sites, Belzec and Sobibor, were soon up and running. By the summer of 1943, when *Aktion Reinhard* was wound down, around 2 million people had been murdered.

Though Hitler had instructed the senior figures who knew about the camps not to discuss them with their wives, Goebbels shared the burden with Magda and she spoke to Ello Quandt about his revelations: 'It's terrible all the things he's telling me now. I simply can't bear it any more. You can't imagine the awful things he's tormenting me with.' But she was sworn to secrecy – 'I have no-one to pour my heart out to. I'm not supposed to talk to anyone' – and stopped herself from giving Ello the whole terrible truth.

Bewildered by what she'd learned, Magda was having doubts about Hitler: 'He no longer listens to reason … And all one can do is stand by and watch what is happening. It's all going to end badly – it can't possibly end otherwise.'[5]

Ilse was at home in Munich when the city experienced its first significant bombing raid; on the night of 20 September 1942, sixty-eight bombers dropped their deadly cargo, killing 140 civilians and injuring over 400. Ilse had no intention of abandoning the city at the first sign of danger. However, by early 1943, she'd had enough of her Munich home; it was too expensive to manage and too big for just her and her son Wolf. Instead, she wanted to convert it into a convalescent home for wounded soldiers. In March, she asked if she could proceed with her plan. The answer was no; Himmler wrote to her and explained that 'the Führer's decision concerning your house is very clear. You should keep the house … and not sell it. You may ask for all the expenses necessary to keep up the house so that you are not burdened in maintaining the valuable piece of property.'[6]

But Ilse knew this was a false promise; any money for the house would have to come through Bormann, and she was well aware of how tricky that would be. So she boxed up her possessions, boarded up the main house and moved into the vacant chauffeur's apartment; her husband's extensive library was stored at their small chalet about 100 miles from Munich.

The city was rocked by another raid in March 1943, much bigger than the previous one; nearly twice as many of its citizens were killed or wounded, while 9,000 were left homeless. Over in Wales, Hess was apparently oblivious to the threat his wife and son were facing. In his letters to Ilse, he focused on Wolf's development, regretting the fact that his talents lay 'in the direction of technical science', when he and Ilse had always hoped that their child would become 'a great poet or musician who would bring happiness to mankind'.[7]

Only once did Hess describe how he felt about what happened to his personal staff, his friends and his family after his departure. Though their persecution angered him, Hess appreciated that Hitler was 'under a nervous strain hard to imagine – a strain responsible for states of excitement, in which decisions have been made which would not have been made in normal times'.[8] He was also 'happy to see' from her letters that Ilse remained loyal to Hitler and that nothing had changed in her *inward relationship* to the man with whose destiny we have been so closely linked in joy and suffering, for more than twenty years'.[9]

One of the many restrictions imposed on civilian life by the pursuit of total war was the ban on the manufacture and sale of cosmetics. As a woman who was fond of her make-up, Eva was less than pleased by this measure, and having made her feelings known, she made sure her supply was not interrupted. Equally, Eva was not affected when the same thing happened with sanitary towels; by the end of the year, there were none available and ordinary women had to come up with home-made alternatives.

The rationing of clothing made no impact on her either. Eva continued to wear three new dresses a day – one for lunch, one for tea, and one for dinner. Like Emmy and Magda, she was able to source her outfits from a handful of German designers and French and Italian fashion houses. The clothing ration that applied to the rest of the population came into effect in 1939. Every individual was given vouchers worth 150 points to last them a year, reduced in 1942 to 120 every sixteen months. Under this system, a winter coat was 100 points, a woman's skirt 20, a blouse another 20, and it cost 40 for a dress or a new pair of stockings.

Despite all her privileges, Eva suffered from Hitler's prolonged absences. On Christmas Day that year, while Gerda spent the afternoon with her kids having 'a birthday party for all the new dolls and for the old rejuvenated ones, complete with cocoa and cake', Eva was all alone at the Berghof. Gerda felt sorry for Eva, but also for Hitler, who had to put up with 'telephone conversations and letters impregnated with this mood of hers instead of something positive that would make him feel happy'.[10]

While Bormann was away almost as much as his boss, Gerda and her husband constantly wrote to each other and their letters demonstrate the intense bond between them. Bormann called her 'the superlative of all the women I know or ever knew'.[11] Contemplating an upcoming visit from him, Gerda was 'overjoyed at the thought of having you here again. So full of longing to have you in my arms and not let you go.'[12] Yet for all the sweet nothings, Bormann could still treat Gerda like she was his servant. During a big reception at their Obersalzburg home, Hitler's chauffeur remembered that at 'about two in the morning Bormann suddenly decided he should wear a smoking jacket' and 'asked for a particular shirt to go with it that he had worn a few days ago'. When Gerda informed him that his shirt was in the wash, her husband 'erupted into a screaming fit'[13] and ordered her to go straight to their Munich residence and bring him back the type of shirt he wanted.

Nevertheless, Gerda increasingly saw herself as a senior figure in the Nazi elite. Her husband had been made secretary to the Führer on 12 April 1943; to get to Hitler you had to go through Bormann first, and he now felt strong enough to move against Gerda's estranged father Walter Buch, who was still head of the Nazi Party Court. In autumn 1943, Hitler put Bormann in charge of party jurisprudence and the court lost its independence. According to Buch, Bormann had the 'power to decide the court's judgements' beforehand. Though Buch 'opposed the change', his protests fell on deaf ears; Hitler had 'stopped listening to him years ago'.[14]

Gerda demonstrated her growing sense of self-importance by befriending Himmler's mistress Hedwig, beginning a correspondence after meeting her. In one letter, she commented on the photographs of Himmler that Hedwig had sent her: 'I have never seen such a relaxed picture of him as these together with his son.'[15] The fact that Himmler was married did not bother Gerda. For her it was the natural order of things: Himmler's behaviour was merely the healthy expression of a man's biological need to reproduce. Her open-minded attitude applied to her own marriage. Bormann never made any secret of the fact that he chased any stray female who happened to wander across his path. During an excursion on a steamer boat, one of Hitler's valets saw Bormann through a half-open cabin door with his trousers round his ankles and his boots still on, having sex with a 'prominent lady'.[16]

Up until 1943, Bormann's infidelities were largely one-night stands or short-term liaisons; once he'd satisfied himself, Bormann lost interest. However, the actress Manja Behrens got under his skin. Born 1914 in Dresden, Manja was the daughter of a lawyer and an actress, and briefly studied English in Prague. Until 1935, she worked as a dental assistant while taking private acting lessons before making her stage debut. Soon after, she appeared in two films: *Stronger than Paragraphs*, where she played a woman in love with the man who murdered her uncle and is faced with a dilemma when the wrong person is arrested and sentenced to ten years; and *Susanna in the Bath*, a sexed up melodrama where an art teacher imagines her nude, paints the results, exhibits the picture and causes a scandal.

Before she could make another movie, Manja's screen career abruptly ended when she rejected Goebbels's attempt to seduce her, telling him she'd rather clean stages than go to bed with him. Without any more film work, she went back to the theatre, did a couple more plays and was introduced to Bormann at a ball in 1940. He found her attractive but nothing happened. They met again in similar circumstances in October 1943; he was overwhelmed by desire, and confessed to Gerda a few months later that he 'fell madly in love with her'.[17] With his usual bull-headed determination, he kept pestering Manja until she gave in.

But Manja was concerned about Gerda's feelings. She needn't have worried. Gerda was glad to welcome Manja into the family – 'I am so fond of M ... and the children too love her very much, all of them' – and was excited at the prospect of establishing a polygamous household together:

> One year M has a child, and the next year I do, so that you will always have a wife that is mobile. Then we'll put all the children together in a house on a lake, and live together, and the wife who is not having a child will always be able to come and stay with you in Obersalzburg or Berlin.

To put this arrangement on a proper legal footing, Gerda suggested they draw up a new marriage contract that would give Manja the same rights as Gerda, something she believed could be repeated on a national scale as part of regime policy to boost the birth rate: 'It would be a good thing if a law were to be made at the end of this war ... which would entitle healthy, valuable men to have two wives.'[18] Keen to put her ideas into practice, Gerda invited Manja to stay with them in Obersalzburg, but the threesome proved unsustainable, Manja struggled to adjust and fled the love nest. By 1944, she was working in an armaments factory doing fifteen-hour shifts.

After her husband's assassination, Lina spent the summer recovering at Fehmarn. Having decided to make her future in the Protectorate, she put her Berlin house on the market and returned to Prague on 7 December 1942. Technically, her Czech manor house belonged to the Reich, but when Hitler gave her permission to stay there indefinitely, she declined his offer; Lina didn't want to own it herself, fearing it would cost too much for to manage on her widow's pension and any income she might earn, so instead she rented the estate.

Rather than dwell on Heydrich's death or wallow in self-pity, Lina showed her resilience and determination to keep fighting. In a letter to her parents, she said her decision to return to the scene of the crime was 'a political commitment' and she was proud of the fact she was 'perhaps the only woman in public life who has not disappeared into anonymity through the death of her husband'.[19] On a trip to Denmark, she argued with the SS chief there about his policies, and was planning similar interventions in Norway and France. Alarmed, Himmler put the brakes on; it was simply too dangerous for Lina to go wandering around Europe. Confined to her estate, Lina concentrated on developing the grounds. She added an orchard, a vegetable patch, and kept rabbits and poultry. Jewish labourers from the Theresienstadt camp were shipped in to landscape the gardens and turn them into an English-style park with a stream.

Life without her husband was made more palatable by his SS chauffeur, who was particularly good with her two sons, and a riding companion of Heydrich's – an SS officer and ex-policeman – who acted as her financial and legal advisor, regularly joined the family for dinner and taught the kids to swim and ride horses. At weekends, he and Lina would hunt hare and pheasants in the forest. To help look after the children, Lina employed a full-time live-in governess, while the house was kept ship-shape by the domestic staff, who did their best not to incur her wrath. One of them remembered that Lina 'liked ordering people around … if she hadn't slept well, she would go about shouting at everybody, telling them they were lazy and so on, even the SS guards. When she was in a good mood she ignored us all.'[20]

On 24 October 1943, Lina experienced another sudden and violent death. Her two boys – Klaus was 9 and Heider was 8 – were riding their bikes round the gardens in the late afternoon. The main gates were open as a visitor was expected and Klaus and Heider zipped in and out of them. After a bit, Heider went back to house, but Klaus stayed out on his bike. At 4.45 p.m., Klaus whizzed past the SS guard, who tried to stop him, and sped into the road, where a truck suddenly appeared out of nowhere and drove straight into him. Lina and the SS guard carried her unconscious son into the house; he was covered in blood and had serious injuries to his neck and chest. One of Lina's Jewish workers was a doctor and he examined Klaus before her personal physician arrived. It was too late; Klaus died within thirty minutes of the collision. He was buried on the estate in a metal casket, dressed in his Hitler Youth uniform.

The long delays that affected the correspondence between Ilse and her husband made life difficult for both of them. On 15 January 1944, Hess complained that it was over four months since he'd received a letter from her, and asked her to send him some more books because they were 'of the greatest value' and helped relieve the monotony of his 'solitary confinement'.

The real reason why Hess was so keen to exercise his mind was that his amnesia had returned: 'I may as well tell you: I have completely lost my memory. The whole of the past swims in front of my mind in a grey mist. I cannot recollect even the most ordinary things.'[21] Though his confession disturbed her, Ilse refused to admit defeat. Having consulted a number of doctors, she reassured her husband that his memory would return after the war was over.

Meanwhile, during June and July, Munich was subjected to a series of massive raids that left thousands dead and hundreds of thousands homeless. Reflecting on the 'destruction of our beautiful, beloved Munich', Ilse was struck by the fact that Hitler had inspected the devastation and 'stood before the rubble deeply shaken'. She wondered how he could bear to stand by as 'one after another of the things closest to his heart is annihilated' while waiting for the right moment to strike back and snatch the victory that Ilse still believed was within his grasp: 'It is 1944 and we will never give up hope.'[22]

That same July, Hamburg was razed to the ground; on the 24th, 1,500 residents were killed along with 140 animals in Hamburg zoo. Three nights later, 787 aircraft dropped loads of incendiaries, creating a terrifying firestorm that accounted for an estimated 40,000 victims. Emmy had grown up in Hamburg and she lost family members and friends, while three of her husband's nieces died in the conflagration.

The capital was also under fire. From March until the end of the year, there were sixteen major raids. It was all too much for Emmy. She was 'unhappy and desperate' and 'crushed by the stupidity of this war'. Rather than let these feelings of hopelessness paralyse her, she did what she could to alleviate the suffering. Each time Emmy was in Berlin, she visited 'the wounded in hospitals to bring them cigarettes, books and other little comforts'.[23] For the bombed out homeless, she donated linen, clothing and furniture from the guest lodge at Carinhall.

On 24 November, during yet another attack, a bomb struck Magda and Goebbels's Berlin residence: 'The top floor is burned out completely. The house is full of water … and all the rooms are filled with pungent smoke.' When Magda drove in from their country house to inspect the damage she passed through some of the city's poorest districts, which had borne the brunt of the assault with 'terrible' results.[24] Having assessed the smouldering remains, Magda and her husband spent the night in the bunker beneath the wrecked building.

To combat the stress and tension of being constantly under threat, tackle her depression and blot out her sense of foreboding, Magda re-engaged with Buddhism, which had intrigued her for a while when she was young. Whether it helped her cope is hard to say; certainly she needed all the Zen-like calm she could muster when Goebbels threw a tantrum that Christmas. According to Rudolf Semmler, Goebbels's PA, 'the traditional movie session' featuring 'an American film' was compromised because the 'big decorated Christmas tree' had been placed in front of the screen. On seeing this, Goebbels lost 'all self-control. Then Frau Goebbels arrived … we could hear the row going on behind closed doors.'[25] Magda was unable to stifle his rage and Goebbels stormed out of the house to spend Christmas Day on his own.

While Magda and her husband were fighting, Emmy was busy with charitable activities, sending 'clothes and toys to thousands of children of numerous families whose fathers had been killed in action during the war'[26] and enclosing a card signed by both her and Goering. This was not simply a wartime measure. The leading Nazi wives had been giving generously to the needy at Christmas time since 1933 when Hitler opened the Winter Relief Agency to fight 'hunger and cold'. Its network of nationwide district branches and staff of over a million volunteers accepted cash donations as well as food, clothing and heating supplies.

Christmas was the focal point of the campaign: SS and SA men dressed up as Santa Claus and dished out presents to street urchins; members of every Nazi organisation – especially the youth and women's groups – stood on busy intersections with their collecting tins, went door to door selling badges in the shape of Christmas decorations, as well as handcrafted gifts at markets and seasonal festivals, and went carol singing. In addition, the agency provided hundreds and thousands of free Christmas trees. Emmy, Magda, and the other wives made their gestures of goodwill on the Day of National Solidarity, which was held on the first Sunday in December, setting up stall in a prominent public place and distributing presents from the piles of goodies heaped up next to them.

By 1939, the agency was harvesting nearly twice as money as it had in 1933, but much of it came from a compulsory 10 per cent tax on workers' incomes that was increasingly resented as people struggled to make ends meet. By the winter of 1943, there was little enthusiasm left for the charity drive; the Allied bombing campaign had sucked the joy out of Christmas and there was a joke going round that offered advice to shoppers looking for the ideal gift: 'Think practically, give coffins.'[27]

Goering had promised the German people that they'd never be bombed so he was held responsible for their flattened cities. At the same time, his and Emmy's luxury lifestyle had lost its popularity. It had ceased to be endearing; it was just insulting. Goering's excessive weight and expanding waistline were no longer sources of mirth but evidence of his greed, and people strongly disapproved of Emmy's conspicuous consumption. In April, an SS man criticised her for inviting the wives of eighty generals for coffee and laying on an obscene amount of food: 'The table fairly groaned under the weight of delicacies.'[28]

At the beginning of 1943, food rations had been reduced by roughly a third from the levels set in 1939, which were 2,570 calories a day for regular civilians, 3,600 for members of the armed forces and 4,652 for those engaged in heavy labour. Ration cards for different items were issued on a monthly basis and amounted to 10kg of bread a month, 2.4kg of meat, 1.4kg of fats, including butter, and 320g of cheese. On paper these quantities were sufficient, but the problem was supply; there were severe shortages of meat, fresh fruit and vegetables, sugar was scarce and people's diets relied more and more on bread – the quality of which deteriorated all the time – and potatoes.

As part of his total war initiative to stamp out wasteful indulgence, Goebbels closed down the half a dozen high-end restaurants in Berlin, including Horcher's, Emmy and Goering's favourite eatery. Goering was furious and fought to keep it open for another six months but in November 1943 Otto and his staff decamped to Madrid and opened a restaurant there. Before the war, Goering would have won this tussle with Goebbels; not any more. Goering had become damaged goods.

Goering's steady loss of power and influence – during 1943 he'd ceded control of the war economy to Albert Speer – had a dire effect on Emmy's efforts to help her Jewish friends. Rose Korwan was an actress who'd met Emmy in the early 1920s and worked with her in Weimar and in Berlin. As the persecution of Germany's Jews worsened, Emmy claimed that she 'tried not to lose sight of her and stay close to her just precisely because she was a Jewess'. When Rose was no longer permitted to perform, Emmy gave her a weekly allowance and encouraged her to flee the country, but Rose had fallen in love with a local Jewish man and refused to budge.

In March 1943, when transports to the East were leaving Berlin, Rose married her boyfriend and asked for Emmy's protection after he was arrested for arguing with an SS man and not wearing his yellow star. Emmy called Himmler, who was reluctant to help: 'You must realise Frau Goering ... that millions of German women have their husbands at the front and do not know what has happened to them. How can you expect that I can concern myself with the fate of one particular Jewess?'

Emmy implored him to do her a 'personal favour', and Himmler agreed to look into it. An hour later, he rang Emmy back and told her that Rose's husband would be dispatched to Theresienstadt, 'one of our very best camps', and assured her that he would 'be very well there'. When Rose heard the news, she asked Emmy if she could accompany him. Not wanting to push her luck, Emmy told Goering to ring Himmler about it, and:

> After some equivocations, Himmler agreed to send the woman to the camp. Everything would be all right, he assured us. He would personally see to it that the couple got a room, and even someone to clean it for them. The promise set both our minds at rest.[29]

But Himmler was lying through his teeth. A mutual friend of Emmy and Rose went to the station to see the couple off, but the train they were put on steamed off in the opposite direction. On hearing this troubling news, Emmy asked her husband to intervene again but Himmler would not take his call. Instead, a note was delivered confirming that Rose and her husband had arrived safely at Theresienstadt. Unable and unwilling to challenge Himmler further, Goering left the matter there; meanwhile, Rose and her husband were on their way to the gas chambers.

According to one of the Jewish prisoners working on Lina's estate outside Prague, she 'strode about like an Amazon, whip in hand' and 'loved the crack of it against her riding boots. The impression was she was cruel and arrogant'. Lina spat at her workers, called them 'Jewish pig' and though she never assaulted anyone herself, she would get her SS guards to do it for her if she spotted anybody slacking off: 'She had the

SS man … beat our comrade … until his back drew blood' because he was 'unable to run with his fully laden trolley'.

Lina housed the prisoners in the stables, where they were 'all crammed together in the smallest possible space', while 'the bugs ensured that we got no rest after each day's 14–18 hours toil. The food was deficient in all respects.' None of them had any doubts about who was responsible for their miserable existence; the 'inhuman treatment' and 'the constant threat of deportation to Auschwitz if the job was not carried out satisfactorily' was the 'exclusive handiwork of Lina Heydrich'.[30]

In January 1944, Lina's Jewish labourers were sent East to the camps and were replaced by fifteen female Jehovah's Witnesses from Ravensbrück. In 1933, Lina's husband had announced that any Jehovah's Witness – there were 25,000 of them in Germany – could be taken into custody by the Gestapo. In 1935, it was the first religious organisation banned by the Nazis. Over the years, 10,000 were imprisoned and over 1,000 killed; in the camps they wore a purple triangle and were especially harshly treated because of their stubborn adherence to their faith.

During July 1943, Margaret was in Berlin with the German Red Cross supervising the opening of an SS-run hospital for those 'hurt by the bombings in the West'. In mid August, she inspected her railway transit facilities and declared that they were in 'perfect condition'. On 3 September, four days before her fiftieth birthday, Margaret expressed her conviction that Germany would prevail: 'Our country is neither destined to, nor can, go under.' She was more concerned about her domestic situation, wondering 'about all the things that are going to happen to me in the next year of my life. And I don't mean in this war.'[31] Himmler's adulterous relationship was a never-ending source of grief and Margaret fretted about the corrupting influence it was having on Gudrun: 'She is only 14 and should not know more about life's difficulties. She already hears so many things she should not know about.'[32]

Though Himmler's visits to Lake Tegernsee were never longer than a three-day stopover, he compensated by increasing the volume and frequency of the packages he sent to his wife and daughter. On Mother's Day, there were flowers for Margaret. Sweets, candied fruits, brandy-filled chocolate beans, cans of condensed milk, and packets of glucose and marzipan arrived with the mail. Alongside these treats, Himmler sought to reinvigorate the intellectual exchange that had been a feature of his correspondence with Margaret until he got involved with Hedwig. As before, history books were at a premium. One parcel that Margaret received from him contained biographies of Empress Constance, who was Queen of Sicily during the Middle Ages; the King of the Vandals, who conquered Carthage; and Bismarck. Another included a glossy SS annual that had photographs of soldiers, workers and farmers engaging in sport and folk-dancing, plus several books on Japan.

On 6 August, Gudrun's birthday, Himmler wrote a wistful letter to Margaret that revisited the day 'fourteen years ago' when she gave him 'our sweet little daughter, with so much pain and in danger of your life'. The memory prompted him to sign off with 'special affection and ... many kisses'.[33] This uncharacteristic outpouring, combined with his diligent present giving, suggests he might have been having regrets about Hedwig, perhaps realising that he had more in common with Margaret than with his younger lover. Or was he just guilty now that Hedwig was expecting their second child?

Himmler was certainly worried about how isolated Hedwig was in her forest home and he wanted to find her somewhere to live close to Obersalzburg; however, he had a cashflow problem. While the SS's wealth grew and grew, his private income remained relatively static, so he turned to Bormann – the party's paymaster – for a loan. Bormann was happy to have one of his rivals in his debt and came up with the money. Himmler bought Hedwig a modest cottage near Berchtesgaden, not far from the Nazi reservation.

On 3 July 1944, at the Hohenlychen clinic, Hedwig gave birth to a daughter under the watchful eye of Professor Gebhardt. Sadly for her, Himmler could not be there, as he was a guest of honour at an extravagant wedding – the party went on for three days – that was being held at the Berghof. One of Himmler's protégés, Hermann Fegelein, a dashing but sadistic SS cavalry officer, was getting married to Eva's younger sister

Gretl. Six months later, as the Soviet army massed on the borders of the Reich, Fegelein deserted Gretl and was preparing to flee Berlin with another woman and some stolen gold bars when he was apprehended by the SS and executed.

At around 12.45 p.m. on 20 July, a bomb hidden in a suitcase and planted under a table exploded during a conference at Hitler's HQ. It blew out the windows, sending glass flying through the air and shattered the table, scattering sharp splinters everywhere. In all the smoke and confusion, Hitler was momentarily trapped under fallen beams. According to an account he gave afterwards, 'I was able to get up and go on my own. I was just a little dizzy and slightly dazed.'[34] However, his forehead was bloody from a cut, the hair was burned off the back of his scalp, there was a saucer-sized burn on his calf, his right arm was so swollen he could hardly lift it and there were burns and blisters on his hands and legs; more seriously, both his ear drums had burst, which temporarily deafened him and took some time to heal. The attempted coup by a conspiracy of army officers, intelligence operatives and concerned civilians was fatally compromised by Hitler's miraculous survival, and within twenty-four hours its leaders were either dead or under arrest. Nevertheless, it sent shockwaves through the Nazi elite.

Eva was on a swimming excursion at Lake Königsee when the bomb went off; the second she knew what had happened, she wrote him a letter: 'Darling, I am beside myself. I am dying of fear. I feel close to losing my mind ... I have always told you that I will die if anything happens to you.'[35] Not far away at Obersalzburg, Gerda was deeply shocked: 'How could that fellow put his briefcase with the bomb down there, how did he get it into HQ at all? I've been racking my brains about it a lot.'[36] On her estate outside Prague, Lina wasn't surprised by the attack, given her husband's belief that the officer corps was a nest of traitors capable of anything. At Lake Tegernsee, Margaret was appalled: 'What a disgrace. German officers wanted to bump off the Führer ... nothing like this ever happened in the history of Germany.'[37]

Emmy – who'd last seen Hitler on Edda's sixth birthday in early June – was more cautious in her appraisal: 'I cannot pass judgement on these men or congratulate their actions,' while her demoralised, lethargic and fatalistic husband did 'not disapprove of the bomb attempt itself as much as the manner in which it had been carried out',[38] implying that the oath of loyalty the army plotters had made to Hitler was too sacred to break whatever the circumstances.

In Wales, Hess heard the news on the radio. According to his orderly, Hess became 'extremely talkative with much gesticulating in a very exhilarated manner. He appeared very pleased that the Führer had escaped assassination.'[39] Earlier in the year, Hess had abandoned all hope and on 4 February he made a feeble attempt to commit suicide by stabbing himself in the chest with a bread knife, a flesh wound that required two stitches and left a tiny scar. Having refused food for the next eight days, he suddenly announced that his amnesia had lifted again. Now Hitler had escaped death, Hess felt more like his old self, for the time being at least.

Hess's long-suffering friend, Professor Haushofer, was caught up in the retribution that followed the assassination attempt, like hundreds of others who were arrested because they had offended Hitler at one time or another. Professor Haushofer spent a gruelling month in Dachau before being released. On 25 July, his son Albrecht managed to evade the Gestapo when they came knocking on his door and hid out for nearly six months until they caught up with him on 7 December. Two days later, Albrecht was driven straight from Munich to Berlin and slung in the dreaded Moabit prison.

Magda was in the Dresden clinic during the attempt on Hitler's life, recovering from the surgery she'd had to treat a problem with her trigeminal nerve, which had paralysed the right side of her face and caused her awful agony. The condition had bothered her for months and the therapy she was getting failed to improve it. After delays and complications – including Hitler's concern that facial surgery might ruin her looks – Magda had the operation that spring. As predicted, it was only partially successful. Her features were still twisted and she was in serious pain; a prolonged period of convalescence beckoned.

But suddenly Magda was galvanised by Hitler's brush with death. Clearly, Fate had spared him for a reason and she began to believe that victory, or at the very least an honourable outcome, was possible. Magda bought into all the talk of the wonder weapons that were going to reverse the course of the war. While the regime did manage to unleash its V1 and V2 rockets over the south-east of England – spreading fear, panic and carnage – it was too little, too late, and the promise that even more decisive weapons were on the way sounded increasingly hollow.

Another false assumption that Magda clung to was the conviction that the Allied coalition would collapse the closer it got to German territory; after all, how could the world's foremost capitalist state – America – and the previous holder of that accolade – the UK – stay on friendly terms with Stalin's Soviet Union?

These ideas sustained Magda for a while, but for a woman as intelligent as she was, the dire reality of the military situation was impossible to ignore. However blinded she may have been by her faith in Hitler, Magda was no fool. The Soviets were pushing relentlessly forward, closing in on Warsaw and penetrating the Balkans. Mussolini had fallen and much of Italy was in Allied hands. After the D-Day landings, the Allies had finally broken out of the coastal regions and with the German army in headlong retreat the way to Paris was open.

The weight of events once again undermined her physical, emotional and psychological health; Magda booked herself back into the clinic, as if she was already preparing for the end.

13

DEAD END

In the summer of 1944, Gerda and her children made the short journey to Berchtesgaden to visit Hedwig's new cottage. Pretty much alone with her two small infants, Hedwig appreciated the company. Gerda thought Hedwig seemed pleased with the house and its location, and was struck by how 'ridiculously like her father'[1] Hedwig's daughter was, just like the pictures Hedwig had showed her of Himmler as a child.

After tea, Hedwig invited them all to the attic to see something special: furniture made from human body parts. Gerda's eldest son, Martin Adolf Bormann – who was home from school for the holidays – remembered how Hedwig 'clinically and medically' explained the process behind the construction of a chair 'whose seat was a human pelvis and the legs were human legs – on human feet'.[2] Hedwig also had copies of *Mein Kampf* bound with human skin that had been peeled off the backs of Dachau inmates. 'Shocked and petrified', Martin Adolf and his siblings went outside with their mother, who was 'equally stricken'. Gerda told them that when Himmler tried to give Bormann a similarly unique edition of *Mein Kampf* he refused to take it; Gerda said it was 'too much for him'.[3]

Gerda had been living in a Nazi bubble since she was a teenager, and in the otherworldly seclusion of Obersalzburg for nearly a decade. Until recently, the war had seemed a faraway thing. Though she was still 'utterly convinced of our victory', Gerda was now having to confront the prospect of defeat. She viewed the war as a 'struggle between

Light and Darkness', and 'a fight of Good against Evil' that resembled the myths and fairy tales that had always fascinated her. Bormann shared her apocalyptic vision; defeat would mean the 'extermination of our race' and 'the destruction of its culture and civilisation'. Faced with such horrors, Gerda refused to accept this outcome – 'it cannot possibly be the meaning of history that Jewry should make itself the master of the world' – and urged her husband to ensure that every German child realised 'that the Jew is the Absolute Evil in this world'.[4]

Margaret was in Berlin during August. There was less for her to do at the German Red Cross, so she 'spread a lot of happiness' distributing clothing to bombed out citizens, even though 'standing in cellars on flagstones for four hours every day is none too easy for me'.[5] At Lake Tegernsee, she supervised construction of an air-raid shelter; the workers came from Dachau and Margaret complained to camp officials about their poor quality.

The letters between her and her husband kept going back and forth, and the packages for her and Gudrun kept coming with rare luxuries like soap and chocolate. In mid November, Himmler was at Lake Tegernsee, and he and Margaret discussed the difficulties Germany faced; both agreed that they would be overcome and 'the war would end favourably'.[6] Himmler departed after three uneventful and unexceptional days, promising that he'd try to make it back for Christmas.

On 3 December, Magda and her husband were honoured by a visit from Hitler. It had been over four years since he'd come to their home. At that moment, with the Allies inexorably pushing forward, it was a deeply symbolic gesture that ensured that they would remain with him no matter what. Hitler arrived at tea-time. Rudolf Semmler, Goebbels's PA, recalled how 'the children received him in the hall with bunches of flowers in their hand' and 'Goebbels stood to

attention with his arm stretched out as far as it would go. The children made their little curtsies and Hitler said how surprised he was at the way they had grown.'

Hitler gave Magda some flowers – a 'modest bunch of lily-of-the valley' – and 'explained that it was the best that could be found', as Goebbels 'had closed all the flower shops in Berlin'. Hitler was accompanied by a servant, an adjutant, six SS officers and a bodyguard. He brought his own tea in a thermos flask and his own cakes. He only stayed half an hour, but having 'enjoyed the family atmosphere', and the chance to escape his 'monastic life for half an afternoon', Hitler 'promised to come again soon'. Delighted and bursting with pride, Magda remarked that Hitler 'wouldn't have gone to the Goerings'.[7]

While Germany starved, Emmy and her family had one final feast at Carinhall to celebrate Goering's birthday on 12 January 1945. They polished off the caviar from Russia, duck and venison from his forests, Danzig salmon, the last of the pâté de foie gras, and washed it all down with vodka, claret, burgundy, champagne and brandy.

At the end of the month, a Soviet tank entered the forests round Carinhall. Emmy, Edda and the other women left the next afternoon and headed for the relative safety of Obersalzburg, where the house had an underground shelter with twelve rooms. Following close behind was Goering's art collection. Over the next two and a half months, two special trains, eight freight cars and over a dozen box cars shunted hundreds of valuable works between various locations in Bavaria and Austria, where they were unloaded and hidden away. Nine freight cars ended up parked on the tracks at Berchtesgaden station, close to Obersalzburg. From their cargo, Goering removed two paintings of the Madonna and four miniature angels by Hans Memling, a fifteenth-century German artist, and gave them to Emmy as a nest egg, something to sell if she fell on hard times.

As the Allies drew closer and nobody appeared to be in charge any more, the locals thoroughly ransacked Goering's train, taking carpets, rugs, tapestries and paintings, and carting off gold coins, sugar, coffee, cigarettes and expensive liquors.

By early January 1945, Himmler had made Hohenlychen his almost permanent base. The roof of the clinic had a Red Cross symbol on it so it wouldn't be bombed, and the ever-loyal Professor Gebhardt was on hand, as was Himmler's Swedish masseur; his persistent stomach ailments were causing him serious grief and he needed to rest. As a result, Himmler did not make it to Lake Tegernsee for Christmas. Instead, he phoned and talked to Margaret. She remembered that 'he had a cold again ... he was sick' and 'in very delicate health'.[8]

Himmler also wrote her a sentimental letter: 'This is the first time we have not celebrated Christmas together; but just yesterday I was thinking so much of you.'[9] He also sent her a silver tray, different coloured silks – blue, black and white – a handbag, some underwear and some stockings: on 9 January he mailed her coffee, gingerbread cookies, liver pâté and a book on the Prussian army.

In her diary, Margaret tried to maintain a positive outlook; she noted that her husband was 'happy and in good form' when they spoke on the phone and she was proud that 'all of Germany looks up to him'. Margaret was also relieved that her difficult stepson Gerhard had finally found his calling – 'he is very courageous and loves it with the SS' – having joined the organisation's military wing. Nevertheless, she was not taken in by false hope: 'The war situation is unchanged and very grave.'[10]

On 6 January, Lina had a private meeting with Himmler in Berlin that lasted an hour and forty-five minutes. They discussed the security situation in the Protectorate and the risks she faced staying there; Lina had received a threatening letter earlier that month and communist partisans were causing more and more disruption.

But Lina returned to her estate, and a few weeks later she wrote to her parents about her plans. For the moment, she was staying put: 'I wouldn't know where we could be safer than here, to flee, as other women do, is out of the question for me.' Ultimately, it didn't matter where she was. Whether in the Protectorate or in Germany, defeat would mean the end for her, as 'the Russians will know where to find us to liquidate us' or the 'British and Americans will come. And with them the Jews. With our Jewish laws we burned our bridges. The Jews will be able to get at us. There is no point in deluding ourselves.'[11]

Eva was in Berlin until 9 February, then returned again for good on 7 March. She explained her decision to stay with Hitler to his faithful secretary Christa Schroeder: 'I have come because I owe the Boss for everything wonderful in my life.'[12]

Bormann also remained in Berlin. Aside from there being no question of him leaving his master's side, he was still running the party machine with his usual hyper-efficiency and productivity, refusing to accept the inevitable. Gerda saw him in February then returned to Obersalzburg. Despite everything, she continued to believe that 'one day the Reich of our dreams will emerge ... even if we no longer survive'.[13]

On 25 February Magda asked one of Hitler's physicians for enough poison 'for herself and her six children'. It was not an easy request for her to make. According to Semmler, she 'could not bear the thought of ending the lives of her children'; the very idea of it drove her 'crazy with grief and pain'.[14] Yet Magda saw no future. She knew that what had been done in Hitler's name would never be forgiven or forgotten, and the Soviets were unlikely to show her family any mercy. On 4 March, her husband informed Hitler that they intended to stay put 'even if Berlin is attacked and surrounded'.[15] Understanding what that meant, Hitler hesitated before giving his approval.

Goebbels's diary entries for that month had a routine, businesslike quality about them. He was still running his Propaganda Ministry, and on the 16th he hosted a reception for all his staff. On the 21st, he was studying 'the latest film statistics', which were 'very good despite all the difficulties. It is surprising that the German people still wants to go to the cinema at all.'

Magda barely featured in Goebbels's notes. He was irritated when she 'got one of her headaches' on the 8th, and annoyed when she retired to bed feeling unwell on the 27th because she'd 'over-done it' organising the move from their country estate to Berlin. By 4 April they were settled in the capital and spent 'a somewhat melancholy evening during which one piece of bad news after another descends on our house. One sometimes wonders desperately where it will all lead.'[16]

Over the night of 7–8 January 1945, 645 Lancaster bombers attacked Munich and Ilse's house received a direct hit. Salvaging what she could, Ilse took her son Wolf and headed for the Bavarian Alps, where they found shelter in a small village. There, Ilse would patiently see out the rest of the war, waiting for the moment danger passed and she could turn her attention back to her husband and their future together.

In Wales, Hess was lost in his own world, passing the time reading novels by obscure eighteenth-century German novelists and marvelling at the 'infinite breadth of form and style in character and presentation'.[17] Knowing he was currently beyond harm, Ilse could imagine a life ahead of her, even if the regime collapsed and Hitler was no more.

For Albrecht Haushofer there would be no future. In the early hours of 23 April, Albrecht – who'd been languishing in jail since the previous December – and fifteen other prisoners were assembled in the yard, given back their personal effects and asked to sign release forms. Any hopes that this meant freedom were quickly dashed when they saw thirty-five SS men armed with machine guns standing outside the gate.

An SS officer informed them that they were being transferred to another facility and his men would escort them to the station. When they got close, Albrecht and fellow inmates were directed towards a stretch of bombed out wasteland. They were put up against a wall and executed. According to his father, Professor Haushofer, Albrecht was shot in the back of the neck.

In March, Lina had an unexpected visitor: Himmler turned up at the house looking tired and dishevelled, and asked her for a hot bath and breakfast. Refreshed, he chatted with her and played with her children. When Lina tried to pin him down on the state of the war and the prospects of reversing the Allied advance, he was evasive, which led her to assume the worst. But Lina was not yet ready to abandon the estate she'd worked so hard to maintain and in which she'd invested so much of herself.

Himmler skulked back to Hohenlychen. All his grand aspirations, his dreams of fostering a rebirth of the German spirit and forming a new aristocracy to govern a racial paradise, were in tatters. By the end of March, American troops were closing in on his fantasy SS castle at Wewelsburg. Himmler evacuated his staff and on the 31st demolition teams arrived, dynamited the castle's west and south towers and set the interior on fire by lighting curtains and anything else that was flammable.

When they left, the locals spent two days looting the smouldering remains, emptying the wine cellar and clearing out the on-site museum, which contained skulls, coins, knives, ancient pottery, Viking swords, Bronze Age helmets, Scythian bronze arrowheads and the fossil of an ancient marine reptile, a 9ft-long ichthyosaur.

After visiting Himmler at Hohenlychen on 22 March, Hedwig made her way back to Berchtesgaden. Her last call from him was on 19 April. They discussed 'personal matters' and the fact that the situation was 'more difficult every day'. Himmler said he'd call her again but never did. He ended the conversation with the 'hope that God would protect her, the children, and Germany'.[18]

At Lake Tegernsee, Margaret received a final phone call from her husband around Easter time. Once again, the main topic was his guts: 'He is very ill again, and had trouble with his stomach.'[19] On 20 April Margaret, her daughter, her sister Lydia, an aunt and several other female relatives crammed themselves into their car and left their home behind. Margaret's driver was heading for the South Tyrol, a region of Austria on the border with Italy that had already been identified as a safe haven with its mountains and secluded valleys. As the Allies neared Berchtesgaden, Hedwig followed in the same direction, taking her children with her.

In early April, Karl Wolff – Frieda's ex-husband – dropped in on Lina to warn her that Soviet forces were not far off and local resistance was mounting. It was time to leave. By the middle of the month, Lina had packed up the house, slaughtered all her livestock, and bought a circus caravan to transport her family's belongings and her dead son's casket. Also in her luggage was the bloodstained uniform her husband had been wearing when he was assassinated.

On the day of departure, the lady of the manor gathered her staff together, thanked them and promised them a small gratuity after the war. Lina, her three children and their governess, plus a certain amount of baggage, squeezed into two cars. With the caravan behind them, they set off for Germany. However, within a few miles, the convoy was attacked by Soviet aircraft. The caravan was blasted off the road. Lina rescued her dead son's damaged casket and what was left of his remains was hastily reburied in the woods.

En route, Lina left her other son and eldest daughter in the care of some friends who promised to get them to Fehmarn when the time was right. Then Lina, with her 3-year-old daughter, carried on through Bavaria to Lake Tegernsee, where they took refuge at Frieda Wolff's house – the two SS wives together again – until US troops turfed them out at the beginning of May.

The atmosphere at Hitler's birthday party on 20 April was more downbeat than usual. A month earlier, the Soviet army had reached the outskirts of Berlin. Their assault began four days before Hitler's closest followers gathered to wish him many happy returns of the day. That morning, Soviet artillery started shelling the city centre, within range of the bunker.

A sombre mood descended on proceedings and most of his guests – including Goering and Himmler – made a hasty exit. Hitler retired early to bed. Eva, however, was determined to have some fun. According to one of Hitler's young secretaries, 'a restless fire burned in her eyes'; Eva wanted 'to dance, to drink, to forget'. Wearing a new dress – 'made of a silvery blue brocade' – she swept towards her apartment in the Reich Chancellery, gathering up Bormann and anybody else she came across. In her living room, Eva cracked open the champagne and dug out her gramophone; she found a record – the popular wartime hit 'Blood in Red Roses Speaks of Happiness to You' – and played it over and over again as 'she whisked everyone into a desperate frenzy'.[20]

While terrified residents tried to flee the city, one woman was desperately trying to get in. Hanna Reitsch was Germany's most famous female pilot and a committed Nazi; she somehow found somewhere to land in the devastated capital and make it to the bunker unscathed on the 26th. She was offering to airlift people out of Berlin. Hitler refused, as did Eva, who handed Reitsch a letter for her sister Gretl in which she asked her to destroy all her private papers and correspondence with Hitler, and said that she was 'glad to die at the side of the Führer; but most of all glad that the horror now to come is spared me. What could life still give me? It has already been perfect.'[21]

Magda also gave Hanna Reitsch a letter, addressed to Harald Quandt – her son from her first marriage – who had served in the infantry throughout the war and was currently a British POW. Written with an eye to posterity, it reads like a last piece of propaganda, courtesy of the First Lady of the Reich. In the letter, Magda laid out her reasons for the course she had chosen:

> For me there is no alternative. Our beautiful idea is being destroyed, and with it goes everything in life I knew to be fine, worthy of admiration, noble and good. Life will not be worth living in the world that will come after Hitler and National Socialism. Therefore, I have brought the children with me. They are too precious for the life that will come after us.

Having extolled their virtues, she asked God to 'grant' her 'the strength to accomplish the last and most difficult task of all … to be true unto death to the Führer'.[22]

Magda's words reflected her unique position in Hitler's entourage, her personal connection to him and her proximity to power. But her motivation was not that different from the scores of other women who chose suicide during the last days of his rule. Over the course of 1945, 7,000 people killed themselves, of whom 3,996 were women. Many justifiably feared they would be raped by Soviet soldiers. At least 100,000 were sexually assaulted, and some small towns and villages in the path of the advancing Soviet army committed mass suicide rather than face its wrath.

In Berlin, women carried cyanide and razor blades in their handbags or on their person. During April and May, the city witnessed 5,881 suicides. In an upmarket Berlin suburb, the wife of an army captain killed herself and her 8-year-old daughter. She'd made the decision to use poison that February and told her husband that 'she feared that she and her child would fall into Russian hands' and 'would end her life before that happened'.[23]

At Obersalzburg, Gerda received her last letters from her husband and some of Hitler's early watercolours. When Bormann managed to reach her on the phone, he told her not to worry as he had a car ready to whisk him out of Berlin at a moment's notice, and assured her that they'd see each other again.

Though Bormann had overseen the construction of a network of underground shelters at Obersalzburg – work began in August 1943 and 3,000 labourers, mostly Italian, built 4 miles of tunnels and bunkers with walls 5ft thick – and the one beneath his house was large enough for his whole family and their staff, he wasn't leaving anything to chance. Gerda's escape plan had been worked out in advance, her destination the South Tyrol. She acquired a school bus and painted a Red Cross on the roof. Aside from eight of her own nine children – her eldest son was making his own way home from his elite Nazi boarding school and would end up missing the bus – Gerda had collected seven other stray infants. Along with her sister-in-law, Gerda and the equivalent of a kindergarten class set off on their trip. She was carrying with her Bormann's precious typewritten copy of *Hitler's Table Talk*, the manuscript he had so diligently compiled from the countless hours he'd spent hanging on Hitler's every word.

Goering went straight to Obersalzburg after Hitler's birthday on 20 April. The day before he'd said goodbye to Carinhall: any art too big to carry was buried in the grounds, demolition teams mined the building and blew it to pieces. The following morning, he was reunited with Emmy and Edda at their mountain retreat.

Unaware of what was happening in Berlin, Goering's egomania prompted him to interpret the silence and lack of news from the bunker as proof that Hitler was dead, making him the new Führer. On the 23rd, he sent Hitler a telegram; as his anointed successor, should he now assume control? If the Führer was alive, however, Goering hoped he would 'decide to leave Berlin and come here'.

Emmy never commented on her husband's last-ditch grab for supreme power, as futile as it was ludicrous. Having heard nothing by 6 p.m. that evening, Goering got back on the line: 'In view of your decision to remain at your post in fortress Berlin, do you agree that I take over, at once, the total leadership of the Reich; with full freedom of action at home and abroad.'[24]

Hitler had shrugged off Goering's first telegram; given the confusion, it was an understandable error of judgement. The second message pushed him over the edge. Feeling hurt and wounded, Hitler ordered Goering's arrest and Bormann was able to activate the SS unit stationed at Obersalzburg. They immediately surrounded Goering's house. Emmy and Edda were separated from him, with a guard stationed outside their room. Before they were parted, Goering told Emmy it was a mistake that would be resolved the next day.

But the following morning, Wednesday, 25 April, at around 9.30 a.m., 359 Lancaster bombers and sixteen Mosquitos pulverised Obersalzburg. Emmy, her husband, Edda, Emmy's sister, and their staff – a maid, a nurse, a governess and an adjutant – were allowed to go into the shelter beneath the house while their SS captors watched over them. During a lull in the bombing, they all transferred to the main Obersalzburg bunker where the Berghof residents were gathered.

Then the second wave hit half an hour later. When Christa Schroeder emerged from hiding, she saw that the Eagle's Nest had been destroyed and the Berghof had been 'badly damaged'. The walls still stood but the roof 'hung in ribbons' and 'doors and windows had disappeared. Inside the house the floor was thickly covered with debris and much of the furniture had been demolished. All the ancillary buildings had been destroyed, the paths scrambled to rubble, trees felled at the root. Nothing green remained, the scene was a crater landscape.'[25]

Scared as she was, Emmy realised this was a crucial moment; with their lives hanging in the balance, she turned to the SS officer in charge of them and gave a virtuoso performance, evoking a pact she'd made with Hitler on her 'wedding day' when he 'promised to grant me a wish'. If for any reason, Hitler considered it necessary to execute her husband, he'd agreed to have Emmy and Edda 'shot at the same time'.[26] This gave the SS man pause for thought. Though he'd received a communiqué from Bormann ordering him to kill the traitors, he was getting cold feet. A compromise was reached. His SS unit would accompany Goering and family to his Austrian castle 150 miles away; it took their convoy of vehicles thirty-six hours crawling along jam-packed roads to get there.

The Goerings' Obersalzburg house had been wrecked by the bombing. A US soldier noticed part of the roof in the swimming pool and two dead bodies floating on the surface. On the bottom of the pool, he saw something glistening in the sun. He dived in and recovered a Roman-style gladiator's sword that had been crafted by Napoleon's personal armourer; the soldier sold it in 1978 to a private collector for an undisclosed sum.

Bormann's house had been hit as well; 1,000 watercolours by Rudolf von Alt – the prolific landscape painter who had inspired Hitler to become an artist – were found unscathed in the underground shelter. After the war, von Alt's paintings were supposed to hang in the galleries of the grandiose museum Hitler was planning to build in Linz. Over 350 of these salvaged works disappeared without a trace.

At the Berghof, French and American troops helped themselves to the copious supplies of alcohol, the artwork and anything that had Hitler's initials on it; his stationery, silverware, porcelain, crystal glasses and goblets. Several days later, a US colonel inspected the site: all that remained standing was the fireplace and the toilet.

Nearby Berchtesgaden was also targeted by the raid and Hedwig's cottage was badly damaged. Scavengers removed the entire bedroom suite, a chandelier, a desk and a small tapestry, but they left Himmler's library untouched.

After Hitler's birthday on 20 April, Himmler headed straight back to Hohenlychen to resume the peace initiatives in which he had been engaged since the beginning of the year. Himmler had approached the International Red Cross through Swedish intermediaries in the vain belief that the Western Allies and the Nazis would join together to fight the Bolsheviks. To demonstrate his good intentions, Himmler authorised the release of some camp survivors, the dwindling number of whom were being driven from place to place on pitiless forced marches in which hundreds perished.

On the 28th, Reuter's news agency exposed Himmler's treachery. While Goering's betrayal had disappointed Hitler, it wasn't a complete surprise; the man he'd admired, trusted and valued had ceased to exist some time ago and it was only his lingering affection for his old comrade that prevented him from jettisoning Goering sooner. But Himmler was a real shock, a body blow that sent Hitler into an apocalyptic fury, and he condemned Himmler to the gallows. However, at this late point, the chances of the order reaching anybody capable of carrying out the death sentence was almost zero. For the time being, Himmler was safe at Hohenlychen, waiting for the Allies to offer him a role in their imminent struggle with Stalin.

On 29 April, Eva and Hitler became husband and wife; with a stroke of a pen his secret mistress – who was a mystery to the majority of Germans

– sealed her place in history and gained a form of immortality. In the hours before the wedding, Hitler had written his last will and testament: 'I have now, before ending this earthly existence, decided to take as my wife the girl who, after years of loyal friendship, has voluntarily returned to the almost besieged city to share her fate with mine. It is her wish to join me in death as my wife.'[27] At the ceremony, attended by Magda, Goebbels, Bormann and a selection of the staff, Eva wore a silk taffeta dress and her finest jewellery. Though the bunker was being rocked by shellfire that made the walls shake, Hitler's chauffeur remembered that the mood was 'festive'. There was champagne and sandwiches, and the 'conversation turned to earlier experiences' as they 'reflected with nostalgia on the past'.[28]

On the 30th, Hitler spoke about the future over lunch. Eva said goodbye to Magda, the two rivals united by their decision to die with their beloved Hitler. Then Magda had a private talk with him. Afterwards, she told his valet about her last moments with Hitler: 'I fell to my knees and begged him not to take his own life. He lifted me up benevolently and explained to me quietly that he had no choice.'[29]

At 3.15 p.m., Hitler and Eva retreated into their shared quarters. His valet and Bormann waited outside for a suitable time before entering. On seeing Hitler and Eva dead on the sofa, Bormann 'turned white as chalk'. Hitler had taken poison – hydrocyanic acid, a clear liquid with the scent of bitter almonds – then shot himself in the temple with his 7.65mm pistol, which lay on the floor near his feet. Eva was slumped next to him, her legs tucked under her. She was wearing 'a black dress of light material'. According to the valet, the poison had left its mark on her; Eva's 'contorted face betrayed how she had died'.[30] She was 34 years old.

Having wrapped the corpses in carpet, Bormann, the valet, the chauffeur and two SS bodyguards carried them outside and into the Reich Chancellery garden. Petrol siphoned from the tanks of the cars in the bunker garage was poured over Hitler and Eva as Soviet artillery shells pounded into the earth nearby and strong winds whistled around them. After repeated attempts to ignite a match failed, Bormann set fire to some papers and tossed them into the pit. The mourners gave a final salute and hurried inside. Five and a half hours later, Hitler and Eva's blackened bones were buried in a shell crater.

For the next twenty-four hours, the survivors existed on autopilot, wandering around in a daze. Magda sunk into a deep gloom. Her husband, Bormann, and what remained of the leadership cadre went through the motions. A request to negotiate peace with the Soviets was rebuffed. They named Hitler's successor – Admiral Donitz, head of the navy – and formed an emergency cabinet. When the play-acting was done and Goebbels had made a few last jottings in his diary, Magda readied herself for the final act. Her children were given cocoa laced with a powerful sedative and fell almost instantly asleep.

Nobody knows for sure what happened next. Nobody who might have been in the children's room when they died lived to tell the tale. From the reminiscences of those close to the scene, several versions of the truth emerged. There is general agreement that the SS physician Dr Stumpfegger was involved in the murder of Magda's children, but there are differences of opinion over her exact role. Several accounts claim that she was in the room at the time and may even have administered the poison herself. But this seems unlikely. Would Magda really have crushed cyanide into her children's mouths? Since moving into the bunker, she was almost incapable of being near them. One of Hitler's young secretaries remembered that Magda 'hardly had the strength to face her children with composure now. Every meeting with them made her feel so terrible that she burst into tears.'[31]

However strong-willed she was, by then Magda was a shadow of her former self. She simply could not cope with the horrific reality of the choice she'd made. And why should she when there was an experienced professional ready and willing to do it for her? Hitler's valet recalled seeing her waiting 'nervously' outside the room 'until the door opened and the Doctor came out. Their eyes met, Magda Goebbels stood up, silent and trembling. When the SS Doctor nodded emotionally without speaking, she collapsed.'[32]

Afterwards, Magda allegedly sat in her room, ashen-faced, playing solitaire and chain smoking. At 8.40 p.m., her and Goebbels's funeral pyre was ready. Wearing their golden Nazi party badges, they walked arm in

NAZI WIVES

arm to the bunker exit and took a step into the garden. Magda bit on her capsule. Her husband shot her in the head to make sure, swallowed his poison and turned the gun on himself. Their bodies were shifted into a shallow grave and doused in petrol. The air was calm enough to light a match. Magda and Goebbels went up in flames: the fire burned all night.

Bormann was in one of two groups that decided to make a break for it. They left the battered bunker and disappeared into the ravaged city where death waited on every street corner. But Bormann had only one thought in his mind: survival.

PART FOUR

HOLDING ON

14

CAPTIVES

Contemplating the fall of Nazism a few weeks after the war ended, Hess struck an optimistic note in a letter to Ilse. The ideals they'd followed for the last twenty-five years would have their day again: 'History has not ended. It will sooner or later take up the threads apparently broken off for ever, and knit them together in a new pattern.' As for Hitler, the time they'd shared with him had been 'full of the most wonderful human experiences' and it was a privilege to have participated 'from the very beginning in the growth of a unique personality'.[1]

Hess was on his way to the International War Crimes Tribunal in Nuremberg, where he would appear alongside Goering and a handful of other senior figures. The ghost at the proceedings was Bormann, who was tried in absentia. Despite the fact several witnesses testified that he died in Berlin, the Allied authorities were not convinced. After leaving Hitler's bunker, Bormann had tried to negotiate his way through the battle-scarred city – where fighting still raged – in the company of the SS doctor who'd poisoned Magda's children. As they made their way, they met up with three Panzer tanks and fell in with them. They were joined by Hitler's valet and his chauffeur and were making slow but dogged progress when they ran into a Soviet anti-tank barrier and came under heavy attack. According to Hitler's chauffeur, 'the Russians opened up with everything they had. A second later, a hellish tongue of fire bust out'[2] and Hitler's valet saw Bormann and the doctor 'tossed in the air like dolls by the explosion'.[3] Fleeing the scene, neither of Hitler's subordinates stopped to check if Bormann was alive or not.

Shortly after, Arthur Axmann, a Nazi Youth leader, 'came across the bodies of Martin Bormann and his companion'. Axmann told the Americans that 'they lay close together without movement'. Initially, he thought 'they were unconscious or sleeping' but when he bent to examine them he noticed 'they were not breathing'. Seeing no visible wounds, Axmann assumed Bormann 'had taken poison'.[4] But the lack of a corpse led to speculation, which fuelled doubts, and a consensus quickly emerged that Bormann had somehow survived and was on the run. Investigators were especially keen to speak to Gerda about his possible whereabouts.

But Gerda had no idea where her husband might be or whether he was dead or not. Gerda's school bus party had made it over the Alps and reached the South Tyrol, where they were met by the Nazis' regional boss, who had secured a place to stash all Gerda's sensitive material and found them a home in a small village in a valley 30 miles from Bolzano.

Though safe for the time being, Gerda was in dreadful agony. Her sister-in-law, who had made the journey with her, observed that 'Gerda was getting worse. She was normally a very quiet person ... now she couldn't hide her pain.'[5] Together, they found a local Italian doctor who immediately recognised the seriousness of her condition; Gerda was suffering from the advanced stages of ovarian cancer and needed an operation as soon as possible. By then, the Allies were on her trail. A distraught parent in Munich had approached the authorities and told them that Gerda had kidnapped his child and taken it to the Tyrol. Two intelligence agents tracked her down and informed the British unit stationed in the area. Having consulted the doctor who diagnosed Gerda, a British army major – who thought Gerda was 'a very nice woman'[6] – turned up on her doorstep.

Gerda panicked, thinking he was going to take her to a concentration camp, but the major assured her that she was in no danger. Instead, she went straight to a hospital for POWs in Merano. Surgery took place but without effect. Facing her imminent demise, Gerda sought solace in religion and converted to Catholicism. She died on 23 March 1946, a few months shy of her thirty-seventh birthday. Aside from the correspondence between her and her husband covering the years 1943–45 (which was found in Berlin and offered a striking contrast to the general view of her as a gentle, introverted soul) Gerda left no trace of herself behind.

The one item of real value stored among her possessions was Bormann's copy of *Hitler's Table Talk*, which Gerda had brought with her from Obersalzburg. The Italian official in charge of her property sold the manuscript to Françoise Genoud, a Swiss-French banker and Nazi spy who laundered money for them during the war. Genoud translated the document into French – and probably made minor adjustments to the text along the way – then his version was acquired by a British publisher, who brought out the English language edition in 1953.

Though its accuracy and authenticity as an exact record of Hitler's monologues is questionable, Bormann had succeeded in capturing his master's voice, fulfilling his mission to present future generations with the opportunity to experience what it was like to be at the Berghof listening to Hitler deliver tedious and long-winded lectures on his favourite topics.

Following Gerda's instructions, her many children were placed in the care of Rev. Theodor Schmitz, a German army Catholic chaplain. Though several of them died young, the rest were fostered by ordinary Italian families. Gerda's eldest, Martin Adolf – who was eventually reunited with his siblings after staying incognito with a farmer and his wife – became a Jesuit priest.

Gerda's father Walter Buch, who had set his daughter on the Nazi path, was picked up by the Allies at the end of April 1945. Due to Buch's long association with Hitler, they treated him as a major player. But Buch denied that he had much influence, deprived of power because his son-in-law loathed him and undermined any authority he might have had. Buch was also tight-lipped about his own devotion to Hitler, avoiding making any personal statement about his allegiance; according to Buch, Hitler had succeeded because of his 'persuasive power and his love for the German people' and their 'need for a leader'. During several interrogations, Buch insisted that he was 'a man who for seventeen years was forced to do against his will a job which he didn't like. I kept asking to be relieved of my functions, and to be permitted to return to my original position as a regular army officer.'[7]

Yet the Allies were not buying his excuses and they kept Buch locked up until November 1949. Only 67, but with nothing left to live for, the old soldier took what he considered to be the honourable way out: shortly after his release, Gerda's father slit his wrists and threw himself in a river.

Gerda's husband, however, continued to live on, if only in the imaginations of those trying to track him down. After Nuremberg, there were alleged sightings of Bormann in northern Germany, Denmark, Italy and Spain. Then from around 1952, attention shifted to South America and there were claims that he was at various times in Argentina, Chile and Peru. The CIA had an open file on him, wrote regular reports, followed leads, kept tabs on obscure informers and tracked anybody who may or may not have come into contact with Bormann since the war. The discovery of Adolf Eichmann – who masterminded the logistics of the Final Solution – in Argentina, his kidnap by the Israeli secret service and subsequent trial in Jerusalem, focused minds on the Nazi diaspora in South America, which included the Auschwitz camp doctor Joseph Mengele, and added to the rumours about Gerda's husband.

In the late 1960s, a number of writers and investigative journalists went in search of Bormann, piecing together any clues that might point them in the direction of his lair; several of them claimed they found incontrovertible proof of his existence, while one actually said he'd been face to face with Bormann. Together, these writers helped promote the idea that Bormann was at the head of a powerful secret organisation – a global network of Nazis – plotting to bring about the Fourth Reich, a notion that inspired a number of best-selling novels at the time.

In December 1972, construction workers on a building site in Berlin found two skeletons with their skulls intact, near to where Bormann was last seen; dental records and facial reconstruction confirmed that the bones belonged to him. Further examinations revealed the cause of death. It seems that the Soviet barrage had incapacitated Bormann – perhaps burying him under rubble – and, unable to move, he took cyanide rather than be captured by Soviet soldiers. The mystery surrounding Bormann's fate was solved and the spectre of Gerda's husband was finally laid to rest.

In the early summer of 1945, Ilse was taken into custody by French troops and spent fourteen days as their guest, during which she was well treated, before being moved to a location close to Nuremberg. The Allied authorities were hoping she might be able to help them break through the wall surrounding her husband, whose amnesia was back with a vengeance. Hess's short-term and long-term memory were shot, or at least they appeared to be. In the dock, he cut a bizarre figure, reading novels, muttering to himself and sleeping, while in his cell he refused food and threw violent tantrums.

The team of psychiatrists working on Hess were inclined to believe him – one of them described Hess's condition as 'hysterical amnesia' – but were still not 100 per cent sure. One person who had their doubts was the American in charge of the prisoners, Colonel Burton Andrus: 'From the moment the man in the old coat and the flying boots began talking about chocolate,' which Hess thought had been poisoned, 'I made up my mind that his madness was a sham.'[8]

Real or not, the Allies had no option but to take Hess's amnesia seriously. Ilse advised an American officer that the best way to draw him out was to concentrate on his personal life rather than his political activities. She provided the officer with eighty family photos, including recent ones of their son Wolf, and suggested 'as possible therapy for her husband the use of classical music',[9] preferably Mozart's *The Magic Flute* or Rossini's *Barber of Seville*.

Although they didn't try this, the Allies were running out of time and ideas. A plan to have Ilse and Wolf visit him was frustrated by Hess's refusal to see them under any circumstances. Desperate, the Allies resorted to a form of shock therapy, putting Hess in a room with a succession of people who ought to have been very familiar to him. Goering went first. On seeing his old comrade, Hess's bemused reaction was 'Who are you?' Goering took this response as an insult, replying 'You ought to know me. We have been together for years.' Hess conceded that Goering's name was familiar but that was all. Exasperated, Goering pressed on: 'Don't you remember that I visited your family and your wife? I saw you and your wife together repeatedly. You also visited my family with your wife.' Hess shook his head helplessly and blamed his amnesia, which was like 'a fog, behind which everything has disappeared'.[10]

Two of Hess's secretaries failed to register. Even Professor Haushofer drew a blank. Haushofer was no stranger to the Allies and was picked up at his farmhouse and taken to Nuremberg. He swore to do everything in his power to break through to his old friend: 'I am prepared to see him even in the critical state of mind he is in now … I am prepared … to go in front of the Devil's eye and talk to him.'[11]

Rather than confront Hess directly, as Goering had done, Professor Haushofer tried to coax him out of his shell. He showed Hess a picture of Ilse — whom Hess recognised — told him that Ilse had shown him all their letters, which meant he'd 'remained in contact' with Hess's 'spiritual life and … feelings',[12] and talked to Hess about his mother. Yet when the professor brought up the subject of Ilse and Hess's home in Munich, Hess denied ever living there. The shutters had come down again.

The encounter deeply disturbed Professor Haushofer, who was already at a very low ebb. A few days before his meeting with Hess, he'd had a minor heart attack, and his interrogators had been extremely hard on him. They wanted Haushofer to admit that his theories had underpinned Hitler's genocidal imperialism. He thought this accusation was absurd given that Hitler 'and his disciples' had 'little knowledge of world events'. At the same time, Professor Haushofer had 'been happily married to a non-Aryan for the last fifty years'; once Hess's protection was gone, he was under constant threat. His inquisitors weren't persuaded and implied guilt by association, showing the professor one of his journals that had articles about the USA being the home of 'Jewish plutocrats'. The effect was instant; his interrogator reported that 'on reading it, Haushofer breaks down emotionally, tears came into his eyes and he could barely speak'.[13]

Eventually Professor Haushofer was released, but he faced the prospect of being re-arrested at any moment. He was 76. His son Albrecht had been brutally murdered, and now his surrogate son – who had both shielded him from and exposed him to great danger – appeared to be a lost soul wandering through perpetual darkness. In March 1946, Professor Haushofer and his wife Martha took a walk in the woods. About a half a mile away from their house, they stopped under a willow tree. They both took poison, then Haushofer hanged Martha from a branch and died at her feet. Their lifeless bodies were found the next day.

On 30 November 1945, Hess suddenly rose out of his slumber and announced to a stunned courtroom that his amnesia was fake – 'simulated' for 'tactical' reasons – and now his 'memory' was 'again at the disposal of the world'. If this wasn't startling enough, he proceeded to 'assume full responsibility for everything that I have done, everything that I have signed, and everything that I have co-signed'.[14]

It seemed that Hess had fooled everybody, including Ilse. However, the effort required to sustain the charade for such long periods over many years and convince the phalanx of experts who poked and prodded him that his amnesia was genuine, was not without consequences for Hess's mental health. To trick his captors he had to trick himself as well, which was a dangerous game, as he acknowledged in a letter to Ilse: 'When I was in England, playing the part of a man who had lost his memory, I learned many things by heart as a means of saving myself from the fate which I was carefully pretending to have suffered.'[15] His behaviour in captivity suggests, however, that the role absorbed him to such an extent that he became a victim of the condition he was trying to simulate. Within weeks of his dramatic statement in court, Hess was stumbling about in the shadows again.

On 1 October 1946, Hess was given life in prison. The fact that he flew to the UK when he did, before the mass murder of the Jews had begun in earnest, saved his neck. Goering and eleven others were sentenced to death by hanging.

Once Emmy and her husband had reached their castle in Austria in the dying days of the war, and their SS escort vanished into thin air,

Goering was removed by the Americans. As Emmy watched him depart her sciatica flared up: 'As I began to brush my hair, my right arm suddenly dropped inertly and I felt a violent pain. It was the beginning of a paralysis. Two years went by before I was able to use my arm properly.' Not long after, Emmy and her 7-year-old daughter Edda were dispatched to Goering's Bavarian castle, only to find it had been stripped bare by US troops: 'What a state the house was in! It was absolutely empty! Not even an electric bulb had been left in it. I later learned that the Americans had taken away twelve lorry loads of furniture.'[16] To add insult to injury, a GI conned her out of some emeralds by telling her that her husband was going to be set free.

On 19 November 1945, one of the Nuremberg psychiatrists brought her a letter from Goering, the first she'd received since they'd been parted. In it, Goering was unconcerned by his own situation. Instead, his worries were focused on Emmy; 'I am desperate when I think of what you have to suffer on my account, only because you are my wife. The only thing that worries me and weighs me down, is the thought of you.'[17]

Five days later, Emmy, her sister and her niece were dumped in Straubing prison in a cell with a straw mattress and a commode. Edda arrived after three days with her teddy bear and running a high temperature. It took a couple of weeks before she was on her feet again. Over the New Year, they were lodged with some Catholic nuns, then moved to a chalet in a forest with a chambermaid, though the building was no more than a hut with no electricity or running water. These basic living conditions were an inconvenience, but what troubled Emmy most was the lack of contact with her husband. At her wits' end, she wrote a passionate letter to Colonel Andrus, begging him to let her visit Goering: 'I haven't seen my husband for nearly a year and a quarter and I am longing so terribly for him that I don't see any way out; I need strength to carry on without my husband. A few minutes when I see him and could hold his hand would help me no end.'[18]

Her request was refused. The Nuremberg officials did not want to give a further boost to Goering's morale. In captivity, Goering had been forced to go cold turkey and quit his addiction to painkillers. As a result, he'd lost weight and regained his fighting spirit. Rather than wilt under cross-examination in court or during lengthy interrogations, Goering came out all guns blazing, questioning the legitimacy of the tribunal and arguing that the war crimes charges were bogus because waging war was inevitably criminal.

He'd also become the ring leader of the other high-profile prisoners – with the exception of Albert Speer, who chose to denounce Hitler and everything he stood for – and tried to coordinate a united front. Emmy was proud of her husband's defiance and told yet another of the Nuremberg psychiatrists that Goering wanted to show the world that he had nothing to be ashamed of and wasn't 'backtracking like a coward'. When her visitor asked her about the Final Solution, Emmy simply stated that 'Hitler must have been insane.'[19]

For all his bluster, the evidence against Goering was overwhelming and clearly demonstrated his involvement in the extermination of the Jews. He was made particularly uncomfortable by revelations about gruesome experiments that were performed on camp inmates for the benefit of the Luftwaffe.

Emmy and Edda were finally permitted to visit Goering on 12 September 1946. They were allowed half an hour with the prisoner, who was chained to a guard. The three of them were divided by a glass wall; Emmy and her husband engaged in trivial chit-chat. Edda read him poems she'd written.

Over the next couple of weeks, they returned to see him eight times. Their final meeting was on 7 October. Emmy put on a brave face and told Goering that he could 'face death with a clear conscience now' having done all he could 'at Nuremberg' for his comrades and 'for Germany'.[20] But outside the prison, Emmy let her guard down; the thought of her beloved being strung up like a piece of meat was tearing her apart. Another visiting wife recalled that 'there were tears in her grey-green eyes. They rolled down her cheeks. She looked utterly desolate and helpless.'[21]

Yet Goering's last words to her were 'They will not hang me.' The idea of dying that way offended him. He'd asked to be executed by firing squad but his request was denied. So on the evening before he was due to climb the scaffold, at around 10 p.m. on 15 October, Goering took cyanide. It will never be known for sure how Goering got hold of the poison; in his suicide note, he claimed he'd had it with him since he was arrested, secreted on his person. This is unlikely given the number of searches Goering was subjected to before entering his Nuremberg cell. Probably one of the American guards he'd befriended smuggled it in for him. When Emmy told Edda what had happened she had her own theory: 'An angel came from the ceiling of his cell to give him the poison.'[22]

Goering's ashes were dumped in an unknown spot somewhere outside Nuremberg. Reflecting on the manner of his death, Emmy could not comprehend how 'such a man' – who had 'always given so much to others, who had radiated understanding' and was 'devotion and goodness incarnate' and a 'model of compassion and fidelity' – could have been treated so harshly.[23]

Emotionally crushed and physically compromised, Emmy received medical care during the months immediately following Nuremberg. On 29 March 1947, she was considered well enough to join around 1,000 other women – including concentration camp staff, prostitutes and wives of SS men – at Göttingen, a former labour camp for Soviet women, which was separated by a barbed wire fence from thousands of male prisoners. The facility had five low barracks, floodlights, sirens and roll-call in the middle of the night.

At first, Emmy was in kept in the clinic, but then moved to a hut that had 'two enormous rats'. One of her fellow inmates was Henriette Hoffmann, whose husband Baldur von Schirach had avoided the death penalty at Nuremberg. During the war, Henriette had fallen from grace after she challenged Hitler about the mistreatment of Jews she'd witnessed while on a trip to Holland. Hitler took her complaints badly and Henriette was no longer welcome; the child prodigy had disappointed 'Uncle Adolf'.

Henriette remembered that Emmy was one of the few women who took her appearance seriously and was the only inmate who 'looked splendid, like a famous actress playing Faust's Gretchen in prison'. Emmy had one nightdress with her – which resembled 'an evening gown' – and as she was 'a glutton for cleanliness' she 'washed it at least three times a week, although it was a complicated job. She would not entrust it to anybody in the wash house and washed it herself, in a charming little wash bowl as smooth as silver.'[24]

A few weeks after Emmy was installed at Göttingen, Ilse arrived; Henriette recalled that she 'wore her hair long and looked like an itinerant preacher'.[25] Ilse shared a hut with sixteen other prisoners – according to her they were all 'wonderful'[26] – and she was especially fond of an old woman who'd worked as a cleaner at Hess's party HQ in Munich. Her mood was lifted further when her request to have her son Wolf with her was granted, and Emmy was reunited with Edda soon after.

Meanwhile, Hess had been transferred to Spandau prison in Berlin with six others on 18 July 1947, at 4 a.m. The jail covered 8 acres, had two outer rings of electric fences, nine concrete watchtowers and an inner wall that was over 26ft high. Hess occupied a cell that was 8ft long and 5ft wide, freshly painted with a metal bed, a mattress, a chair and a table, a commode, a bar of soap and a towel on a shelf, and a barred window.

Hess and Ilse continued to correspond, both keeping the tone light; Ilse told him that she'd retained her 'sense of humour' and formed 'a splendid literary study circle' with some other women, and they were tackling the work of the poet Rilke. Yet time moved slowly. By Christmas 1947, there was still no sign of an end to her confinement. But Ilse was more worried about Emmy's well-being than her own; not only was Emmy 'ill', she had also 'been through more than I have in the last two years'.[27]

Ilse was right; Emmy was struggling to deal with her protracted incarceration and that October she wrote an indignant letter to a government minister about the injustice of her situation: 'I am completely un-political ... my only fault is that I am Hermann Goering's wife. You cannot possibly punish a woman for loving her husband and being happily married to him.'[28]

Both Emmy and Ilse were waiting to appear before denazification courts. While the Allies concentrated on prosecuting major figures and those closely associated with the Final Solution, the West German judiciary assumed responsibility for the hundreds of thousands who'd worked with the regime. Every suspect was ranked according to five categories of guilt, of which Category (I) – Major Offender – was the most serious.

The courts were generally quite lenient. Given that it was impossible to recruit totally new legal personnel, many of the judges involved had Nazi sympathies – by September 1950, when the process was being wound down, over 950,000 people had been tried, of whom 270,000 were pardoned.

In March 1948, Ilse finally appeared before a denazification tribunal and was completely exonerated. Hess's flight and its consequences had saved his life; now it spared Ilse any further retribution for her years of unwavering dedication to Hitler.

Emmy went to trial two months after Ilse. The proceedings lasted two days. Sixteen witnesses testified on her behalf; Jewish friends she'd helped, residents from the retirement home for actors that Emmy had founded, famous female movie stars, and even her old sparring partner Gustav Gründgens. But Emmy was too high-profile a figure to be discharged with just a slap on the wrist. As the judge observed, Emmy had 'not only shared in a large number of personal honours, but also the exceedingly luxurious lifestyle of her husband'.[29] She was placed in Category (II) – Offender – and sentenced to one year behind bars, which she'd already served. Thirty per cent of her assets and property were seized, and she was banned from acting for five years.

When news of the verdict got out, there was shock and dismay. How could Emmy Goering, who'd flaunted her power so blatantly for so many years, have got off so lightly? In Stuttgart, 300 women gathered to express their anger and disgust.

15

REMEMBERING AND FORGETTING

On 13 May 1945 Margaret and her daughter Gudrun were discovered in the Tyrol and taken into custody by the Allies. They spent two nights at an American-run hotel near Bolzano, one night in Verona, flew to Florence, and ended their journey in a British-run camp and interrogation centre near Rome, where they were the only female prisoners.

Margaret remained ignorant about her husband's fate until 20 August when she was interviewed by Ann Stringer, an American reporter with the United Press. Once it was obvious that the Allies were not going to do business with him, Himmler tried to lose himself among the thousands heading west. However, he was arrested by British soldiers and on 23 May, just as his captors realised who they were dealing with, he took cyanide.

On hearing this news, Margaret barely reacted. Stringer remembered that when she informed Margaret 'that Himmler was buried in an unmarked grave' she 'showed no surprise, no interest. It was the coldest exhibition of complete control of human feeling that I have ever witnessed.' What Stringer didn't realise was that Margaret would have considered it beneath her dignity to display emotion in front of an American journalist.

Margaret had seen press coverage about the death camps and knew her husband would be blamed; facing the prospect of having to account for his actions, she chose to plead ignorance, and told Stringer that she was 'just a woman' who 'did not understand politics'.[1]

From Rome, she and Gudrun were transported to Nuremberg. On arrival, Margaret was strip-searched and 'a vial of potassium cyanide was found stitched into the shoulder padding of her coat'. Margaret and Gudrun were placed in a bare cell with two planks for beds. Recognising that Nuremberg jail wasn't exactly an ideal environment for a teenage girl, Colonel Andrus attempted to make Gudrun's time there as normal as possible: 'I was determined that the girl's education should go on. We shopped around Nuremberg city ... to find school-books and water-colours for the child. She showed her appreciation by shyly sending me a painting she'd done surrounded by yellow and blue flowers.'[2]

Nevertheless, Gudrun was interrogated on 22 September 1945; she was asked about her final meeting with her father and whether she travelled round a lot in the war. Gudrun replied that she'd spent 'the last five years' either 'at home' or at 'school'. She talked briefly about her tour of the Dachau herb plantation, and when she was questioned about whether her parents had ever discussed their post-war plans, or anything else of significance, Gudrun's response was unequivocal: 'My mother never told me anything.'[3]

Four days later, it was Margaret's turn in the hot seat. Unsurprisingly, her interrogator was primarily interested in her husband's organisation of the Final Solution and how much Margaret knew about what was going on. At first, she claimed that Himmler never discussed the extermination camps with her, but after persistent probing she confessed that she knew some 'existed' but couldn't remember who told her about them – 'maybe' Himmler – she wasn't certain. Pushed further, Margaret admitted that she'd visited Ravensbrück – 'I have seen the concentration camp for women myself' – but didn't say when or why she went; Ravensbrück's grounds included a herb garden, though not as big as the one at Dachau, and German Red Cross nurses were employed there. Margaret didn't mention Ravensbrück in her diary, but she probably inspected the camp when she was on one of her official trips, either on her way to Poland in 1940 or to Latvia in 1942.

As to whether her husband was the driving force behind the annihilation of the Jews, Margaret shifted the blame on to Hitler: 'I think that these matters were determined by the Führer.' Otherwise, Margaret was keen to stress that her separation from Himmler meant she only saw him '15 or 20 times' during the entire war and for merely three days at a time. When it came to Hedwig, however, she was reluctant to go into detail. She pretended not to recall her first name or how many children she had, though Margaret did concede that Himmler was not a 'faithful' husband.[4]

Hedwig had made it to Austria at the end of the war but was easy to find. She was interrogated on 22 May 1945, during which she described Himmler as 'an idealist with tremendous faith in Germany and in the Führer'. Her interrogator observed that Hedwig was 'an attractive woman in her early thirties' and concluded that she was an 'unassuming woman rather than a forceful or calculating one'.[5]

Considered of no importance, Hedwig was released. She did not face a denazification hearing and settled down in Bavaria, where she kept in touch with some of Himmler's old colleagues and members of his family. In 1953, Hedwig decided to cut all connections to her past, moved to Baden-Baden, married and worked as a secretary, glad to be forgotten. Hedwig gave one interview before she died in 1994 and insisted that she knew nothing about what Himmler did during the war; there was no mention of the human furniture she'd stored in the attic of her Berchtesgaden home.

Lina and her youngest daughter were staying with Frieda Wolff at Lake Tegernsee when the war finished and were promptly ejected by US troops who wanted to commandeer Frieda's house. For a short while Lina and her daughter slept in their car before finding beds in a local hospital. Having given her child to friends for safe-keeping, Lina embarked on the long haul back to Fehmarn; she went by train from Tegernsee to Munich, by bicycle to Augsburg, hitched to Stuttgart, then took a train via Hanover to the Baltic coast. She arrived at her parents' house on 7 September 1945 and registered with the British authorities administering the region.

About a year later, Lina heard some unsettling news. She was wanted by the authorities in Prague for crimes against humanity. Scared that the British might hand her over, Lina procured false papers and went south, landing first in Munich before crossing the border into Austria where she worked as a milkmaid on a farm. Lina hated every minute, gave up, and returned to Fehmarn.

On 19 October 1947, the People's Special Court in Prague – which had heard testimony from workers on Lina's Czech estate – sentenced her to life in prison with twenty years' hard labour for starving prisoners and letting her SS guards beat them. The Czech authorities applied to have Lina extradited but the British declined to cooperate. Instead, they picked her up themselves.

Lina's denazification trial took place on 29 June 1949; she was designated as a Category (IV) – Follower – and let off without a custodial sentence. Perhaps her husband's assassination was considered punishment enough. Even by the standards of the denazification tribunals it was a strangely generous judgement given the indictment against her in Prague and Heydrich's instrumental role in shaping and directing the Final Solution, which had been systematically exposed during the 1947–48 trials of the surviving Einsatzgruppen leaders. Lina was surprised by the court's clemency: 'I became one of the few Nazi women who never got locked up, and I was a bit sorry not to have had to do some time.'[6]

Nevertheless, Lina appealed, and in January 1951 she was downgraded to Category (V) – Exonerated – and permitted to keep her assets, including her and Heydrich's Fehmarn villa. Lina converted it into a guesthouse and restaurant. Many of her visiting trade were SS veterans and through them she was introduced to a charitable organisation called Silent Help that had been formed by a core of twenty or thirty members in November 1951 to 'help all those who, as a consequence of wartime and post-war conditions, have forfeited their liberty through imprisonment, internment or similar circumstances'.[7]

Founded by Helene Elisabeth von Isenburg, a staunch Catholic and neuropath whose late husband had been a fervent Nazi and professor of family and family research in Munich, Silent Help raised money for former SS men – whether concentration camp staff or high-ranking officials – who were rotting in jail, secured them representation and paid their legal fees, pestered the authorities about their treatment and helped them adjust to civilian life after release.

Though Lina would have recognised the faces and names of the SS stalwarts who stayed at her guesthouse, her friends from her Berlin days were not among them. Schellenberg had re-invented himself as an international man of mystery and assisted US agents in their efforts to catch Nazis on the run. Max de Crinis, the euthanasia expert, and his wife Lilli poisoned themselves on 2 May 1945. Herbert Backe – who was in charge of the production and distribution of food during the war and was responsible for starving millions to death – hanged himself in his cell at Nuremberg on 6 April 1947; his wife Ursula was the only one of Lina's close-knit group who stayed in touch and helped out Lina's son Heider; he lodged with Ursula while studying engineering at Hanover University in the early 1950s.

Heider graduated and went on to work for the Dornier aircraft company. Lina's youngest daughter Marte married a local farmer and opened a small fashion shop in Fehmarn. Her other daughter Silke became a model, lived for a while in Mexico, but later returned to Fehmarn and settled down. Ever concerned about her finances, Lina launched a series of legal challenges over her right to receive the full pension owed to a widow of a German general killed in action – which was equivalent to that paid to the wife of a government minister. Despite the detailed evidence presented in court about Heydrich and the Holocaust, Lina won her case.

From as early as 1949, when Lina gave an interview to a journalist from *Der Spiegel*, she rarely missed an opportunity to talk about her husband. In 1951, she was contacted by Jean Vaughan, a writer and Nazi sympathiser, who wanted to collaborate with her on a book about Heydrich. They wrote to each other for several months. In some of their exchanges, Lina answered his specific questions, and in others she presented fragments of detail alongside more lengthy reflections.

Lina's recollections were hesitant at times, her thoughts muddled, especially when it came to the Final Solution. Her starting position was denial. Her husband was innocent of that particular crime, based on the fact that the extermination programme began after his assassination: 'As to the orders concerning the Jews in Russia, they were issued from the highest places, as far as I know, and I don't know whether they were already issued in the lifetime of my husband. But the more I think about it, the more I doubt it.' In that sense, Lina was glad Heydrich 'died in 1942' and was able to keep 'his faith and his ideal'.

Lina also pointed out that Heydrich had no authority over the camp system, which was overseen by Himmler and run by a specific branch of the SS. Heydrich might have been responsible for putting people in cages but once they walked through the camp gates his power over them ended; as Lina put it, 'never is a judge held responsible for the condition of the prison'. Yet she couldn't shake the disquieting feeling that her husband must have been aware of Himmler's mission and may well have been involved in the planning stages. But even if Heydrich was aware of the horrors to come, he didn't share any of it with her: 'He kept an absolute silence, and if he knew of what was to happen, he certainly succeeded in keeping it from us.'[8]

The process of raking over the recent past unsettled Lina and she broke off her correspondence with Vaughan. The events were still too fresh, the emotions too raw to process, Lina needed more time and distance before she could erect a monument to her husband.

After Nuremberg, Margaret and her daughter Gudrun were detained in a women's camp until November 1946; sick, depressed and dysfunctional, they were both admitted to a Church-administered mental hospital, alongside 2,500 epileptics and 800 other patients, while Margaret awaited denazification.

Between 1948 and early 1953, Margaret was involved in three different trials with three different outcomes. In 1948, she was placed in Category (III) – Lesser Offender. In 1952, following an appeal, this verdict was reduced to Category (IV) – Follower. Her reclassification was met with howls of protest – after all, she was Himmler's wife – and

Margaret was bumped up to Category (II) – Offender – which meant forfeiting any property or money linked to her husband and losing the right to vote. Margaret was not happy with this decision and for several years she battled to get the various widow and state pensions she thought were owed to her.

By then, Margaret had moved to a small apartment in Munich; she wanted a quiet life and was content to disappear into obscurity. Her old friends and colleagues were dead. Ernst-Robert Grawitz, her boss at the German Red Cross, used a grenade to obliterate himself and his family. Professor Gebhardt of the Hohenlychen clinic was arrested for his gruesome experiments on camp inmates and in the autumn of 1946 he joined other members of his profession – including Karl Brandt, whose wife had been such a close companion of Eva's – at Nuremberg for what was known as the Doctors' Trial. Professor Gebhardt was sentenced to death and executed on 2 June 1948.

More heartening for Margaret was the return of her stepson Gerhard from nearly a decade in the Soviet Union. Gerhard – who'd joined the military wing of the SS in the last months of the war – was captured by Soviet troops and deposited in a labour camp. The Soviet authorities knew about his connection to Himmler and gave him a twenty-five-year sentence. After Stalin's death, the authorities began slowly emptying their sprawling network of camps and Gerhard was freed in 1955. He headed for Munich and stayed with Margaret for a year before striking out on his own. He married, worked as a truck driver, and kept in touch with both his stepmother and stepsister.

Gudrun's relationship with Margaret had become strained; unlike her mother, she was not ready to bury the past. Having graduated high school, Gudrun left Margaret and trained to be a dressmaker. But building an independent life for herself was not easy. When her employers or co-workers discovered who she was, Gudrun was out of a job. Struggling to make ends meet, she moved back in with Margaret when her health went into steady decline.

Gudrun did find some validation, however, among the ranks of Silent Help, and worked tirelessly on its behalf for over forty years. Gudrun entered the SS self-help association when it was established and its members treated her with a degree of respect and admiration that bordered on reverence.

At the same time, Gudrun helped to set up a barely legal neo-Nazi group for her own generation called the Viking Youth. In 1958, Gudrun attended a gathering of SS veterans and fellow travellers held in Austria near an ancient Celtic site deep in the Bohemian forests. Gudrun was the guest of honour at what would become an annual celebration of her father's achievements; she considered it her 'life's work to show' Himmler 'in a different light'. Though he was 'branded as the greatest mass murderer of all time', she wanted 'to try and revise this image' and 'get the facts straight about what he thought and what he did'.[9]

Her mother died on 25 August 1967; she was 74. Margaret's silence about her husband and their lives together meant she was largely ignored by historians, who concluded that their marriage was effectively over by 1935. Only recently, after her correspondence with Himmler and portions of her diary entered the public domain, has it been possible to gain some insight into this strange sphinx-like woman, who was determined to take her secrets with her.

Other than a brief three-year marriage of convenience to a Finnish theatre director, Heydrich was the only man in Lina's life; she confessed to a women's magazine in 1967 that 'even today I still dream about my husband nearly every night. He wants to separate himself from me. He wants to leave me. I reproach him that he has deserted me. Almost every night it is the same.'[10] In 1969, Lina's Fehmarn guesthouse burned down when the thatched roof caught fire, but thanks to the insurance payment she was able to purchase a new, smaller property and resume her business. Her main concern, however, was safeguarding Heydrich's legacy. Lina was obsessed by the idea that he was being treated unfairly by posterity. In a letter to a Dutch historian, she bemoaned the fact that her husband was being judged so harshly for committing acts that he thought were 'an unavoidable political necessity', and pointed out that it was easy to condemn 'the decisions of those times from today's warm bed'.[11]

To help create a more balanced assessment, Lina spoke at great length to a number of historians. Given that she wanted to be taken seriously, Lina only agreed to work with candidates she approved of on the basis that they were going to be thorough, objective and interested in the real truth about her husband. Her most unusual encounter was with Shlomo Aronson, an Israeli academic from Tel Aviv. After covering the trial of Adolf Eichmann, Aronson decided to study Nazism in greater depth and went to Germany, where he enrolled at the Free University in Berlin and completed a thesis about the early days of the SD and the Gestapo in Munich. Aronson put to one side any hostile feelings he may have had towards Heydrich's widow and sought Lina out. Despite her anti-Semitism, Lina was prepared to indulge Aronson and gave him many hours of her time.

Lina also talked to Heinz Höhne, who became interested in the SS when he wrote a series of articles for *Der Spiegel* about former SS men who'd avoided denazification and held prominent positions in West German society. This investigation inspired Höhne to embark on his monumental, ground-breaking and definitive study of the SS; Lina was a willing interviewee and provided him with brutally frank anecdotes about Margaret and her husband. In the early 1970s, Lina gave another grandstanding performance to the American author John Toland, who was writing a biography of Hitler.

Nevertheless, Lina was still not satisfied with how Heydrich was being represented. Alongside these scholarly tomes, there were a raft of other books about Heydrich that portrayed him as Hitler's executioner and the most evil man in the Third Reich, an ice-cold sadist and butcher; the uber-Nazi. It was all too much for Lina to tolerate without fighting back, so she wrote her own book. Candid and disarmingly honest – as if she was presenting the unvarnished truth – Lina's account of her life with Heydrich featured no guilt or doubt or regret about what she was recounting. She was unapologetic about their ideological convictions and shameless about their racism and anti-Semitism, while at the same time downplaying Heydrich's direct involvement in the Final Solution.

Ultimately, she wanted the reader to appreciate that Heydrich was a supremely gifted individual. There was his talent as a musician – 'if things had not gone so horribly wrong, I would not be the widow of a war-criminal but without doubt the wife of a brilliant violinist'[12] – his athletic prowess, his courage, his diligence and work ethic, his intellect and powers of reason, and his patriotism; in the end serving Germany was the most important thing for him. He was in short, a great man. Lina's appeals fell on deaf ears. Her book – *My Life with a War Criminal* – which was published by a small German imprint in 1976, made little impact and has never been translated into English. Undeterred, she kept talking to whoever wanted to listen.

Lina died on 14 August 1985; she was 74. Not long before she passed away, Lina gave a brief TV interview. Sitting straight-backed and motionless in a book-lined study, poised and polished, her clothes conservative but smart, staring straight ahead with an unblinking stare and delivering her answers in a dry emotionless tone, she let the world know that she was proud to be Lina Heydrich.

THE FINAL YARDS

A fter her spell at Göttingen prison camp, Ilse settled in Munich and reconnected with former friends and acquaintances like Winifred Wagner. Though the Queen of Bayreuth was not taken into custody, she went through two denazification hearings. At the first, in 1947, Winifred was placed in Category (II) – Offender; at her re-trial in 1948, she was rewarded with a lower ranking, Category (III) – Lesser Offender. Nevertheless, her reputation was tainted and she gave up running the festival.

Winifred's social circle included Emmy and Edda – Emmy was full of admiration for Winifred and wrote that 'my child and I love and respect this wonderful woman with all our hearts'[1] – but ultimately, Winifred was closer to Ilse; unlike Emmy, they'd experienced the Nazi movement's early years together, and to them the 1920s seemed like an innocent and carefree time when Hitler was more easy-going and approachable, before his dreams became an appalling reality.

Though over the years Ilse and Winifred saw less of each other, they kept in touch by letter, exchanging gossip about surviving members of Hitler's clique and criticising their memoirs, and debating the merits of each year's festival programme. In 1975, five years before her death, Winifred gave an ill-judged interview during which she extolled Hitler's virtues and practically declared her love for him.

On 14 December 1955, *Der Spiegel* printed a short announcement: Ilse had opened a guesthouse and rooms were available at reasonable nightly rates. She had converted an old farmhouse high in the Bavarian Alps; it had stunning views and a room set aside for her husband that contained his books, his manuscripts and papers, a radio, and some of the toys he and Wolf used to play with together. Ilse had reserved this private space for Hess because she was convinced that one day he'd walk out of Spandau. However, she didn't expect the Allies to reconsider his life sentence unless they were forced to.

To help gain publicity for her cause, Ilse produced *Rudolf Hess: Prisoner of Peace* in 1954, the first of a series of collections of her correspondence with her husband. According to one of his fellow inmates, when Hess learned about the book he 'became feverishly excited', delighted that he had gone into print before any other of the Spandau prisoners.

On the basis of Hess's letters to her – in *Prisoner of Peace* and later editions – a casual reader might think that Ilse's husband enjoyed his incarceration; his monastic life seemed to suit him as he worked on his patch of the Spandau garden, revelled in the odd classical recital played on the chapel organ by another one of the prisoners, and read voraciously, consuming the stacks of books Ilse kept sending him – on one occasion he ordered as many as sixty. Hess delved into history, musical biography, architecture, astronomy and nuclear physics, while keeping a close eye on current events. But this was only half the story. From 1950 onwards, Hess was as difficult and disruptive as he had been in the UK and at Nuremberg. He refused to sleep. He wouldn't work. He wouldn't eat. He kept everyone awake at night with his moaning and groaning. His amnesia made regular appearances, like an annoying neighbour you can't quite get rid of.

Once again, his jailers had to decide whether it was all an act or not. Albert Speer – who was serving a twenty-year sentence – thought it was; on 1 July 1956, Speer noted in his diary that he saw Hess emerge from his cell looking 'relaxed and cheerful' but as soon as he realised Speer was watching him, Hess's 'expression changed in a fraction of a second. Suddenly a tormented, suffering man confronted me. Even his gait changed abruptly. His springy step became stiff and faltering.'[2]

Matters came to a head after one of his fellow inmates was released early due to ill health. During November 1957, there were rumours that Hess was eating small amounts of laundry detergent to give himself stomach cramps. Towards the end of the month, while he was performing his gardening duties, Hess tried to commit suicide and was found in his cell lying under his bed-sheets covered in blood.

The medical staff patched him up and the next day Hess told Speer what had happened:

> There was no guard in the vicinity, I quickly smashed my glasses and used a piece of glass to open the veins of my wrist. For three hours nobody noticed anything. I lay in the cell and had plenty of time to bleed to death. Then I would have been freed of my pain forever.[3]

On the outside, Ilse was striving to get him released. In 1956, she appealed to the UN, then in 1957 to the European Commission for Human Rights. Her argument was simple: Hess had risked everything to be an ambassador for peace and the sixteen years he'd already spent in captivity was surely sufficient punishment for his Nazi activities, not to mention the effect it had on his well-being.

On 1 October 1966 Hess became the sole prisoner at Spandau when Speer and Baldur von Schirach left the jail. Both had done their allotted time. Speer would return to his wife Margarete and become a best-selling author. Von Schirach was not so blessed. Henriette had divorced him in 1950; she remarried and spent the rest of her colourful life offending people with her provocative opinions.

Ilse and her son Wolf – who had qualified as an engineer and was married with children – realised that this was a crucial moment in their quest to liberate Hess. Not only did Hess's solitary confinement highlight his predicament, the eyes of the media were on him. On the 10th, Ilse and Wolf issued a 'Declaration to all Thinking People in the World' that condemned Hess's 'cruel' imprisonment for being 'hitherto unknown in the annals of modern law',[4] and sent it to the pope, the UN Human Rights Commission and the World Council of Churches.

At the beginning of 1967, Ilse formed the Freedom for Rudolf Hess Support Association and issued a petition for her husband's release that gained over 40,000 signatures from people in forty different countries, while the association's rallies drew an average crowd of around 500. At the same time Ilse fired off letters to politicians, intellectuals, bishops, journalists and historians asking for their backing. Many of them went on record to say they agreed with her.

During November 1969, Hess was incapacitated by a perforated ulcer and was transferred to the British Military Hospital in Berlin on 8 December. His condition was critical. Now it looked like he might actually die, Hess wrote to the Spandau director and asked if Ilse and Wolf could visit him; after twenty-eight years, Hess wanted to see his wife and child again.

On 24 December 1969 Ilse and Wolf arrived at the hospital. Forty reporters and photographers were waiting for them. Ilse was wearing a fawn, camel-hair coat and a scarf round her head. Once inside, she removed her outer garments to reveal a two-piece suit and a blouse with a white collar. She and Wolf took the lift to the third floor. Ilse had brought her husband a large bunch of winter flowers but was not permitted to give them to him. During the half-hour meeting that followed, Ilse, Wolf and Hess were flanked by four prison directors and a warden.

As Ilse and her son entered the room, Hess spontaneously leapt up to greet them, remembered that they weren't allowed to touch and made a hand-kissing gesture instead. For a moment, the atmosphere was charged with emotion, and Wolf could tell his mother was 'on the edge of tears',[5] but Ilse held her feelings in check and they began chatting about Hess's health, Wolf's engineering career, and other family members. It all went by in a flash; Ilse recalled that 'time passed very quickly, and before the conversation really got into its stride visiting time was over'. As they left, Ilse gave the Spandau director her husband's Christmas presents; a sandalwood box of Mousson lavender soap, pale blue cotton pyjamas and a recording of Schubert.

Hess recovered and returned to Spandau, against the wishes of the Western powers – Britain, America and France – who shared jurisdiction over Hess with the Soviets. They'd decided that it was no longer necessary to keep him locked up. But the Soviets felt differently. They thought Hess was just as culpable as the other defendants at Nuremberg, considering the longevity of his service to Hitler and his influence on the movement and its ideology, and were angry he'd been spared death. As for his so-called peace mission, it was only undertaken to make it easier for Hitler to crush the Soviet Union.

The Soviets also pointed out – quite correctly – that Hess remained an unreconstructed Nazi. Hess's extensive prison writings are full of contempt for liberal democracy, which he thought was feeble and corrupt, US-style capitalism, which was soulless and culturally barren, while communism was just as awful as always. His anti-Semitism was alive and well, and in the future, Hess firmly believed that Nazism would again capture hearts and minds; commenting on the prospects of converting young people to the cause, Hess was confident that when 'they become more detached from the past events, and when normal times return, they will again resume an attitude that will correspond to *ours*'.[6]

On this basis, the Soviets rejected any suggestion that Hess should be released. As a minor concession, they agreed he could receive one visitor a month for an hour at a time. Undaunted, Ilse kept up the pressure. In 1973, she delivered a complaint to the European Commission for Human Rights at Strasbourg which claimed the British government had contravened Article Three of its Human Rights charter. Her appeal was rejected in May 1975.

On 2 February 1977, Hess tried to sever an artery with a knife. On 28 December 1978, he suffered a stroke that left him almost blind. At the end of his tether and 'convinced that I have only a short time to live', Hess wrote to the Spandau directors on 4 January 1979 and asked to be released 'because of my poor state of health, and because I would like to see my grandchildren'.[7] His request was denied.

In the early 1950s Emmy got a modest apartment, which she shared with her daughter Edda, and enjoyed a pleasant existence, sustained by her memories: 'The years have gone by. Edda and I like Munich very much. Fate has brought me many sorrows but also incomparable happiness. My marriage was a gift from God and my daughter is my whole life.'[8]

Yet Emmy was not entirely satisfied. Ever since US personnel had emptied her husband's various castles and storage facilities, Emmy had resented the appropriation of Goering's immense collection of art; the Allies found a total of 1,375 paintings, 250 sculptures, 108 tapestries, 75 stained-glass windows and 175 other objets d'art. But that wasn't all of it. Numerous valuable pieces were stolen; Goering's silver-topped baton; a gold-handled sword awarded to Emmy on her wedding day; several priceless diamond-encrusted daggers; and the paintings by Memling that Goering had removed from his art train and given to Emmy.

What hurt most was the loss of the *Madonna and Child* by Cranach the Elder, which the city of Cologne presented to Edda on the day of her birth and took back after the war. Emmy agitated unsuccessfully for its return until Edda stepped into the fray. Edda had passed her *Abitur* and studied law at Munich University. In 1964, she put her newly won knowledge to use and persuaded the courts to give her back the painting, beginning a four-year wrangle with the Cologne authorities that eventually ended in victory for them; Edda's most prized possession was gone for good.

Emmy died on 8 June 1973, aged 80, and was buried at the Waldfriedhof cemetery in Munich. It was a relatively low-key, quiet affair, in keeping with the life she'd led since moving back to the city after her denazification tribunal.

After Emmy's death, Edda inhabited a neo-Nazi milieu. Her only relationship of any significance was with a wealthy journalist and Nazi follower who'd bought Goering's yacht *Carin II*. During frequent media appearances – she did a three-hour interview for Swedish TV – Edda stubbornly defended her father, and continued to cherish him until her death in 2018: 'I loved him very much, and it was obvious how much he loved me. My only memories of him are such loving ones. I cannot see him any other way.'[9]

Like her daughter, Emmy never denied her love for Goering and was distressed that so many people thought he was a monster; as far as she was concerned, he wasn't guilty of many of things of which he'd been accused. To set the record straight, in 1967 she wrote a book – *My Life with Goering* – that attempted to paint a more flattering picture of the man she adored, and give her perspective on his actions. Nowhere in the book did Emmy address her husband's decisive role in Hitler's rise to power, his development of the Luftwaffe as an instrument of terror aimed at civilians, or his management of the war economy; 'a woman in love thinks only of her partner's success, and it is of little importance to her how he obtains it'. Nor did Emmy dwell on his addictions or his insatiable appetite for material wealth. Instead, she described him as a perfect husband and father whose only crime was his loyalty to Hitler, which itself was a product of Goering's noble character, duty-bound to follow the Führer's orders however wrong-headed they might be; besides, trying to get Hitler to change his mind was like 'baying at the moon'.

Nevertheless, there is an uneasiness in her text, a sense of uncertainty and incomprehension about what the Nazis did and to what extent she and her husband were responsible. Emmy admitted that 'one never knows whether one has acted rightly or wrongly', and she was haunted by the disturbing thought that she was partly to blame: 'I often wonder now if we should not ... have been a little more vigilant, and when we saw injustices being done if we should not have put up stronger resistance, especially to Adolf Hitler over the Jewish question.'[10]

On 24 February 1981, a federal court quashed a civil action brought against the West German government by Ilse's lawyer in 1977 on the basis that Hess's detention was unconstitutional. Another door had slammed in Ilse's face. That October, she saw her husband for the last time and it must have been heart-breaking for her to see him in such terrible shape, affected by pleurisy, a dodgy heart, skin rashes and knotted intestines.

In 1984, Ilse wrote the introduction to a book by her son about Hess's predicament. Ilse described how she and her husband always had a sympathetic attitude towards the British that encouraged Hess to believe he would receive a fair hearing rather than the 'inhuman treatment'[11] the British subjected him to: Ilse sincerely hoped they would finally see the error of their ways. The British authorities were already on her side, and together with their French and American partners made another approach to the Soviets about granting Hess his freedom, citing his advanced age and deteriorating health. The Soviets were unmoved and blocked their proposal.

Ilse was in her 80s by now and the accumulated stress of running the campaign and banging her head against a brick wall was weighing her down. As she took a back seat, Wolf maintained the momentum, staging candlelit vigils and protests outside Spandau, while one particularly aggrieved neo-Nazi hurled a petrol bomb into the prison. There was renewed hope that the Soviets might reconsider their inflexible position when their new premier, Mikhail Gorbachev, signalled his desire to reform the communist regime. But in the end, Hess took matters into his own hands.

On 17 August 1987, Hess was tending to the Spandau garden and asked the guard if he could retrieve something from the tool shed. The guard agreed and left Hess to his own devices. Seven minutes later, the guard went to check on his prisoner and found him sprawled awkwardly across the tool-shed floor. He was stone dead.

Apparently, Hess had stood with his back against the wall, taken hold of an extension cable, tied it to the window handle, wound the loose end round his neck and slid slowly downwards, legs stretched out, the noose tightening all the time until it strangled him to death.

Ilse and Wolf immediately cried foul. How could a frail, weak 93-year-old man have managed to kill himself like that? Ilse demanded a second autopsy and accused the British of murdering her husband. But Hess had tried to commit suicide on four previous occasions, and there is no hard evidence to suggest that this wasn't his fifth attempt. The official autopsy was carried out on the 19th and confirmed that Hess had died by his own hand. The case was closed and Spandau demolished.

Hess's body was flown to an airstrip north of Nuremberg and handed over to Wolf. He took it straight to Munich for a second autopsy, performed on 21 August, which failed to find an alternative cause of death. On the 22nd, Wolf met Ilse to discuss plans for a secret burial; the local authorities in Wunsiedel, where the Hess family had a plot, refused to accommodate Hess's coffin. The following day, Wolf had a heart attack.

Eventually, the police performed the burial over the course of three nights, depositing Hess's corpse in an undisclosed location. In March 1988, the authorities caved in to Ilse's demands and his body was dug up and interred in the Hess communal grave at Wunsiedel.

The ugly nature of her husband's death and the trauma surrounding it left Ilse exhausted, and in the early 1990s she went into a nursing home. Her son Wolf recovered from his heart failure but was never quite the same again; he died in 2001. He was only 63 years old.

On 7 September 1995, Ilse passed away. She was 96. The ceremony at her funeral was performed by Gerda's eldest son, Martin Adolf Bormann, the trained Jesuit priest who'd spent his adult life trying to make sense of the misery his father had helped cause, arranging encounter groups for the victims and perpetrators of Nazi persecution. The mourners included Gudrun Himmler, ever faithful to her father and still heavily involved with neo-Nazi organisations; Gudrun died in 2018, clinging to the belief that Himmler had done no wrong.

Ilse's funeral was held at the Wunsiedel cemetery and she was buried next to her husband in the Hess family plot. On 21 July 2011, they were separated again. Ilse and Hess's grave had become a neo-Nazi shrine that attracted a steady stream of pilgrims. The local mayor was tired of them turning up in his town to pay homage to their fallen heroes and decided to act. Ilse and her husband's gravestone was removed; Hess's remains were exhumed and cremated, and his ashes were scattered in the sea.

CONCLUSION

On paper, Gertrud Scholtz-Klink was the most powerful woman in Hitler's Germany. Born in 1902, Scholtz-Klink qualified as a nurse, joined the Nazi party in 1930 and fully supported its plans for women. In 1934, she was made Reich Women's Leader and put in charge of the Nazi Women's League; over the next few years, she became head of the Women's Bureau – set up to get women into work – and established the Nazi Mothers' Service, which taught women about their duties and responsibilities as mothers.

These organisations intruded on the lives of millions of women, and Scholtz-Klink tackled her many tasks with tremendous zeal. She designed posters and invented slogans, wrote dozens of books and pamphlets, gave hundreds of speeches at meetings and rallies, went on lecture tours, broadcast on the radio, and talked to foreign journalists.

Yet Scholtz-Klink was never in the running to be First Lady of the Reich. She was never on display at receptions or high-profile public events. She never obtained the same exalted status as the other leading women. The wives of the Nazi elite ignored her; there is no record of Scholtz-Klink ever receiving an invitation from any of them. Crucially, Hitler couldn't stand her.

The top Nazi wives were able to enjoy their many privileges and their gilded lifestyles because Hitler allowed them to. His interest in them was bound up with his need for an extended family – he took great care choosing Christmas and birthday presents for the wives and their children – and the fact that he was more relaxed and comfortable in the company of women, as long as they openly and unconditionally adored him, didn't discuss politics and conformed to the stereotypes he found attractive.

Any power the top Nazi wives had was entirely dependent on his goodwill. One false move was enough to ruin them; Hitler could reduce them to nothing with a wave of his hand. Ilse understood what it meant to incur his displeasure, as did Emmy in the final weeks of the war, while Magda felt the consequences of his anger during her separation from Goebbels.

Each of the women in this book had a different relationship to Hitler, his ideology and the Nazi regime. During the twelve years of his rule, Magda was consistently portrayed as the Reich's leading lady. The grotesque final hours of her life, full of nightmarish images and bloody tragedy, cemented her reputation as the archetypical Nazi wife. But Magda's actions were not determined by her devotion to Hitler's philosophy – she subscribed to his main ideas but began questioning them as early as 1936 – and once the war started, aside from the odd moments of euphoria when she glimpsed victory, her attitude was largely negative. Obeying her husband's wishes was also of secondary importance; pleasing Goebbels was never Magda's sole motivation, and under different circumstances she would have divorced him.

In the end, it was Magda's emotional and psychological attachment to Hitler that governed her behaviour. What made Magda different from the other women was the nature of this relationship. From the beginning, Hitler appeared to feel as strongly about her as she did about him. It seemed they were a perfect match, an idea that was given greater allure by the fact that they could never be together, creating a seductive fantasy that trapped her in Hitler's deadly embrace.

Next to Magda stands Carin Goering, whose connection to Hitler was both personal and political. Though she did not commit suicide, she seemed to consciously choose martyrdom. Given her awful health problems, an early end was always possible. If she'd wanted to live to a ripe old age, Carin could have pursued a life of leisure, a sedate existence taking long vacations in warm climates and seeking out clean mountain air. But she took a different path and threw herself into the Nazi movement, expending every ounce of energy on the struggle, dragging her husband through hell and back, all to help bring about Hitler's revolution. The effort was too much for her. But Carin's sacrifice was not forgotten; she was sanctified by the Nazi regime and held up as a shining beacon for German women to follow.

Though Carin and Magda became icons, Gerda was the closest of all the wives to the Nazi ideal of womanhood; she fitted the image created by the propaganda machine. Her husband once reminded her that 'as a Nazi child' she was 'dyed in the wool'.[1] And he was right; Gerda was exposed to Hitler before she was even a teenager, brought up by a rabidly Nazi father, married off to a Nazi hard man, and sealed away from the outside world. She lived and breathed Hitler's ideology. It was second nature to her, and Gerda's early death ensured that her beliefs were never compromised.

Lina only met Hitler once at a reception in the early 1940s and exchanged a few words with him. Nevertheless, her dedication to his mission was total and unwavering. Any doubts Lina had were related to the state of her often tense marriage, while her criticisms were directed at those she thought were failing to do their duty properly. There's no doubt that if Lina had been given real power she would have used it ruthlessly, without hesitation or remorse; a merciless warrior ready to wipe her foes off the face of the earth.

For all their differences, Lina and Margaret had one thing in common; they were both snobs who looked down their noses at most of humanity. But Margaret was from another generation to Lina, her character had been shaped by the end of the imperial era and her experiences in the First World War. Though she appeared to endorse her husband's ideas, she rarely expressed an opinion of her own. When she did, it was usually a petty complaint about a particular individual. Margaret's ingrained pessimism meant she was never able to share Himmler's utopian visions. In her own mind, she always tried to do the decent thing, conduct herself properly and act in a morally correct manner. However, she was fundamentally incapable of appreciating the suffering of others and lacked the imagination to truly comprehend the horrors that her husband inflicted on millions of people.

Emmy was the least interested in Nazism and would have played out her days on the stage if she hadn't met and fallen in love with Goering. Her wilful blindness about what that meant was not accidental and was typical of many Germans who benefited from the regime and preferred to ignore its brutal excesses and look the other way, rationalising their lack of resistance and passive complicity. Though Emmy firmly disapproved of the Nazis' radical anti-Semitism, she shrugged helplessly as the persecution intensified, deceiving herself about what was happening in the East. Emmy's excuse was that she was theatre folk, part of a select and distinctive breed that existed apart from everybody else, for whom the concerns of the 'real world' were an irrelevance.

Ilse also saw herself as part of a unique tribe; she was an idealist. Her whole identity was wrapped up in her beliefs; she was the movement's patron saint, who'd held on to her warped principles throughout all her trials and tribulations. It never occurred to Ilse that she might be wrong.

A few years before her death, a German film crew got into Ilse's nursing home hoping to interview the Grand Old Lady of Nazism. They found Ilse sitting in a crowded room and managed to come away with a few minutes of footage. Watching her skilfully fend off their questions with monosyllabic, non-committal answers, a twinkle in her eye and a smile on her lips, it's hard to shake the feeling that despite everything that had happened, Ilse still believed it had all been worthwhile.

NOTES

INTRODUCTION

1. Fromm, *Blood and Banquets*, p. 248.

PART ONE

Chapter 1

1. W. Hess, *My Father Rudolf Hess*, p. 30.
2. I. Hess, *Prisoner of Peace*, p. 81.
3. Görtemaker, *Eva Braun*, p. 74.
4. Reiche, *Development of the SA in Nürnberg*, p. 26.
5. Bormann, *The Bormann Letters*, p. 34.
6. Irving, *Goering*, p. 47.
7. Ibid., p. 55.

Chapter 2

1. Reiche, *Development of the SA in Nürnberg*, p. 48.
2. L. Mosley, *The Reich Marshal*, p. 118.
3. Toland, *Hitler*, p. 199.
4. Knopp, *Hitler's Henchmen*, p. 184.
5. NA: IMT – RG 59:73088690.
6. Bormann, *The Bormann Letters*, p. 93.
7. Irving, *Goering*, p. 70.
8. Ibid., p. 88.

Chapter 3

1. Toland, *Hitler*, p. 950.
2. Schwärzwaller, *Rudolf Hess*, p. 78.
3. Manvell and Fraenkl, *Hess*, p. 38.
4. Wagner, *Heritage of Fire*, p. 31.
5. Schwärzwaller, *Rudolf Hess*, p. 78.
6. Hoffmann, *Hitler Was My Friend*, p. 148.
7. Von Schirach, *The Price of Glory*, pp. 178–9.
8. Sigmund, *Women of the Third Reich*, p. 132.
9. Himmler and Wildt (eds), *The Private Heinrich Himmler*, p. 30.
10. Ibid., p. 49; Longerich, *Heinrich Himmler*, p. 106.
11. Himmler, *The Himmler Brothers*, p. 79.
12. Ibid., pp. 66 and 83.
13. Longerich, *Heinrich Himmler*, p. 107.
14. Himmler, *The Himmler Brothers*, pp. 69 and 71.
15. Irving, *Goering*, p. 93.
16. Whiting, *The Hunt for Martin Bormann*, p. 50.
17. Von Lang, *Bormann*, p. 36; Whiting, *The Hunt for Martin Bormann*, p. 45.
18. Himmler, *The Himmler Brothers*, p. 112.
19. Ibid., p. 118.

Chapter 4

1. Wyllie, *Goering and Goering*, p. 37.
2. Heydrich, *Mein Leben mit Reinhard*, p. 23.
3. Knopp, *The SS*, p. 120.
4. Read, *The Devil's Disciples*, p. 216.
5. Wagener, *Hitler*, pp. 241, 255 and 258.
6. Ullrich, *Hitler: A Biography*, p. 284.
7. Himmler, *The Himmler Brothers*, p. 132.
8. Toland, *Hitler*, pp. 229–30.
9. L. Mosley, *The Reich Marshal*, p. 164.

Chapter 5

1. E. Goering, *My Life with Goering*, pp. 11–12 and 14.
2. Ibid., pp. 52 and 54.
3. Ibid., pp. 8 and 12.
4. Dederichs, *Heydrich*, p. 52.
5. Deschner, *Heydrich*, p. 57.
6. D'Almeida, *High Society in the Third Reich*, p. 37.
7. H. Goering, *Germany Reborn*, p. 129.
8. Gerwath, *Hitler's Hangman*, p. 68.
9. Riefenstahl, *A Memoir*, pp. 124 and 168.
10. Himmler, *The Himmler Brothers*, p. 58.

PART TWO

Chapter 6

1. E. Goering, *My Life with Goering*, pp. 28 and 46.
2. Fromm, *Blood and Banquets*, p. 197.
3. Reuth, *Goebbels*, p. 183.
4. Guenther, *Nazi Chic?*, p. 151.
5. Ibid., p. 132.
6. Ibid., p. 172.
7. Ibid.
8. Sigmund, *Women of the Third Reich*, p. 23.
9. Wyllie, *Goering and Goering*, p. 101.
10. E. Goering, *My Life with Goering*, p. 56.
11. Hillenbrand, *Underground Humour in Nazi Germany*, p. 25.
12. E. Goering, *My Life with Goering*, p. 78.
13. Von Schirach, *The Price of Glory*, p. 87.
14. Fromm, *Blood and Banquets*, p. 66.
15. E. Goering, *My Life with Goering*, p. 83.
16. Hoffmann, *Hitler Was My Friend*, p. 141.
17. Sigmund, *Women of the Third Reich*, pp. 158–9; Knopp, *Hitler's Women* p. 19; Görtemaker, *Eva Braun*, p. 92.
18. Görtemaker, *Eva Braun*, p. 98.
19. Kempka, *I was Hitler's Chauffeur*, p. 13.
20. Klabunde, *Magda Goebbels*, p. 233.
21. Hoffmann, *Hitler Was My Friend*, p. 165.
22. Wagner, *Heritage of Fire*, p. 141.
23. D. Mosley, *A Life of Contrasts*, p. 130.
24. Ibid.
25. Hillenbrand, *Underground Humour in Nazi Germany*, p. 28.
26. Ludecke, *I Knew Hitler*, p. 378.
27. Romani, *Tainted Goddesses*, p. 159.

Chapter 7

1. Schwärzwaller, *Rudolf Hess*, p. 90.
2. Schroeder, *He Was My Chief*, p. 8.
3. Ibid.
4. Kempka, *I was Hitler's Chauffeur*, p. 39.
5. Schroeder, *He Was My Chief*, pp. 9–10.
6. Von Lang, *Bormann*, p. 52.
7. Linge, *With Hitler to the End*, p. 93.
8. Bormann, *The Bormann Letters*, p. 35.
9. Wagner, *Heritage of Fire*, pp. 85–87.
10. I. Hess, *Prisoner of Peace*, p. 129.
11. Manvell and Fraenkl, *Doctor Goebbels*, p. 59.

12. NA: IMT – RG 238: 57322925.
13. Görtemaker, *Eva Braun*, p. 100.
14. Schroeder, *He Was My Chief*, p. 19.
15. MC: US/MISC/14; Brandt, 'The Brandt Interview', p. 22.
16. Von Lang, *Bormann*, p. 96.
17. Hoffmann, *Hitler Was My Friend*, p. 202.
18. Von Lang, *Bormann*, p. 116.
19. Toland, *Hitler*, p. 415.
20. Manvell and Fraenkl, *Doctor Goebbels*, p. 47.
21. Semmler, *Goebbels*, p. 36.
22. Riefenstahl, *A Memoir*, p. 163.
23. Irving, *Hess*, p. 57; Schwärzwaller, *Rudolf Hess*, pp. 143–4.
24. Ibid., p. 108.
25. Pryce-Jones, *Unity Mitford*, pp. 138–9.
26. I. Hess, *Prisoner of Peace*, p. 144.
27. Ibid. p. 22.
28. Von Schirach, *The Price of Glory*, p. 155.
29. Speer, *Inside the Third Reich*, p. 179.
30. Ernst, 'Rudolf Hess (Hitler's Deputy) on Alternative Medicine'.
31. Semmler, *Goebbels*, p. 35.
32. Taylor, Timm and Hern (eds), *Not Straight from Germany*, p. 319.
33. Semmler, *Goebbels*, p. 35.

Chapter 8

1. USHMM: Doc: 1999. A.0092; *Frau Marga Himmler Diaries 1937–1945* (trans), p. 10.
2. Höhne, *The Order of the Death's Head*, p. 164.
3. Von Schirach, *The Price of Glory*, p. 61.
4. Pryce-Jones, *Unity Mitford*, p. 157.
5. L. Heydrich and J. Vaughan *Correspondence*, 7 March 1951 from Real History www.fp.co.uk and Höhne, *The Order of the Death's Head*, p. 165.
6. Ibid., p. 166.
7. USHMM: M. Himmler, pp. 11–12.
8. Höhne pp. 128–9.
9. L. Heydrich and J. Vaughan, *Correspondence*, 12 December 1951; Williams, *Heydrich*, p. 69.
10. Schellenberg, *The Schellenberg Memoirs*, p. 34.
11. L. Heydrich and J. Vaughan, *Correspondence*, 12 December 1951.
12. Ibid.
13. Bassett, *Hitler's Spy Chief*, p. 99.
14. USHMM: M. Himmler, p. 9.
15. Ibid.
16. L. Heydrich and Jean Vaughan, *Correspondence*, 7 March 1951.
17. Longerich, *Himmler*, p. 233.
18. McDonough, *The Gestapo*, p. 180.

19. Gerwath, *Hitler's Hangman*, p. 112.
20. MacDonald, *The Killing of SS Obergruppenfuhrer Reinhard Heydrich*, p. 14.
21. Ibid.
22. Schellenberg, *The Schellenberg Memoirs*, pp. 35–6.
23. Ibid.
24. USHMM: M. Himmler, p. 11.
25. Ibid., pp. 2 and 5.
26. Lambert, *The Lost Life of Eva Braun*, p. 346.
27. USHMM: M. Himmler, p. 14.

Chapter 9

1. E. Goering, *My Life with Goering*, p. 92.
2. Meissner, *Magda Goebbels*, p. 140.
3. Read, *The Devil's Disciples*, p. 491.
4. Wagner, *Heritage of Fire*, p. 203.
5. USHMM: M. Himmler, pp. 15–16.
6. Ullrich, *Hitler: A Biography*, p. 609.
7. Döhring, Krause and Plaim, *Living with Hitler*, p. 126.
8. E. Goering, *My Life with Goering*, p. 81.
9. Heydrich, *Mein Leben mit Reynard*, p. 71; Knopp, *The SS*, p. 131; Heydrich, *Mein Leben mit Reynard*, p. 81.
10. Friedländer, *Nazi Germany and the Jews*, p. 115.
11. Ullrich, *Hitler: A Biography*, p. 632.
12. Von Lang, *Bormann*, p. 116.
13. Linge, *With Hitler to the End*, p. 94.
14. USHMM: M. Himmler, pp. 17–18.
15. K. Himmler p. 189.
16. Ibid..
17. Himmler, *The Himmler Brothers*, p. 244.
18. USHMM: M. Himmler, p. 19.
19. www.history.com/this-day-in-history
20. Goebbels, *Diaries 1939–1941*, pp. 4 and 14.
21. Speer, *Inside the Third Reich*, p. 220.
22. USHMM: M. Himmler, p. 21.
23. Gerwath, *Hitler's Hangman*, p. 139.
24. USHMM: M. Himmler, p. 23.
25. E. Goering, *My Life with Goering*, pp. 2–3.
26. I. Hess, *Prisoner of Peace*, p. 15.
27. Irving, *Hess*, p. 57.
28. D. Mosley, *A Life of Contrasts*, p. 145.
29. Pryce-Jones, *Unity Mitford*, p. 235.
30. D. Mosley, *A Life of Contrasts*, p. 142.

PART THREE

Chapter 10

1. Goebbels, *Diaries 1939–1941*, p. 109.
2. Fox, 'Everyday Heroines', p. 28.
3. Goebbels, *Diaries 1939–1941*, p. 79.
4. USHMM: M. Himmler, p. 24.
5. Ibid., p. 23.
6. Ibid., p. 24.
7. Bryant, *Confronting the 'Good Death'*, p. 38.
8. Kater, *Doctors Under Hitler*, p. 129.
9. Stephenson, *Women in Nazi Germany*, p. 34.
10. Schellenberg, *The Schellenberg Memoirs*, p. 86.
11. Ibid., p. 265.
12. L. Mosley, *The Reich Marshal*, p. 312.
13. USHMM: M. Himmler, p. 24.
14. Ibid., p. 25.
15. Ibid., pp. 25 and 27.
16. Schroeder, *He Was My Chief*, pp. 160–1.
17. Goebbels, *Diaries 1939–1941*, p. 157.
18. Ibid., p. 171.
19. USHMM: M. Himmler, p. 26.
20. Ibid., p. 30.
21. I. Hess, *Prisoner of Peace*, pp. 12 and 19–24.
22. Ibid., p. 25.
23. Toland, *Hitler*, p. 665.
24. I. Hess, *Prisoner of Peace*, p. 14.
25. Ibid. p. 27.
26. Goebbels, *Diaries 1939–1941*, pp. 364 and 367.
27. Hillenbrand, *Underground Humour in Nazi Germany*, p. 39.
28. Hutton, *Hess*, p. 110.

Chapter 11

1. Döhring, Krause and Plaim, *Living with Hitler*, pp. 140–1.
2. Schroeder, *He Was My Chief*, p. 112.
3. Hutton, *Hess*, p. 100.
4. McGinty, *Camp Z*, p. 181.
5. Schellenberg, *The Schellenberg Memoirs*, p. 203.
6. Kurlander, *Hitler's Monsters*, p. 120.
7. Goebbels, *Diaries 1939–1941*, p. 408.
8. Gerwath, *Hitler's Hangman*, pp. 189–90.
9. Williams, *Heydrich*, p. 101.
10. Deschner, *Heydrich*, p. 191.
11. Schellenberg, *The Schellenberg Memoirs*, p. 239.

12. USHMM: M. Himmler, p. 29.
13. Himmler, *The Himmler Brothers*, p. 199.
14. USHMM: M. Himmler, p. 30; K. Himmler, p. 211.
15. USHMM: M. Himmler, p. 30.
16. Himmler, *The Himmler Brothers*, p. 218.
17. Himmler, *The Himmler Brothers*, pp. 233–4.
18. Ibid., p. 232.
19. USHMM: M. Himmler, pp. 30 and 32.
20. Knopp, *The SS*, p. 160.
21. Williams, *Heydrich*, p. 160.
22. Ibid., p. 176.
23. McGinty, *Camp Z*, p. 299.
24. Ibid., p. 300.
25. I. Hess, *Prisoner of Peace*, p. 43.
26. Ibid., p. 46.
27. Schwärzwaller, *Rudolf Hess*, p. 190.
28. I. Hess, *Prisoner of Peace*, p. 43.
29. Goebbels, *Diaries 1942–1943*, pp. 175 and 218.
30. Meissner, *Magda Goebbels*, p. 213.
31. Gerwath, *Hitler's Hangman*, p. 270.
32. Williams, *Heydrich*, p. 189.
33. Dederichs, *Heydrich*, p. 145.
34. Gerwath, *Hitler's Hangman*, p. 199.
35. Ibid., p. 279.
36. USHMM: M. Himmler, p. 32.
37. Ibid., p. 33.

Chapter 12
1. Stephenson, *Women in Nazi Germany*, pp. 56–7.
2. Goebbels, *Diaries 1942–1943*, p. 260.
3. Ibid., p. 309.
4. Ibid., p. 138.
5. Klabunde, *Magda Goebbels*, p. 301; Meissner, *Magda Goebbels*, pp. 224–5.
6. Schwärzwaller, *Rudolf Hess*, p. 179.
7. I. Hess, *Prisoner of Peace*, pp. 44–45.
8. Ibid., p. 46.
9. Ibid.
10. Bormann, *The Bormann Letters*, pp. 37–8.
11. Ibid., p. 6.
12. Ibid., pp. 8–9.
13. Kempka, *I was Hitler's Chauffeur*, p. 43.
14. NA: IMT – RG 238:57318818.
15. Himmler, *The Himmler Brothers*, p. 249.
16. Knopp, *Hitler's Hitmen*, p. 158.
17. Bormann, *The Bormann Letters*, p. 39.

18. Ibid., pp. 42 and 45.
19. Dederichs, *Heydrich*, p. 167.
20. Ibid., p. 163.
21. I. Hess, *Prisoner of Peace*, p. 47.
22. Görtemaker, *Eva Braun*, p. 219.
23. E. Goering, *My Life with Goering*, p. 106.
24. Goebbels, *Diaries 1942–1943*, p. 524.
25. Semmler, *Goebbels*, p. 115.
26. E. Goering, *My Life with Goering*, p. 146.
27. Perry, 'Nazifying Christmas', p. 604.
28. Irving, *Goering*, p. 518.
29. L. Mosley, *The Reich Marshal*, p. 365.
30. Dederichs, *Heydrich*, p. 164.
31. USHMM: M. Himmler, p. 34.
32. Ibid., p. 35.
33. Himmler, *The Himmler Brothers*, p. 259.
34. Ohler, *Blitzed*, p. 192.
35. Sigmund, *Women of the Third Reich*, pp. 174–5.
36. Bormann, *The Bormann Letters*, p. 66.
37. USHMM: M. Himmler, pp. 35–6.
38. E. Goering, *My Life with Goering*, p. 112.
39. Irving, *Hess*, p. 395.

Chapter 13

1. Bormann, *The Bormann Letters*, pp. 119–20.
2. Knopp, *Hitler's Hitmen*, p. 146.
3. Lebert and Lebert, *My Father's Keeper*, p. 113.
4. Bormann, *The Bormann Letters*, pp. 67, 37, 173 and 104–6.
5. USHMM: M. Himmler, p. 36.
6. NA: IMT – RG 238: 57323277.
7. Semmler, *Goebbels*, pp. 174–5.
8. NA: IMT – RG 238: 57323277.
9. Himmler, *The Himmler Brothers*, p. 277.
10. USHMM: M. Himmler, p. 36.
11. Dederichs, *Heydrich*, p. 167.
12. Schroeder, *He Was My Chief*, p. 146.
13. Bormann, *The Bormann Letters*, p. 177.
14. Semmler, *Goebbels*, pp. 185–6.
15. Goebbels, *Diaries: Final Entries 1945*, p. 45.
16. Ibid., pp. 192, 83, 254 and 317–18.
17. I. Hess, *Prisoner of Peace*, p. 48.
18. NA: IMT – RG 238: 6242149.
19. NA: IMT – RG 238: 57323277.
20. Junge, *Until the Final Hour*, pp. 159–60.

21. DNTC: IMT – Vol. 004 – Subdivison 8/Hitler Section 8.15.
22. Ibid.
23. Goeschel, 'Suicide at the End of the Third Reich', p. 164.
24. L. Mosley, *The Reich Marshal*, p. 378.
25. Schroeder, *He Was My Chief*, p. 188.
26. L. Mosley, *The Reich Marshal*, p. 382.
27. NA: RG 242: 6883511.
28. Kempka, *I was Hitler's Chauffeur*, p. 70.
29. Ibid., pp. 89–90.
30. Linge, *With Hitler to the End*, p. 199; Kempka, *I was Hitler's Chauffeur*, p. 78.
31. Junge, *Until the Final Hour*, p. 174.
32. Linge, *With Hitler to the End*, p. 207.

PART FOUR

Chapter 14

1. I. Hess, *Prisoner of Peace*, p. 49.
2. Kempka, *I was Hitler's Chauffeur*, p. 95.
3. Linge, *With Hitler to the End*, p. 210.
4. Kempka, *I was Hitler's Chauffeur*, p. 152.
5. Whiting, *The Hunt for Martin Bormann*, p. 35.
6. Farago, *Aftermath*, p. 163.
7. NA: IMT – *RG 238: 573188178*.
8. Andrus, *The Infamous at Nuremberg*, p. 73.
9. NA: IMT – RG 238: 57323137.
10. Ibid.
11. NA: IMT – RG 238: 57322925.
12. NA: IMT – *RG 238: 57323137*.
13. NA: IMT – RG 59: 73088690; RG 238: 57322925.
14. Irving, *Hess*, pp. 496–7.
15. I. Hess, *Prisoner of Peace*, p. 38.
16. Goering, *My Life with Goering*, p. 135.
17. DNTC: IMT –Vol. 014 Subdivision 35/Goering Section 35.03.
18. Andrus, *The Infamous at Nuremberg*, p. 161.
19. Persico, *Nuremberg*, p. 297.
20. Sigmund, *Women of the Third Reich*, p. 63.
21. Von Schirach, *The Price of Glory*, p. 87.
22. E. Goering, *My Life with Goering*, p. 159.
23. Ibid.
24. Von Schirach, *The Price of Glory*, pp. 134 and 137.
25. Ibid., p. 138.
26. I. Hess, *Prisoner of Peace*, p. 89.
27. Ibid., p. 96.

28. Sigmund, *Women of the Third Reich*, p. 64.
29. Ibid.

Chapter 15
1. Crasnianski, *Children of the Nazis*, p. 16; Himmler, the Himmler Brothers, p. 287.
2. Andrus, *The Infamous at Nuremberg*, pp. 69 and 139.
3. NA: IMT – RG 238: 57323267.
4. NA: IMT – RG 238: 57323277.
5. NA: IMT – RG 238: 6242149.
6. Dederichs, *Heydrich*, p. 171.
7. Knopp, *The SS*, p. 336.
8. L. Heydrich and J. Vaughan, *Correspondence*, 7 March 1951.
9. Lebert and Lebert, p. 106.
10. Dederichs, *Heydrich*, p. 175.
11. Ibid., p. 174.
12. Knopp, *The SS*, p. 120.

Chapter 16
1. E. Goering, *My Life with Goering*, p. 87.
2. Speer, *Spandau*, pp. 216 and 291.
3. Ibid., p. 343.
4. Posner, *Hitler's Children*, p. 62.
5. Ibid., p. 65; W. Hess, *My Father Rudolf Hess*, p. 288.
6. Schwärzwaller, *Rudolf Hess*, p. 16.
7. Posner, *Hitler's Children*, p. 69.
8. E. Goering, *My Life with Goering*, p. 168.
9. Posner, *Hitler's Children*, pp. 212–13.
10. E. Goering, *My Life with Goering*, pp. 15 and 95.

CONCLUSION
1. Bormann, *The Bormann Letters*, p. 49.

BIBLIOGRAPHY

ARCHIVE SOURCES

Donovan Nuremberg Trials Collection, Cornell University Library (DNTC).
Institute for Contemporary History, Munich (ICH).
Musmanno Collection, Gumberg Library, DuQuesne University (MC).
National Archives, Washington DC (NA).
Swiss Federal Archives, Bern (SFA).
United States Holocaust Memorial Museum (USHMM).

Books

Alford K.D., *Nazi Plunder: Great Treasure Stories of World War II* (De Capo Press, 2000).
Andrus, B., *The Infamous at Nuremberg* (Leslie & Frewin, 1969).
Ascheid, A., *Hitler's Heroines: Stardom and Womanhood in Nazi Cinema* (Temple University Press, 2003).
Bach, S., *Leni: The Life and Work of Leni Riefenstahl* (Knopf/Doubleday, 2007).
Bassett, R., *Hitler's Spy Chief: The Wilhelm Canaris Story* (Cassell, 2005).
Bird, E., *The Loneliest Man in the World: The Inside Story of the 30-year Imprisonment of Rudolf Hess* (Sphere, 1974).
Black, M. and Kurlander, E. (eds), *Revisiting the 'Nazi Occult': Histories, Realities, Legacies* (Camden House, 2015).
Bloch, M., *Ribbentrop* (Abacus, 2003).
Boak, H., *Women in the Weimar Republic* (Manchester University Press, 2013).
Bormann, M., *The Bormann Letters: The Private Correspondence between Martin Bormann and his Wife from January 1943–April 1945* (Weidenfeld and Nicolson, 1954).
Bramwell, A., *Blood and Soil: Walther Darré and Hitler's Green Party* (Kensal Press, 1985).
Bridenthal, R., Grossmann, A. and Kaplan, M. (eds), *When Biology Became Destiny: Women in Weimar and Nazi Germany* (Monthly Review Press, 1984).

Browning, C. and Matthias, J., *The Origins of the Final Solution: The Evolution of Nazi Jewish Policy 1939–1942* (William Heinemann, 2004).

Bryant, M., *Confronting the 'Good Death': Nazi Euthanasia on Trial 1945–1953* (University of Colorado Press, 2005).

Calic, E., *Reinhard Heydrich: The Chilling Story of the Man who Masterminded the Nazi Death Camps* (William Morrow Company Inc., 1985).

Cocks, G., *Psychotherapy in the Third Reich: The Göring Institute* (Oxford University Press, 1985).

Crasnianski, T., *The Children of the Nazis: The Sons and Daughters of Himmler, Göring, Höss, Mengele and others – Living with a Father's Monstrous Legacy* (Arcade Publishing, 2018).

D'Almeida, F., *High Society in the Third Reich* (Polity, 2008).

De Courcy, A., *Diana Mosley* (Vintage, 2004).

Dederichs, M., *Heydrich: The Face of Evil* (Greenhill, 2009).

Deschner, G., *Heydrich: The Pursuit of Total Power* (Orbis, 1981).

Dietrich, O., *The Hitler I Knew: Memoirs of the Third Reich's Press Officer* (Skyhorse Publishing, 2010).

Döhring, H., Krause, W.H. and Plaim, A., *Living with Hitler: Accounts of Hitler's Household Staff* (Greenhill, 2018).

Dornberg, J., *Munich 1923: The Story of Hitler's First Grab for Power* (Harper & Row, 1982).

Douglas-Hamilton, J., *Motive for a Mission: The Story Behind Hess's Flight to Britain* (Macmillan, 1971).

Evans, R., *The Coming of the Third Reich* (Penguin, 2004).

——*The Third Reich at War: How the Nazis led Germany from Conquest to Disaster* (Penguin, 2009).

——*The Third Reich in Power: 1933–1939* (Penguin, 2006).

Farago, L., *Aftermath: Bormann and the Fourth Reich* (Hodder and Stoughton, 1975).

Fest, J., *Inside Hitler's Bunker: The Last days of the Third Reich* (Pan, 2004).

——*Speer: The Final Verdict* (Weidenfeld & Nicolson, 2001).

——*The Face of the Third Reich* (Penguin, 1979).

Fisher, M.J., *A Terrible Splendor: Three Extraordinary Men, A World Poised for War, and the Greatest Tennis Match Ever Played* (Crown Publishers, 2009).

Friedländer, S., *Nazi Germany and the Jews 1933–1945* (Phoenix, 2009).

Fromm, B., *Blood and Banquets: A Berlin Social Diary* (Carol Publishing Group, 1990).

Gadberry, G., *Theatre in the Third Reich, the Pre-war Years: Essays on Theatre in Nazi Germany* (Greenwood, 1995).

Gerwath, R., *Hitler's Hangman: The Life of Heydrich* (Yale University Press, 2011).

Gilbert, G., *Nuremberg Diary* (Da Capo Press, 1947).

Goebbels, J., *The Diaries of Joseph Goebbels: Final Entries 1945* (ed. H. Trevor-Roper) (GP Putnam's Sons, 1978).

—— *The Goebbels Diaries 1939–1941* (ed. and trans. F. Taylor) (Sphere, 1982).

——*The Goebbels Diaries 1942–1943* (ed. and trans. L. Lochner) (Doubleday, 1948).

Goering, E., *My Life with Goering* (David Bruce & Watson, 1972).

Goering, H., *Germany Reborn* (Elkin Mathews and Marrot, 1934).

Goeschel, C., *Mussolini and Hitler: The Forging of the Fascist Alliance* (Yale University Press, 2018).

Görtemaker, H.B., *Eva Braun: Life with Hitler* (Penguin, 2011).

Graber, G., *The Life and Times of Reinhard Heydrich* (McKay, 1980).

Grange, W., *Hitler Laughing: Comedy in the Third Reich* (University Press of America, 2006).

Grunberger, R., *A Social History of the Third Reich* (Penguin, 1974).

Guenther, I., *Nazi Chic? Fashioning Women in the Third Reich* (Bloomsbury, 2004).

Gun, N., *Eva Braun: Hitler's Mistress* (Meredith Press, 1968).

Hake, S., *Popular Cinema In the Third Reich* (University of Texas Press, 2001).

Hamann, B., *Winifred Wagner: A Life at the Heart of Hitler's Bayreuth* (Granta, 2005).

Haste, C., *Nazi Women* (Channel 4 Books, 2001).

Hayman, R., *Hitler and Geli* (Bloomsbury, 1997).

Heins, L., *Nazi Film Melodrama* (University of Illinois Press, 2013).

Helm, S., *If This is a Woman: Inside Ravensbrück, Hitler's Concentration Camp for Women* (Abacus, 2015).

Henderson, N., *Failure of a Mission 1937–1939* (GP Putnam's Sons, 1940).

Herzog, D., *Sex after Fascism: Memory and Morality in Twentieth-Century Germany* (Princeton University Press, 2005).

Hess, I., *Prisoner of Peace* (Institute for Historical Review, 1954).

Hess, W., *My Father Rudolf Hess* (WH Allen, 1984).

Heydrich, L., *Mein Leben mit Reinhard: Die Persönliche Biographie* (Druffel & Vowinckel, 2012).

Hillenbrand, F., *Underground Humour in Nazi Germany 1933–1945* (Routledge, 1995).

Himmler, K., *The Himmler Brothers: A German Story* (Macmillan, 2007).

Himmler, K. and Wildt, M. (eds), *The Private Heinrich Himmler: Letters of a Mass Murderer* (St Martin's Press, 2014).

Hoffmann, H., *Hitler Was My Friend* (Burke Publishing, 1955).

Höhne, H., *Canaris: Hitler's Master Spy* (Doubleday, 1976).

——*The Order of the Death's Head: The Story of Hitler's SS* (Penguin, 1969).

Hutton, J.B., *Hess: The Man and his Mission* (David Bruce & Watson, 1970).

Irving, D., *Goebbels: Mastermind of the Third Reich* (St Martin's Press, 1994).

——*Goering: A Biography* (Focal Point, 1989).

——*Hess: The Missing Years 1941–1945* (Macmillan, 1987).

Junge, T., *Until the Final Hour: Hitler's Last Secretary* (Phoenix, 2005).

Kater, M., *Doctors Under Hitler* (Chapel Hill, 1989).

Kelley, D., *22 Cells in Nuremberg* (WH Allen, 1947).

Kempka, E., *I was Hitler's Chauffeur: The Memoirs of Erich Kempka* (Frontline, 2012).

Kershaw, I., *Hitler: 1889–1936 Hubris* (Penguin, 1999).

——*Hitler: 1936–1945 Nemesis* (Penguin, 2000).

——*The End: Nazi Germany 1944–45* (Penguin, 2012).

King, D., *The Trial of Adolf Hitler: The Beer Hall Putsch and the Rise of Nazi Germany* (Pan, 2017).

Kirkpatrick, C., *Women in Nazi Germany* (Jarrolds, 1939).

Klabunde, A., *Magda Goebbels* (Little Brown, 2001).

Knopp, G., *Hitler's Henchmen* (Sutton, 2000).
——*Hitler's Hitmen* (Sutton, 2002).
——*Hitler's Women* (Sutton, 2003).
——*The SS: A Warning from History* (The History Press, 2008).
Kurlander, E., *Hitler's Monsters: A Supernatural History of the Third Reich* (Yale University Press, 2017).
Lambert, A., *The Lost Life of Eva Braun* (Arrow, 2007).
Leasor, J., *The Uninvited Envoy* (McGraw-Hill, 1962).
Lebert, S. and Lebert, N., *My Father's Keeper: The Children of the Nazi Leaders – An Intimate History of Damage and Denial* (Little Brown, 2001).
Le Tissier, T., *Farewell to Spandau* (The History Press, 2008).
Lifton, R., *The Nazi Doctors: Medical Killing and the Psychology of Genocide* (Basic Books, 1988).
Linge, H., *With Hitler to the End: The Memoirs of Adolf Hitler's Valet* (Frontline, 2013).
London, J., *Theatre Under the Nazis* (Manchester University Press, 2000).
Longerich, P., *Goebbels: A Biography* (Vintage, 2015).
——*Heinrich Himmler* (Oxford University Press, 2012).
Lower, W., *Hitler's Furies: German Women in the Nazi Killing Fields* (Vintage, 2014).
Ludecke, K., *I Knew Hitler* (Jarrolds, 1938).
MacDonald, C., *The Killing of SS Obergruppenführer Reinhard Heydrich* (Papermac, 1989)
Manvell, R. and Fraenkl, H., *Doctor Goebbels: His Life and Death* (Frontline, 1960)
——*Goering* (Greenhill, 1962).
——*Hess* (MacGibbon & Kee, 1971).
Meissner, H., *Magda Goebbels: First Lady of the Third Reich* (Nelson Canada Ltd, 1980).
McDill, J., *Lessons from the Enemy: How Germany Cares for her War Disabled* (Lea & Febiger, 1918).
McDonough, F., *The Gestapo: The Myth and Reality of Hitler's Secret Police* (Coronet, 2016).
McGinty, S., *Camp Z: How British Intelligence Broke Hitler's Deputy* (Quercus, 2011)
McGovern, J., *Martin Bormann* (Arthur Barker Ltd, 1968).
Middlebrook, M. and Everitt, C., *The Bomber Command War Diaries: An Operational Reference Book 1939–1945* (Penguin, 1990).
Mosley, D., *A Life of Contrasts: The Autobiography* (Gibson Square Books, 2009).
Mosley, L., *The Reich Marshal: A Biography of Hermann Goering* (Pan, 1977).
Nicholas, L, *The Rape of Europa: The Fate of Europe's Treasures in the Third Reich and the Second World War* (Vintage, 1995).
Ohler, N., *Blitzed: Drugs in Nazi Germany* (Penguin, 2017).
Overy, R., *Goering: The Iron Man* (Routledge, 1984).
Padfield, P., *Himmler: Reichsführer SS* (Papermac, 1990).
Persico, J., *Nuremberg: Infamy on Trial* (Penguin, 1994)
Petropoulos, J., *Art as Politics in the Third Reich* (The University of North Carolina Press, 1996).
——*Artists under Hitler: Collaboration and Survival in Nazi Germany* (Yale University Press, 2014).

——The Faustian Bargain: The Art World in Nazi Germany (Penguin, 2001).

Phipps, E., Our Man in Berlin: The Diary of Sir Eric Phipps 1933–1937 (Palgrave, 2008).

Picknett, L., Prince, C. and Prior, S., Double Standards: The Rudolf Hess Cover-Up (Time Warner, 2001).

Pine, L., Nazi Family Policy 1933–1945 (Bloomsbury, 1997).

Pope, E., Munich Playground (GP Putnam's Sons, 1941).

Posner, G., Hitler's Children: Inside the Families of the Third Reich (Heinemann, 1991).

Pringle, H., The Master Plan: Himmler's Scholars and the Holocaust (Harper Perennial, 2006).

Proctor, R., The Nazi War on Cancer (Princeton University Press, 1999).

Pryce-Jones, D., Unity Mitford: A Quest (Weidenfeld & Nicolson, 1976).

Read, A., The Devil's Disciples: The Lives and Times of Hitler's Inner Circle (Pimlico, 2003).

Regin, N., Sweeping the Nation: Domesticity and National Identity in Germany 1870–1945 (Cambridge University Press, 2007).

Reiche, E., The Development of the SA in Nürnberg 1922–1934 (Cambridge University Press, 1986).

Reiss, C., Joseph Goebbels: A Biography (Hollis & Carter, 1949).

Reitsch, H., The Sky My Kingdom (Bodley Head, 1955).

Reuth, R.G., Goebbels (Constable, 1993).

Rhodes, R., Masters of Death: The SS-Einsatzgruppen and the Invention of the Holocaust (Alfred Knopf, 2002).

Riefenstahl, L., A Memoir (St Martin's Press, 1967).

Romani, C., Tainted Goddesses: Female Film Stars of the Third Reich (Sarpedon Publishers, 1992).

Roseman, M., The Villa: The Lake, The Meeting: Wansee and the Final Solution (Penguin, 2003).

Scheck, R., Mothers of the Nation: Right Wing Women in Weimar Germany (Berg, 2004).

Schellenberg, W., The Schellenberg Memoirs: A Record of the Nazi Secret Service (Andre Deutsch, 1956).

Schmidt, U., Karl Brandt: The Nazi Doctor – Medicine and Power in the Third Reich (Bloomsbury, 2007).

Schroeder, C., He was My Chief: The Memoirs of Adolf Hitler's Secretary (Frontline, 2012).

Schwärzwaller, W., Rudolf Hess: The Deputy (Quartet, 1988).

Semmler, R., Goebbels: The Man Next to Hitler (Westhouse, 1947).

Sigmund, A.M., Women of the Third Reich (NDE Publishing, 2000).

Speer, A., Inside the Third Reich (Phoenix, 1995).

——Spandau: The Secret Diaries (Macmillan, 1976).

Steinacher, G., Nazis on the Run: How Hitler's Henchmen fled Justice (Oxford University Press, 2011).

Stephenson, J., Women in Nazi Germany (Longman/Pearson Education Ltd, 2001).

Strobl, G., The Swastika and the Stage: German Theatre and Society 1933–1945 (Cambridge University Press, 2007).

Taylor, M., Timm, A. and Herrn, R. (eds), *Not Straight from Germany: Sexual Politics and Sexual Citizenship Since Magnus Hirschfeld* (University of Michigan Press, 2017).

Toland, J., *Hitler* (Wordsworth Editions, 1976/1997).

Tooze, A., *The Wages of Destruction: The Making and Breaking of the Nazi Economy* (Penguin, 2007).

Trevor-Roper, H., *The Last days of Hitler* (Macmillan, 1947).

——(ed.) *Hitler's Table Talk: His Private Conversations* (Enigma Books, 1953/2000).

Ullrich, V., *Hitler: A Biography – Volume 1: Ascent 1889–1939* (Vintage, 2016).

Von Lang, J., *Bormann: The Man Who Manipulated Hitler* (Book Club Associates, 1979).

——*SS General Karl Wolff: The Man between Himmler and Hitler* (Enigma, 2005).

Von Schirach, H., *The Price of Glory: The Memoirs of Henriette von Schirach* (Muller, 1960).

Wachsman, N., *KL: A History of the Nazi Concentration Camps* (Abacus, 2015).

Wagener, O., *Hitler: Memoirs of a Confidant* (Yale University Press, 1985).

Wagner, F., *Heritage of Fire* (Harper & Brothers, 1945).

Walters, G., *Berlin Games: How Hitler Stole the Olympic Dream* (John Murray, 2006).

Weale, A., *The SS: A New History* (Abacus, 2010).

Wehler, H.U., *The German Empire 1871–1918* (Berg Publishers, 1985).

Welch, D., *Propaganda and the German Cinema 1933–1945* (IB Tauris, 2001).

Wertham, F., *A Sign for Cain: An Exploration of Human Violence* (Macmillan, 1966).

Whiting, C., *The Hunt for Martin Bormann: The Truth* (Pen & Sword, 1973).

Williams, M., *Heydrich: The Dark Shadow of the SS* (Fonthill, 2018).

Wilson, J., *Hitler's Alpine Headquarters* (Pen & Sword, 2013).

——*Hitler's Alpine Retreat* (Pen & Sword, 2005).

Wyllie, J., *Goering and Goering: Hitler's Henchman and his Anti-Nazi Brother* (The History Press, 2010).

Zwar, D., *Talking to Rudolf Hess* (The History Press, 2010).

JOURNAL ARTICLES AND THESES

Badger, W. and Purkiss, D., 'English Witches and SS Academics', *Prenature: Critical and Historical Studies on the Preternatural*, 6.1 (2017).

Carrier, R., '"Hitler's Table Talk": Troubling Finds', *German Studies Review*, 26.3 (2003).

Fox, J., '"Everyday Heroines": Nazi Visions of Motherhood in Mutterliebe (1939) and Annelie (1943)', *Historical Reflections*, 35.2 (2009).

Goeschel, C., 'Suicide at the End of the Third Reich', *Journal of Contemporary History*, 41.1 (2006).

Harris, V., 'The Role of the Concentration Camps in the Nazi Repression of Prostitutes 1933–1939', *Journal of Contemporary History*, 45.3 (2010).

McDonogh, G., 'Otto Horcher: Caterer to the Third Reich', *Gastronomica*, 7.1 (2007).

Montgomery, J., 'Sisters, Objects of Desire or Barbarians: German Nurses in the First World War', thesis, University of Tennessee, 2013.

Nilsson, M., 'Hugh Trevor-Roper and the English Editions of Hitler's Table Talk and Testament', *Journal of Contemporary History*, 5.1 (2016).

Palumbo, M., 'Goering's Italian Exile 1924–1925', *Journal of Modern History*, 50.1 (1978).

Perry, J., 'Nazifying Christmas: Political Culture and Popular Celebration in the Third Reich', *Central European History*, 38.4 (2005).

Quirin, K., 'Working Women and Motherhood: Failures of the Weimar Republic's Family Policies', *The Gettysburg Historical Journal*, 13.8 (2014).

Roos, J., 'Backlash against Prostitutes' Rights: Origins and Dynamics of Nazi Prostitution Policies', *Journal of the History of Sexuality*, 11.1/2 (2002).

Sigel, R., 'The Cultivation of Medicinal Herbs in the Concentration Camp', Studies, Reports, Documents, vol. 2, *Dachau Review History of Nazi Concentration Camps* (1990).

Silver, J., 'Karl Gebhardt (1897–1948): A Lost Man', *Journal of the Royal College of Physicians at Edinburgh*, 41, (2011).

Timm, A., 'Sex with a Purpose: Prostitution, Venereal Disease and Militarised Masculinity in the Third Reich', *Journal of the History of Sexuality*, 11.1/2 (2002).

Zroka, A.L., 'Serving the Volksgemeinschaft, German Red Cross Nurses in the Second World War', thesis, University of California, 2015.

WEBSITES

Carrier, R., 'Hitler's Table Talk; An Update', www.richardcarrier.info/archives/10978.

Ernst, E., 'Rudolf Hess (Hitler's Deputy) on Alternative Medicine', edzardernst. com?2015?01?rudolf-hess-hitlers-deputy-on-alternative-medicine

Irving, D., 'Frau Marga Himmler Diaries 1937-1945: Himmler's Diary Jan 1934-Dec 1935.

1939: The Vaughan Papers', Real History, www.fp.co.uk.

INDEX